Probation: politics, policy and practice

*Probation: politics,
policy and practice*

TIM MAY

OPEN UNIVERSITY PRESS
MILTON KEYNES · PHILADELPHIA

Open University Press
Celtic Court
22 Ballmoor
Buckingham MK18 1XW

and
1900 Frost Road, Suite 101
Bristol, PA 19007, USA

First Published 1991

British Library Cataloguing in Publication Data

May, Tim
  Probation: politics, policy and practice.
  1. Probation services. Influence of social change. England
  I. Title
  364.630942

  ISBN 0 335 09378 7
  ISBN 0 335 09377 9 pbk

Library of Congress Cataloging-in-Publication Data

May, Tim, 1957–
  Probation: politics, policy, and practice/Tim May.
      p.   cm.
  Includes bibliographical references and index.
  ISBN 0-335-09378-7   ISBN 0-335-09377-9 (pbk.)
  1. Probation – England. 2. Probation – Wales. 3. Corrections –
England. 4. Corrections – Wales.   I. Title.
HV9346.A5M39   1990
364.6'3'0942 – dc20   90-39103 CIP

Typeset by Rowland Phototypesetting Limited
Bury St Edmunds, Suffolk
Printed in Great Britain by
Billing and Sons Limited, Worcester

Contents

Acknowledgements

In personal terms, this book is more than the culmination of three years work: it marks the end and, one hopes, the beginning of change. There are a number of people I wish to thank who, in one way or another, have been with me on my journey. Before I do that, however, I must thank the following for providing comments on drafts of the script: Ian Levitt, Rob Mawby and David Dunkerley; also Dick Hobbs, whose advice to 'add or slaughter' I hope I will never forget; Mike Maguire, who has always been considerate and helpful; David Downes, who provided both constructive and critical comment; Christine Firth with her keen eye for detail; and John Skelton and the staff at Open University Press.

I especially wish to mention Dee, who has experienced some of those years of personal change and with whom it is now a pleasure to share my life. In reading parts of the final draft, Dee also provided a keen eye; her comments were very helpful, whilst her own dedication to particularly demanding work, rightly induces a sense of humility in my own. Mel, Pete, Kate and Tam provided frequent respite which was much needed. Thanks also to Mum and Dad. Frank Lee I thank for encouraging me on my late but determined path to university; my friends at 'The Bell' were good companions, while Louise and Lyn were valuable sources of encouragement, as also Ken and Angus, both of whom know the trials of the writing process.

Finally I must thank the staff of the Treen Service. Quite simply, without their co-operation this book would not have been possible. The 'Chief' not only showed openness in disclosing sometimes sensitive information, but also carefully read and commented on my work. Other members of staff I would like to mention, but the request for anonymity prevents me from doing so. I hope they know who they are. One person in particular was a never ending source of material and put up with my constant requests. Another provided detailed comments on drafts and encouraged me during a process in which praise seemed to be rarely forthcoming. My thanks also to the officer, from whose original idea this work finally evolved.

I make the usual disclaimer on behalf of the above, in that I alone remain responsible for the finished product, which simply aims to cast a little light on territory that is often neglected or misunderstood in times of change.

T.M.

Introduction

This book is about change. More specifically, it is about the effect of changes in the criminal justice system and society in general upon the probation service in England and Wales. Its purpose is to add to an understanding of the nature of these changes, how they are interpreted by the probation service and the process of their implementation. In so doing, it moves from the general to the specific: from the nature of these changes, to an analysis of their consequences within one probation service which, for the purposes of anonymity, is simply called 'Treen'. However, the study also analyses the work of probation personnel in different work settings and considers the appropriateness of these policy changes in relation to the everyday realities of probation work.

Chapter 1 examines the history of the probation service and the changes which brought about its expansion. While histories of the service already exist, this chapter is designed to add to an understanding of contemporary changes. Its core themes are the rise of the service, the expectations placed upon it and the functions of the probation service within the criminal justice system as a whole. In addition, it charts the rising occupational aspirations of probation officers. As a result, the nature of policy change and its effects on the organization of the service and the status of its personnel are examined in historical context.

Chapter 2 examines more contemporary shifts which have led to changes in the traditional role of the service, as outlined in Chapter 1. I shall refer to three levels of change. First, 'macro' changes, that is changes in thinking on crime and the subsequent effect on the service via Home Office policy changes. Second, these are examined in relation to 'mezzo' or organizational level changes, which include the targeting and monitoring of probation work and changes in the service's managerial style. Third, these are examined in terms of their effects on the 'micro' or interactional level: changes in the role and type of probation personnel, organizational accountability being emphasized over autonomy, as well as an alteration in the service's clients. The discussion of ideological and political factors is therefore linked to their effects on organizational and interactional levels of probation work.

Chapter 3 is concerned with the interpretation and implementation of policy changes within the Treen Probation Service, that is the 'mezzo' layer. I shall examine a major policy initiative which took place during the research; the difficulties of its implementation in Treen and the beliefs and reactions of staff to the proposed changes and policy-making in general. In the process, the issues of objectives, targets, monitoring, budgets and the government's Financial Management Initiative and Home Office policy changes are also discussed in relation to the work of the service.

Chapters 4 to 6 consider the beliefs and actions of staff at the 'front line' (probation officers and ancillaries). This covers beliefs concerning the value of probation work, the autonomy and accountability of work in relation to the organization and the changing roles of staff within the service. The everyday contingencies of probation work and the extent to which official policy is 'in-tune' with the working environment are explored in a variety of settings: the courts, probation hostels, day centres, community service and Divorce Court welfare. Chapter 7 then examines the work of seconded prison probation officers.

Until recently, and relative to other agencies in the criminal justice system, little attention has been paid to the probation service from those interested in organizations and the criminal justice system in general. The exception to this is Gwyneth Boswell's (1982) research. She found a lack of consensus amongst probation officers concerning the goals of the service. Not only did members of her sample appear to lack a 'universal sense of purpose'

(1982: 342), their differing goals could be argued to render organizational effectiveness problematic. Nevertheless, the full implications of this conflict were not investigated due to the study relying on interview data alone. Therefore, while Boswell broke new ground, a further understanding of organizational behaviour and conflict would have been achieved by the inclusion of other research instruments. By using participant observation, interviews, a questionnaire and documentary research, an overall picture of change and the service's everyday work would have been obtained. To characterize an organization as lacking in common goals, without a corresponding consideration of the relationship between the environment and its work, fails to acknowledge what I consider to be fundamental: the political and environmental effects on organizational work and change.

I hope that this book goes some way towards redressing this imbalance. Chapter 7 returns to an examination of all three levels of analysis – the macro, mezzo and micro – to consider the findings of Chapters 3 to 6 in relation to the discussion in Chapters 1 and 2. Finally, the Postscript looks at the future of the service through the eyes of members of the Treen Probation Service, to whom this study is indebted.

PART I

The historical and political context

I

An evolving organization and occupation

Offence after offence . . . and sentence after sentence appears to be the inevitable lot of him whose foot has once slipped.
(Part of F. Rainer's letter to the English Temperance Society, 1876; quoted in Jarvis, 1972)

any set of social and economic arrangements which is not founded on the acceptance of individual responsibility will do nothing but harm. We are all responsible for our own actions. We cannot blame society if we break the law. We simply cannot delegate the exercise of mercy and generosity to others.
(Margaret Thatcher speaking to the General Assembly of the Church of Scotland, May 1988; emphasis added)

The 1980s were characterized by rapid change: increased unemployment, the unleashing of market forces and a government ideology motivated by the sanctity of individual liberty and responsibility. Economic efficiency is predicated upon competition. The individual pursuit of ends is guided by Adam Smith's (1776) 'invisible hand': an 'impersonal' regulatory economic force. While opinions vary on the reasons for this change in government thinking, it is undoubtedly having an effect on economic, political and cultural life (see D. King 1987). By the rolling back of the state, individual initiative is no longer stifled and a resulting freedom to choose has as its concomitant increasing individual responsibility. This renewal of *laissez-faire* in the economic sphere has apparently resulted in an increasing authoritarianism in the social sphere (see S. Hall and Jacques 1983; Leys 1984).

The criminal justice system has felt the impact of these changes. Additionally, within criminology, there has been a movement away from the endeavour to uncover the aetiology of crime, towards a focus on the effect of crimes on the victim and the administration of our system of justice. Change has taken place in penal discourse and practice. Rehabilitation of the criminal is no longer the primary aim it once was. There is now a focus on punishment, predicated upon individual responsibility for criminal acts. It is this change in penal thinking and political rhetoric that defines the climate in which the probation service operates. The object of this chapter, therefore, is to examine some of these changes in relation to the rise of the probation service within the criminal justice system; changes in its organization and the emerging professionalism of probation officers.

The emergence of 'mission'

Several histories of the probation service already exist and it is not my purpose to replicate these (see J. King 1969; Jarvis 1972; Bochel 1976; Haxby 1978). However, in order to understand the particular pressures the probation service is currently facing it is important to locate the emergence and changing nature of the service within the environment it operated. This method enables a greater understanding of the probation service in its present context, sharpening insight into contemporary changes.[1]

The probation service evolved in a time of rising concern at the level of moral degeneration of a particular section of the population, namely working-class habitual petty offenders whose patterns of offending were thought to be linked to their drinking habits. For these offenders incarceration, at the centre of penal sanctioning at the time, was not thought appropriate. An alternative form for the moral training of the individual offender, given the nature of their behaviour, was required.

The Summary Jurisdiction Act 1879 provided for conditional discharge for the young or petty offenders, as long as those individuals were of good behaviour and agreed to appear for sentence if required. In addition, they may have been ordered to observe certain conditions the court imposed. Such practices are regarded as forming the beginnings of the probation system and the administration of local initiatives from which sprang police court missions.

However, underlying these changes was the fundamental belief that offending behaviour was the result of rational choice:

> Illegality, like poverty, was an effect of individual choice. Accordingly, punishment took forms appropriate to its object. The proper response to the rational criminal thus constructed was a policy of deterrence and retribution, the former to deny the utility of crime, the latter to reconstitute the social contract after its breach.
>
> (Garland 1985: 17)

This utilitarian calculation, inspired by Bentham's (1830) philosophy, required a careful balance in deterrence and retribution – sufficient to deter criminals but not too much to jettison them down the path of criminality. Therefore, individuals were presumed equal and rational under the law.[2] The administration of Victorian criminal justice not only was characterized by these principal aims, but also contained a third element: reform.

In the USA a Boston cobbler, John Augustus, was widely regarded as being the world's first probation officer. From 1841 to 1859 he took offenders on bail from Boston courts, promising the courts to report on their behaviour before they were recalled for judgment. Following his death, voluntary workers continued this tradition until the Massachusetts Act 1878 provided for:

> such persons as many reasonably be expected to be reformed *without punishment* should be selected to be put on probation.
>
> (Jarvis 1972: 13, italics added)

Penal thinking in Britain also appeared to be moving in the same direction. Even those who attacked 'sentimentalists' for believing in reform, not punishment, considered imprisonment an inappropriate response for the young and petty persistent offender.[3] These beliefs found their legislative expression in the Probation of First Offenders Act 1887. However, the Act did not include the systematic supervision of offenders by an 'authority', despite attempts to introduce such a clause.

Within the discipline of criminology during this time, two schools of thought were predominant: those of the eugenicists and the social environmentalists. Cesare Lombroso's *L'Uomo Delinquente* was published in 1876. By the fifth edition in 1896, it had become three volumes of 1,903 pages, from its original of 252 pages. The focus was upon the idea of a born criminal: a class of individuals whose anti-social behaviour shared common characteristics and whose physical appearances were also similar. This atavist being possessed ferocious instincts symptomatic of inferior animals. By locating a criminal anthropology in the physical appearance of criminals Lombroso's theory paralleled another dominant mode of thought at the time: Social Darwinism. As Radzinowicz has noted of Lombroso's popularity:

> It served the interests and relieved the conscience of those at the top to look upon the dangerous classes as an independent category, detached from the prevailing social conditions.
>
> (Quoted in Jones 1986: 10)

This biological positivism was preceded by the work of the French social statisticians Quetelet and Guerry in the 1830s and 1840s. Their findings were radical in implication, concluding that crime was the result of social causes; a concept less easy to digest than that of a 'dangerous class':

> For the first time in the history of human thought crime came to be viewed as a social fact primarily moulded by that very social environment of which it is an integral part.
>
> (Radzinowicz 1966: 35)

However, this begs the question of how it was that two seemingly irreconcilable explanations of criminal behaviour – the 'eugenicists' and the 'individualizers' – were compatible with the theories of environmentalism and social determination. On the one hand, the individual was the *problem*. On the other, crime was a social fact and was generated by prevailing social conditions. The clue lay, as Garland argues, in the 'analytic primacy of the individual':

> Such a paradox was possible because the 'environmentalists' did not take social relations as their object of analysis and transformation, nor even the phenomenon of crime. Instead, they, like their 'opponents', took as their object *the criminal individual as affected by social factors*.
>
> (Garland 1985: 175, original italics)

As noted, underpinning the Victorian system of penology was the idea of the responsible subject, free to choose illegal activity and to be punished accordingly. Within criminology, the identification of causal factors leading to criminal behaviour was infused with a determinism – the individual pushed into crime by social causes beyond their control – as such, offenders could hardly be construed as responsible for their actions. Criminology's logic, therefore, seemed to deny penal practice. However, the dominant thinking in the moral and political spheres was still that of the free individual. The compromise was to introduce a measure whose logic underlies and gave impetus to the formation of the probation service and the claims to professionalism of its members. Action became the result of choice which may, on occasion, be placed in doubt; a soft determinism prevailed:

> *Responsibility thus became a presumption which was always put in doubt* . . . It replaces a philosophical principle (all men are free and responsible) with a positive psychology (each man must be investigated, his personality assessed).
> (Garland 1985: 187, original italics)

The subject, as defined by the prevailing moral and political ideology, became an object for the *experts'* assessment: the age of *treatment* had begun.[4]

Between 1895 and 1914 the number of criminal sanctions nearly doubled. Inspired by a reforming zeal of the evangelical spirit and a middle-class entrepreneurial philosophy, legislation provided a focus for the 'Puritan combination of a "consciousness of sin" . . . with a generalized compassion towards the 'disadvantaged"' (A. Young 1976: 45). A fusion took place between the charitable and legal spheres. Philanthropy was a medium between Christian conscience and business and a young probation service the buffer between *laissez-faire* individualism and state intervention in the penal sphere. The site for the expression of such beliefs became a legally responsible *subject* who, on occasion, lapses into irresponsibility which requires treatment. The individual becomes the *object* and the probation officer the means for intervention.

The resulting individualization of crime remains to this day one of the principal justifications of probation service work and a core belief underlying the professional status of its members (McWilliams 1987; Boswell 1982, 1989). Such was the strength of belief concerning these ideas and practices that any oppositional debate was 'marked by its absence' (Garland 1985: 168). The consensus around 'welfarism' as a core component of penal strategies and rationale of the probation service, began to be *fully* challenged – in the political sphere – only in the 1970s and 1980s, with considerable effect (see Chapter 2).

It was not until the Probation of Offenders Act 1907 that legislation provided for the appointment of full-time probation officers. Representatives of the Church of England Temperance Society argued that police court missionaries, who were already engaged in social work in the courts, should be appointed. Nevertheless, it was decided that the decisions of magistrates regarding the suitability of individuals to supervise offenders should be elastic, while the duties of probation officers, following an amendment to the Bill, were

> To visit or receive reports from the person under supervision at such reasonable intervals as the probation officer may think fit; to see that he observes the conditions of his recognizance; to report to the Court on his behaviour; to advise, assist and befriend him and, when necessary, to endeavour to find him suitable employment.
>
> (Quoted in Jarvis 1972: 16)

To this day 'advise, assist and befriend' is still widely quoted. Salaries were payable by 'case', reflecting not only the likelihood of the work being part-time, but also some doubt as to the use which would be made by the courts of probation officers. The Act provided the beginnings of a transition from voluntary to public provision, although there was no obligation on local justices to implement the Act: the only proviso was the Probation Rules 1908, which required magistrates of each Petty Sessional Division to meet once a year to appoint probation officers. Under the Act, conditions could also be added to orders which included prohibiting the individual from socializing with other thieves, or if the offence involved alcohol, abstention from intoxicating liquor and the leading of 'an honest and industrious life'. Similar motivations were contained in the subsequent Prevention of Crime Act 1908, only this time in the prison, as opposed to the community (see Garland 1985: 220).

Some commentators on the justice system were arguing that the provision of probation was a matter for the state and not philanthropists (see Bochel 1976: 34). However, the pay, appointment and workloads of officers were locally determined and this autonomy meant a variability in workloads and salaries. This, in turn, led to questions of whether probation work should be under local or central control (a consideration remaining the subject of debate to this day). In reaction to this local variability, the Home Office was issuing Circulars suggesting the increased use of probation on suitable cases (as today) and, following the report of the Departmental Committee on the Probation of Offenders Act 1909, it was also agreed that in most cases fixed annual payments should be made to probation officers.

This era in the formation of the service took its impetus from a convergence between the inappropriateness of existing penal sanctions to a particular class of offenders – habitual, drunken and petty – and a reforming zeal motivated by religious belief. This middle-class movement was charity-based in its organization and moral in its ethos, although operating in a society where the philosophy of self-help and entrepreneurial spirit were paramount:

> The solution for these Victorian pundits was therefore to define these miscreant individuals as being a social problem on account of their moral laxity or failing.
>
> (A. Young 1976: 52)

Nevertheless, the success of probation required greater provision' than that allowed for by charitable organization alone. Legislation provided the framework, but the organization for its effective implementation was to come later.

'Evangelical voluntarism' to the 'public therapeutic'

In 1912 the National Association of Probation Officers (NAPO) was formed; it had three aims. First, the advancement of probation work. Second, the promotion of a bond union amongst probation officers, by the provision of opportunities for social intercourse and the giving of friendly advice. Third, to enable probation officers by collective action, as a result of practical experience, to make suggestions for advancements in probation work and the reformation of offenders.

The formation of NAPO was not without critics. Some, particularly those religiously motivated, saw the association as a self-seeking body, representative of an increasing secularization. Two years later a related issue of voluntary versus professional probation officers was discussed in Leeson's *The Probation System* (1914). These issues began a debate stressing the religious element of the service versus a public body administered and staffed by professionals.

Leeson also raised the issue of central and local control of the service. He suggested the special training of probation officers and the formation of a Home Office department to co-ordinate probation work nationally. To add to this debate the Howard Association's Annual Report (1916) highlighted the unsuitability of many officers, their clients and the short length of orders, and an inadequacy in organization and control of probation work.[5] One year later a deputation from the State Children's Association met the Home Secretary and were also disturbed at the lack of training in reformative methods of many police court missionaries. Educated workers, they believed, were being asked to work with those whose outlook was in the past. Probation officials were reported to be overworked and lacking in co-ordination, while probation supervision was inadequate. In fact by 1920, of the 1,034 Courts of Summary Jurisdiction, only 215 had taken steps to appoint probation officers. This deputation therefore suggested that the Home Secretary should use his influence over justices to appoint those who were 'well educated', of 'high ideals' and with knowledge of the 'best reformative methods' (Bochel 1976: 69).

The evangelical spirit of the police court missionaries was therefore being gradually replaced by the therapeutic approach of the diagnostician (see McWilliams 1983). Governments, spurred on by the above arguments, assumed increasing responsibility in the planning of probation provision to courts. In the process the concept of 'all equal under the law', characteristic of the Victorian era, moved more into the background. As a result, the 'judicial institution' was incorporated into Foucault's (1977) 'continuum of apparatuses' which performed regulatory as well as disciplinary functions over the individual. Normalization became the goal, diagnosis its method and probation its means in the penal sphere. These practices were 'concerned not just to prevent law-breaking, but also to inculcate specific norms and practices' (Garland 1985: 238).

Changes in thinking were also taking place among probation personnel. The missionary ideal, based as it was on the 'stumbling block of drink', justified the coercion of the individual in order to 'save them from themselves'. Thus the end-state – the understanding of 'God's law' – would be enhanced. However, the actual practice of reformative techniques led missionaries to believe that individual behaviour was actually conditioned by this 'stumbling block of drink'. This gave additional impetus to a new movement based on the psychological diagnosis of the individual. The rise of the '"scientific" ontology' of the diagnosticians had begun:

> Once this became widely accepted it meant that the Mission had no ultimate defence left against the determinist ontology of the diagnosticians. The triumph of the 'scientific social workers ensued.

> (McWilliams 1983: 142)

Even so, two important ingredients were missing for the success of this movement: organization and training.

While the Home Office had appointed an official with responsibility for overseeing probation, following the recommendations of the 1909 Committee, the post was in the Children's Division. The 1920 Departmental Committee, appointed by the Home Secretary to inquire into the pay, training and appointment of probation officers, found staff in the Home Office distracted by the workload of other duties. The Committee, reporting in 1922, recommended sufficient staff should be appointed to the Children's Division and an annual report on the probation service should be produced and made available to magistrates, social workers and probation officers. The Committee also recommended that the government should now pay half the cost of providing probation officers, noting a 'saving to the Exchequer' if probation were successful. Further, the Committee suggested the beginnings of a system of control and finance whose form remains to this day: a central government grant but '*without direct interference with the organisation of the work on local lines*' (quoted in Bochel 1976: 88, italics added).[6] The Committee also recommended that each Bench should appoint representatives from its members to form a Committee to organize probation work in the area. Their tasks, the Committee suggested, should include questions of pay and supervision of officers, as well as their appointment.

The Criminal Justice Act 1925 made it mandatory for every criminal court to have a probation officer attached to it. This was the first major Act to facilitate the uniform workings of probation 'organizationally'. Additionally, each petty sessional division became a probation area, while probation work was to be administered by a new statutory body – the Probation Committee – responsible for the pay and appointment of officers. However, the supervision of probation officers' work remained the responsibility of the local Bench unless it had been delegated to an elected Probation Committee or alternatively, under the Home Secretary's powers, took place in a combined area – in which case the Probation Committee assumed responsibility. Salaries, as determined by the committee, would be met by local authorities who no longer had the powers under the 1907 Act to refuse justices' recommendations.[7]

Under pressure from various groups in the criminal justice system and for pragmatic reasons such as cost, governments had acted during this period in implementing the universal provision of a probation service to courts. However, there still existed an uneasy tension between newly recruited probation officers and missionaries from the Church of England Temperance Society. This situation, coupled with increased workloads and duties over the next decade, was to prompt another major review of the service.

An aspiring occupation

During the next decade a considerable expansion took place in probation work. Numbers placed on probation increased from 15,094 in 1925 to 18,934 in 1933, a phenomenon attributed by Bochel (1976), albeit with some caution, to increased numbers of probation officers; increased knowledge on the part of magistrates; closure of reformatory schools and a change in attitudes towards institutions. Not only did government moves appear to facilitate a higher profile for probation in the criminal justice system during this time, but utterances regarding the professional nature of probation officers' work were becoming more frequent. Indeed, during the 1928 Annual Conference of NAPO the future secretary, H. E. Norman, referred to the proceedings of the association as those not of a trade union, but a 'learned society' (Jarvis 1972: 40). Practitioners and their representatives, spurred on by the diagnostic ideal, sought professional status based upon their diagnostic abilities.[8] This movement meant a change in the ethos of probation work:

> The gradual movement from the religious, missionary ideal to the scientific, diagnostic ideal, depending, in part, on notions of professionalism, required that probation work should be something for which people were *trained* to enter rather than *called* to follow.
>
>   (McWilliams 1985: 261, italics added)

Further evidence for the importance of diagnosis came from the field of criminology in the form of Cyril Burt's *The Young Delinquent* (published in 1925). He noted the importance of examining offenders' characteristics and not offences. As a result, he advocated training for probation officers in psychology, all of which was reproduced in Le Mesurier's *Handbook of Probation* (1935).

Official credibility for the training of officers came from the Advisory Committee on Probation in 1930. Legislatively the Children and Young Persons Act 1933 provided not only for a system of supervision of young offenders, but also for inquiries into their home circumstances to be undertaken by probation officers (as well as local authority officers). Once again, given these changes in practice and beliefs, the probation service found itself the subject of a Departmental Committee.

The Departmental Committee on the Social Services in Courts of Summary Jurisdiction began its investigation in 1934 and reported in 1936. Its tasks included inquiries into the practice of probation; methods of reconciliation in matrimonial disputes; social investigations for the courts, and finally, to recommend any necessary changes in the organization of the probation service. It found the Probation Committee system to be inadequate. Many members did not have sufficient contact with their probation officers who were thereby isolated. Others had appointed only part-time officers; many courts were often without officers, while many officers were unqualified, inexperienced or overworked by supervising, on average, between sixty and seventy cases. In addition, 300 petty sessional divisions were without a woman probation officer, whose presence the Committee considered important. The Committee found these facts fair to neither the officers nor the system. While some areas had combined, others remained very small, leading the Committee to conclude that the case for combination was 'unassailable' and that the most effective unit for such combination was the County. However, the Committee remained convinced of the principle in the 1925 Act, which left the control of the service in the hands of justices – despite finding that Probation Committees were 'remote' from officers.

Among the Departmental Committee's proposals was the introduction of a supervisory post, the principal probation officer, which already existed in some areas. The duties of principal probation officers were given as: advising the Probation Committee on technical matters; acting as executive in the organization and administration of the service; liaising between the Probation Committee and other relevant bodies; promoting effective probation work through the provision of reports and enabling those probation officers interested in 'other work' to incorporate this within their probation experiences, thus 'broadening the base of their social endeavours' (Bochel 1976: 138–9). It also recommended that matrimonial work, already undertaken on a voluntary basis by probation officers, should become a statutory duty for the service. (This was implemented by the Summary Procedure Act 1937.)[9] Finally, the Committee noted the importance of training officers and also recommended an increase in the *central control* of the Service. While these recommendations were to be implemented in the Criminal Justice Act 1938, the outbreak of the Second World War prevented its reading. Nevertheless, the service developed along the lines proposed by the Committee and the last police court mission (Middlesex) handed over to the Home Office in March 1941.

Speaking to the 24th Annual Conference of NAPO, the Chair of the 1936 Departmental Committee, Sidney Harris, noted two principles contained in the report: the need for trained social workers to undertake the social work of the courts and the necessity for the probation service to be a wholly *public* service. The emphasis of this wide-ranging report rested firmly on the service's *administration*. If its ethos was to be questioned it was in a favourable light.

Officially, at least, disputes regarding the rationale of therapeutic practices became administrative problems. Concern centred on the execution not on the conception of the task. Practitioners were to implement on behalf of the courts, while a more hierarchical administrative structure was to enhance and facilitate their work, providing a career ladder where none existed before. Sufficient training in diagnostic methods became the means towards the end of rehabilitation, although its full development was still to come in the form of training officers in various practices.

The post-war period: the peak of occupational status

The 1936 Departmental Committee's recommendations were eventually incorporated in the Criminal Justice Act 1948. This Act repealed all past legislation in respect to probation. It set up a new structure of administration for the probation service, restated the powers of the courts in respect to probation and set the duties of probation officers, particularly their new responsibilities for after-care of prisoners. The Act also provided for an increase in Home Office control of local administration and an Exchequer grant to be paid at a rate not exceeding 50 per cent. By 1959 there were eleven inspectors from the Home Office Probation Division, with each newly appointed officer receiving a visit from an inspector. In addition, *ad hoc* visits were made to probation areas. The Probation Rules 1949 also set out the duties of principal probation officers and those of senior probation officers (SPOs), who had been appointed in many areas. While the service became more hierarchical, it was noted that

> The sturdy independence of the individual officer had long held sway, and was to do so long after the Rules had been issued.
>
> (Jarvis 1972: 64)

The Home Secretary had used powers of combination, justified by the presumed increase in efficiency which would result from larger areas of administration. By 1959 there were 104 probation areas in England and Wales – reduced from 292 in 1947 – and by 1962 there were 62 principal probation officers. Further duties were given to probation officers during the 1950s and these included those of 'welfare officer' via the Matrimonial Proceedings (Children) Act 1958.

The development of the probation service led one observer of the criminal justice system to write in 1958:

> If I were asked what is the most significant contribution made by this country to the new penological theory and practice which struck root in the twentieth century . . . my answer would be probation.
>
> (Radzinowicz 1958)

Despite such optimism, concern was expressed at the decline in numbers placed on probation and an increase in recorded crime. Between 1938 and 1947, as a percentage of indictable offences known to the police, those aged over 17 convicted and placed on probation fell from 22 per cent to 11 per cent.[10]

The probation service was now in the middle of the period Bill McWilliams (1986) calls the 'phase of diagnosis'. From the early saving of souls through divine grace, the onus was now on the scientific assessment and treatment of the individual. No longer were offenders 'sinners' but 'patients'. Officers no longer engaged in special pleading on behalf of individuals in the courts, but provided a scientific assessment of their predicament. With the casework method the offender became the subject of professional diagnostic appraisal, all of which drew upon a phase in criminological thought which provided for the treatment of the offender who was in some way maladjusted.[11] Therefore, this period provided social workers with their prime justification for professional status which, in various forms, remains to this day: the skills required in one-to-one intensive casework. However, McWilliams (1986) argues that underlying this 'scientism' is a diguised moral goal regarding appropriate behaviour.

A major review

Increased pressure on probation officers, given the absolute rise in reported crime, led to a demand for their work which was not being met by the supply of officers. This led to demands for increased salaries because not only was greater expertise required, but there was an increase in workloads. While the Home Office were initially reluctant to launch a large-scale inquiry, a Committee was convened in May 1959 under the direction of a QC, Ronald Morison. The Committee's brief was to inquire into 'all aspects of probation in England and Wales and Scotland' and 'the approved probation hostel system in England and Wales and Scotland'. The Morison Committee finally reported in March 1962.

The Morison Report was wide ranging in its content and marked the beginning of two decades of rapid change in the functions and organization of the service. The Committee offered the following definition of probation:

> We understand by probation the submission of an offender while at liberty to a specified period of supervision by a social caseworker who is an officer of the court: during this period the offender remains liable, if not of good conduct, to be otherwise dealt with by the court.
>
> (Home Office 1962: para. 9)

It also emphasized that the court makes a probation order *instead of* a sentence and places a trust in the probationer 'to be of good conduct'. At the same time, the Committee were anxious to dispel the myth that a person is let off if placed on probation and stressed the disciplinary element in submitting to supervision. This was a response to the perceived public demand for tougher sentencing as the crime rate was rising.

Central to the aim of probation was the use of social casework and in this the Committee reinforced the main justification for the professional status of the probation officer:

> To-day the probation officer must be seen, essentially, as a professional caseworker, employing, in a specialised field, skill which he holds in common with other social workers; skills which, if it opens up to him hopes of constructive work which

were not enjoyed by his predecessors of twenty years ago, also
make complex and subtle demands upon him, reflecting, as it
does, growing awareness of the difficulty of his task.

(Home Office 1962: para. 54)

While treatment of the individual remained the central work of the
officer, the Committee also invested the probation officer with
the responsibility for protecting society and regulating the probationer's behaviour by the inculcation of society's norms (Home
Office 1962: para. 54).

Duties 'proliferate'

The Committee noted that the functions of probation officers had
increased considerably, but believed such demands should continue (1962: paras 10, 11.) Thus, the duties of probation officers and
the service's administrative responsibilities grew rapidly over
the next two decades, providing ammunition for the Probation
Division of the Home Office for further expenditure by central
government.

Following the Advisory Council on the Treatment of Offenders
(ACTO) Report *The Organisation of After-Care* (Home Office 1963)
– which stressed the development of welfare work within prisons –
an expanded probation service assumed responsibility from the
Discharged Prisoners' Aid Societies on 1 January 1966. Administratively, at least, this changed the 'long-standing antipathy'
(Haxby 1978: 242) probation officers had towards prisons.[12] The
Criminal Justice Act 1967 further incorporated probation officers
into the prison system by the introduction of parole. This gave
additional responsibilities to seconded probation officers, who also
supervised parolees on licence.[13] The same Act gave the courts
power to suspend a sentence. This did not affect the probation
service at the time, but following the Wootton Report's (Home
Office 1970) recommendation for 'guidance or help' for those on
suspended sentences, the power of courts to make a supervision by
a probation officer part of such a sentence was introduced in the
Criminal Justice Act 1972.

Furthermore, the Children and Young Persons Act 1969 placed
two primary obligations on the courts. First, the protection of the
community, and second, the promotion of the welfare of the child.
If this Act had been fully implemented, the work of the service with
young offenders would have been greatly reduced. As a result of a

change of government, the Act was modified and the probation service is still heavily involved with the 14 to 16 as well as 17 to 21 age groups. There then followed the Criminal Justice Act 1972 and the Powers of Criminal Courts Act 1973 – legislation which considerably expanded the duties and functions of the service. These were designed to make better use of probation resources and reduce the prison population. They included empowering probation committees to set up and fund bail and probation hostels, day training centres and other establishments for use in connection with the rehabilitation of offenders. In addition, courts were now required to consider a social inquiry report (SIR) on offenders under 21 before imposing a custodial sentence, to determine whether any other suitable method existed for their disposal. This same criterion applied to those over 21 who had not previously been sentenced to imprisonment. However, if magistrates were of the opinion that no other suitable method of disposal existed other than prison, they were not required to consider a report, but did have to state their reasons openly in court (Powers of Criminal Courts Act 1973, sec. 20). Community Service Orders, following the recommendation of the Wootton Report, were also introduced. This new sentence, to be administered by the service, empowered courts to order offenders to undertake unpaid work for the community for a period of not less than 40 hours or more than 240 hours.

In response to these increasing demands and allocation of resources, the probation service grew considerably in the period between 1960 and 1978. The number of full-time officers of all grades had increased by 3,553 to a total of 5,186 (in 1988 there were 6,792). At the same time, the administrative hierarchy had increased. The ratio of supervisory to non-supervisory posts increased from 1:6 to 1:3 (or from 13.7 to 22.9 per cent of all officers).[14] A NAPO (1966) Working Party Report believed such moves did not inhibit the professional responsibility or initiative of the probation officer and these posts were considered to enable good professional practice.

These were not the only posts to proliferate in the service. The ancillary grade was introduced by the Home Office in 1971. The purpose was to introduce duties between those of probation officers and clerical assistants. By 1974 there were 373 ancillaries in post. In addition, D. Mathieson (1979) notes that the service had as many accredited volunteers as probation officers. Thus, levels, types and numbers of probation personnel increased considerably over a relatively short period.

Other changes also affected the organization of the service. The Seebohm Committee, who reported in 1968 (mainly noted for recommending unifying local authority personal services into social service departments), recommended changes in social work training (Home Office 1968). As a result, in 1971 the government transferred responsibility for training to the newly formed Central Council for Education and Training in Social Work (CCETSW). The Council soon implemented a policy of recognized courses leading to a Certificate of Qualification in Social Work (CQSW). While the service was represented on the Council, concern was expressed at the possibility of less attention being devoted to probation training in favour of general social work courses; especially as the probation service now exercised less direct control over the training of officers. In December of the same year, a House of Commons Expenditure Committee supported the continuing independence of the service in England and Wales.

A year later the Home Secretary reaffirmed this principle, adding the following:

> The boundaries of probation and after-care areas will have to be adjusted in consequence of local government reorganisation. After consulting the national probation organisations and other interested organisations, I have decided to use my existing powers to establish a probation area for each new county, subject to the possibility of combination of those where the service would otherwise be very small.
>
> (Quoted in Haxby 1978: 24)

The Committee had also noted the maintenance of law and order and questions of its reform was the Home Secretary's responsibility. As such, the responsibility for the probation service within the penal system should remain part of the Home Secretary's duties. Further, the government grant for the administration of local services increased from 50 to 80 per cent. From seventy-nine probation areas at the end of 1971, following local government reorganization in 1974, there are now fifty-six.

Discussion

Government moves to widen the duties of the probation service were often a reaction to several factors. First, the increase in the prison population and hence a need for alternatives to custody.

Second, a perceived public concern at the increase in crime. Third, the higher cost to the Exchequer of incarceration over its alternatives. The main means for tackling such concerns was, as noted, the probation service. At the same time, probation officers' methods of working were based on the skills of casework and it was upon these that their occupational aspirations were based. This was substantiated by the method of diagnostic appraisal. Officers then needed a degree of discretion in the execution of their tasks, which, in turn, rested upon courts' decisions. Officers became the means for the correct training (normalization) of their clients. In the process, better methods towards this end were developed, but rarely was the underlying philosophy questioned.

Administrative changes during this period were designed to enable officers to perform these tasks more effectively. However, increased caseloads and duties meant a proliferation in the size and hierarchy of the service. Nevertheless, the *nature* of some of these tasks also began to change in form with the introduction of alternatives to custody, such as community service, with its corresponding increased component of punishment over the 'conventional' probation order. Indeed, it can be argued that it was the convenience of the geographical spread of the probation service which led to it assuming responsibility for this area of work (Pease 1981). In addition, the service assumed responsibilities in the prison system. This led to concerns over being identified with the 'sharp end' of the penal ladder from which, in its beginning, the service was intended to be an alternative for those for whom imprisonment was thought inappropriate.

At a policy level, it was considered unconstitutional for the executive to interfere with the independent decisions of the judiciary, who were also the local employers of probation officers. The service then became wedged between central government concerns and the sentencing decisions of judges and magistrates. Administrative problems concerning the place of the service within the criminal justice system were also increasingly resolved by more central control and an increasing organizational hierarchy.

As this chapter shows, the history of the service cannot be characterized as revealing either harmonious beliefs among its members, or a uniform development of its organization. However, members did share one common bond: a missionary and humanitarian approach to the administration of criminal justice. As the service developed and assumed responsibilities in other areas of work, the nature of that work changed. This then raised questions regarding the compatibility of this new work and traditional beliefs of officers. Therefore, the implementation of such changes, given both their rationale and speed, raised problems for the occupational ethos of probation officers. In addition, criticisms of the increasing hierarchy became more frequent as many felt this did not facilitate but rather controlled their work. The organization, it was believed, began to emphasize accountability over officers' autonomy. However, not only was the organization criticized, but also the practice of its members began to be questioned and new types of staff were also being employed.

Few studies had been conducted into probation work during the period this chapter covers, but a proliferation of research began to question the effectiveness of probation work. For the first time in the mid-1970s, the idea of objectives and targets began to be considered as applicable to probation work. The ethos of probation officers – based on the original compromise – had enjoyed a period of enhancement. Yet, it was also peculiarly vulnerable to the ideological whims of governments. While soft determinism had a relatively untroubled development, it was also the buffer between responsibility and doubt concerning the autonomy of individual criminal acts. Now the Victorian philosophy of emphasizing responsibility was to enjoy a new lease of life, and change and conflict was to follow.

2

Change and conflict

Basic to the profession of social work is the recognition of the value and dignity of every human being irrespective of origin, status, sex, age, belief or contribution to society.
(Part of the British Association of Social Work 'Code of Ethics', quoted in D. Mathieson 1987: 459)

The first priority [of the service] should be to ensure that, wherever possible, offenders can be dealt with by non-custodial measures and that standards of supervision are set and maintained at the level required for this prupose.
(Home Office Statement of National Objectives and Priorities 1984: section D, part vi (a))

If the 1960s and 1970s had been a period of rapid change, the 1980s were not to provide a respite. Punishment was increasingly emphasized as a core component of alternatives to custody which, as many in the service believed, was at odds with its traditional function in the criminal justice system. Further, the future of the service remained and still remains uncertain especially with the prospect of privatization on the horizon. Differences of opinion have increasingly emerged within its ranks and it is believed that geographical variations in courts' sentencing practices and an expansion of prison places frustrate its attempts in providing alternatives to custody, even though research demonstrates the ineffectiveness of custodial penalties in preventing crime (Brody 1976).[1] The organization is felt to have become not only more hierarchical, but also bureaucratic – more concerned with monitoring and evaluating its members' work. At the same time, the recent history of criminology charts the apparent demise and ineffectiveness of the rehabilitative ideal: the traditional value underpinning its members' work.

This chapter aims to examine these more recent changes, their rationale and the impact they have had on the service and its staff.

Reflections on change

Davies (1976) posed the question of a 'defensive or developmental' service for the future. He considered the service's commitment to development in the face of change 'true to its heritage'. However, he also noted the effect of these changes on probation staff:

> There is now a feeling in some quarters that the changes affecting probation officers now are so fundamental that they may be undermining the morale of employees who came into the Service to *do one job only to find themselves required to undertake another.*
>
> (Davies 1976: 86, italics added)

The research which Davies quotes also found a variability in job satisfaction among long-serving officers. In particular, officers felt the organization's hierarchy did not value their work, and erosion in their autonomy was too high a price to pay for such recognition (Keynon and Rhodes undated). A popular belief was to consider that there had been an erosion of autonomy as a result of the increased hierarchy. However, Kakabadse and Worrall (1978) found no support for this idea. They did find that a major determinant of staff satisfaction was the quality of support and supervision that an organization gave its members. The probation service appeared to have accommodated to administrative change by developing professional supervision, without any change in the feeling of autonomy amongst its officers. Nevertheless, other criticisms by staff of the organization were not uncommon, mentioned in one study by nearly one-third of respondents (see Mawby 1980).

Fullwood (1978) has noted three changes of importance which have had a profound effect on the organization. First, the increased role of non-professional staff in day centres, community service and other areas. Second, the establishment of a unit at the Home Office, which began to examine the work of the service – a hitherto infrequent phenomenon. Third, there was the 'constant search for answers', which led towards monitoring and targeting of probation officers' work. However, while these changes are important, they cannot be considered in isolation from the environment in which the service found itself. They were a response to external or 'exogenous' conditions: changes in the criminal justice system; thinking on the 'crime problem' and economic, political and cultural changes. In order to understand internal or 'endogenous' changes in the service, it is necessary to examine these external conditions. Thus, 'the societal nature of organizational functioning' (Clegg and Dunkerley 1977: 6) is recognized.

The ethos under question?

Box (1987) acknowledges that the 'lurch into prominence' of the service is difficult to explain, but two considerations deserve attention. First, the proliferation of alternatives to custody, and second, the concept of individualized justice, which required background information on the individual, with the result that

> much of the decision-making in the lower courts soon came to be centred on questions concerning the *type* of person who committed the crime, rather than on questions of guilt or innocence.
>
> (Carlen and Powell 1979; 97, original italics)

The emphasis on one-to-one casework methods with offenders was bolstered by this focus. The method and rationale concentrated on the offender who, it was believed, then became empowered (self-determined) to overcome her or his problems and thus lead a law-abiding way of life. In essence, the ethos of the probation service was based upon this method and, as commentators have noted, adherents needed only to refine their methods and therefore, by default, not question its underlying philosophy (Cohen 1985; McWilliams 1986). Bean (1976) concluded his study on rehabilitation by considering the concept a 'shambles', firmly located within its underpinnings of social pathology and individualization of sentencing. He suggested that the scales of justice had tilted during the development of probation, from the 'all equal and responsible under the law' principle, to a 'welfare model of justice'. In the process, social problems became individualized and welfare professionals were given discretionary powers which themselves led to enormous disparity and injustice outside of the courtroom. This discretion, which was 'the essence of rehabilitation' (Bean 1976: 144), simply led to demands for more discretion in the pursuit of effectiveness.

A radical critique

The development of probation officers' occupational ethos was accompanied by a belief in 'professional service' which several authors shared. For example, Durkheim (1957) was optimistic in his appraisal of the professions, giving them a pivotal role in the transmission of ethical standards. Tawney (1921) considered professions a major force against the rampant individualism of the 'acquisitive society'. Carr-Saunders and Wilson (1933) viewed professions as 'rocks' who stood against crude forces of change threatening peaceful evolution and Marshall (1963) placed the nature of professional service at the centre of his analysis. Greenwood (1957), writing in the journal *Social Work*, drew up a list of professional characteristics against which the professional status of an occupation could be measured. So popular was this idea, the article reappeared in 1962 and 1966 (Noscow and Form 1962; Vollmer and Mills 1966). This tradition was then exemplified by Halmos (1970), who went as far to suggest that should communist societies become more affluent and capitalist ones move towards collectivist provision, they would eventually converge into 'personal service societies'.

Despite this body of literature, the proliferation of research within the fields of the sociology of professions, deviance and criminology, began to question the implicit assumptions of the above approaches and, in particular, the neutrality of professional assessments. Theory and research was now questioning the idea that deviance and crime was the outcome of a value-neutral process. No longer could it be assumed those who worked within the criminal justice system were simply responding to deviant acts, instead they were central to the definition of deviance itself:

> Deviancy is the outcome of a process of judgement and evaluation which distinguishes certain forms of behaviour as rule-breaking and attaches penalties to them. The context in which the rules emerge, are applied, and sanctions are inflicted is all important.
>
> (Rock 1973: 21)

This perspective, although not without its problems, began to undermine the professional self-conception of a neutral response to the assessment procedure.[2] However, the lure of individualization remained a powerful one. In addition, from the point of view of organizational accountability, the very nature of the probation officer's task – diagnosis and counselling – did not seem amenable to standardization due to its reliance on the skills of individual workers and their assessment of the personality of the offender which, by definition, is a unique and non-quantifiable concept. Even so, the increased monitoring of probation officers' work could always be justified by alluding to this widening body of research, which questioned the impartiality of their discretion.

Probation officers had traditionally undertaken a 'Home Office Certificate in Training'. Now university courses proliferated and (as noted in Chapter 1) the Central Council for Education and Training in Social Work (CCETSW) was formed in 1971. While represented, the probation service's control was lessened and the type of probation officers recruited also changed. In the climate of radical opinion from the late 1960s and early 1970s, trainees were then questioning more and accepting less. A group of radical social workers formed the organization 'Case Con' in 1970 and referred to large social service bureaucracies as 'Seebohm factories'. This group concentrated their efforts on areas of conflict and the need for changes in practice:

> One important tool of professional social work has been case-work – a pseudoscience – that blames individual inadequacies for poverty and so mystifies and diverts attention from the real causes – slums, homelessness and economic exploitation.
>
> (Part of the 'Case Con Manifesto' in the Appendix to Bailey and Brake 1975)

Epstein (1970) argued that this radicalism resulted from increased education in social work departments and advocated, along with Rein (1970), that social workers should be formed into an educating elite for social action and political activities. Hardker (1977) found some support for this belief in that younger officers were less 'treatment orientated' than their elder, Home Office trained counterparts, but in actual practice the differences were less apparent. Nevertheless, social workers and probation officers were not considered neutral responders. On the contrary, the political nature of their work, as educators and gatekeepers of scarce resources, was paramount. This political challenge to professional knowledge led to the differentiation of the traditional professional (lawyers, doctors, dentists, accountants) from the personal service worker (a facilitating professional) whose knowledge base 'is manifestly political in nature or which at least has strong political implications' (Bennett and Hokenstad 1973: 40).

The tradition of humanism running through the probation service was seen as incompatible with elite professionalism, with its emphasis on the notions of detachment and objectivity, behind which the professional hides and the client suffers. Such a view was further substantiated by the belief that much crime was either an historically informed response against a repressive system, or an understandable one on the part of those who had little and simply reached out for more (Taylor, Walton and Young 1973, 1975). To concentrate on individual therapy in the belief of 'saving someone' was not the means welfare professionals should then use:

> There is no other road to humanisation – theirs as well as everyone else's – but authentic transformation of the de-humanising structure.
>
> (Pearson 1975a: 176)

Practitioners sought to remedy the gap between such political analysis and action within the realm of social work (Corrigan and Leonard 1978) and probation work (Walker and Beaumont 1981, 1985). Pearson (1975a) argued deviance should be firmly placed in the political realm. In applying this to social work training, he wished recruits to turn their attention to help in 'the world of moral and political discourse' (1975b: 43); 'immature radical movements' may have naively castigated psychological aspects of social work ideology, but skills were required in helping people. In this respect, social work training was confusing and not assisting new recruits. Newly acquired knowledge was directed not to clients, but appropriate audiences, such as managers of the service. In the process, new recruits learn to play a part with the consequence that 'social work education ought to be more appropriately described as socialisation' (Millard 1977: 2). While some authors urged the tempering of political aspects of the critique, practitioners should 'refuse the casework ideology' and incorporate deviancy theory in their practice, but not sell out the client 'for the sake of ideological purity or theoretical neatness' (Cohen 1975: 94–5).

The nature of professional discretion was being questioned, within the occupation, with implications for probation officers. According to the critique, the notion of discretion – which was to come under the scrutiny of the employing organization for different reasons – was founded upon a professional ideology. However, this sphere of discretion also enabled probation officers to ameliorate the worst excesses of an unjust criminal justice system:

the boundaries of probation work are still sufficiently diffuse
and broad for a substantial range of campaigning work to form a
legitimate activity within the probation officer's role.

(Beaumont 1985: 95)

Nevertheless, with the changing nature of the organization and
tasks facing the probation officer, this critical stance became harder
to 'maintain in the face of the exigencies of a pressurised job'
(Fielding undated: 9).

Penal pessimism and a new paradigm

Aside from the above critiques, further external influences on
change within the service were to arise. Due to the emerging body
of research alluding to the ever-present crime problem, governments looked to alternative methods for its control and the probation service was to be the main means for the execution of such a
policy. Organizationally, the service reacted by increasing the
monitoring of its officers' work and the targeting of those offenders
who were at the higher risk (to society) end of offending and,
therefore, at risk of receiving custody. As a result, the professional
optimism of the 1960s gave way to a professional pessimism (Pitts
1988). Radzinowicz, who had believed probation to be the major
development in penal theory and practice, was now considering
how effective it was in relation to the crime problem:

how can you expect an officer, with other duties to attend to
and with something like fifty people under his supervision,
seeing them perhaps once a week to start with, once a fortnight
or less thereafter, to have time to get to know and influence
more than a handful of them, or to make much of real impact
on their outlook and circumstances? Must not 'supervision', in
the sense of knowing what people are doing, keeping them out
of trouble, be largely a fiction?

(Radzinowicz and King 1979: 330)

Probation practice also changed in the face of such criticism. Some
moved to community work, emphasizing the political dimension
of crime control. Bottoms and McWilliams (1979), on the other
hand, suggested 'A Non-Treatment Paradigm for Probation Practice'. They, too, alluded to research which added to a growing body
of opinion on the negligible reformative effects of penal innovations (see Croft 1978).

Bottoms and McWilliams viewed crime as a social and not pathological phenomenon. They believed that the ethos of the service had been based upon a medical model of crime control, which was both empirically and theoretically flawed. Harris (1977) had reacted to this situation by suggesting probation officers should distance themselves from the courts and turn their attention to the disadvantaged sectors of society. Haxby (1978) argued for a community correctional service to overcome these problems. However, both authors were criticized by Bottoms and McWilliams. Harris had confused elements of treatment and help: even though he recognized the importance of the latter, given that many probation clients are from deprived backgrounds. Further, his stress on punishment as a primary element of any order – as opposed to treatment – would require a new non-social work agency with the present structure of the probation service remaining intact:

> Such a proposal can only be described as hopelessly unrealistic politically, quite apart from the obvious potential problems about the relationship between the two agencies.
>
> (Bottoms and McWilliams 1979: 163)

Haxby was also criticized for not fully considering the implications of his suggestions. The aetiology of crime, Haxby believed, should be seen as a mixture of personal pathology and individuals' responses to their environment. Thus, a new probation service, separate from local government, should become involved in the community: 'concerned with the pre-conditions which have such an influence on the incidence of the problem [of crime]' (Haxby 1978: 195). The service, he argued, should have a statutory duty in relation to crime prevention. Yet, the tension between this statutory duty and the functions of 'community protest and involvement' (1978: 232–5) are not considered. In addition, the traditional treatment model remained part of his plans. Therefore, Bottoms and McWilliams argued that the time had come

> for a new paradigm of probation practice which is theoretically rigorous; which takes seriously the exposed limitations of the treatment model; but which seeks to redirect the probation service's traditional aims and values in the new penal and social context.
>
> (Bottoms and McWilliams 1979: 167)

This new paradigm brought the concept of help and not treatment to the forefront of probation practice. Instead of clients being passive recipients of expert assistance, they should act as active agents in their own rehabilitation. In the process, the aim of preventing crime, via community involvement, becomes central, as opposed to a by-product of probation work. However, there is no necessary connection between helping offenders and the reduction of crime. As crime is 'predominantly social . . . any serious crime reduction strategy must be socially (rather than individually) based' (Bottoms and McWilliams 1979: 188). The client is then able to identify those areas which are of importance to her or him and not be told by an all-knowing diagnostic professional what is wrong. This paradigm created

> the opportunity for the potential re-emergence of the probation service's traditional core values rather than their demise. But of course, these values cannot reappear in the same guise as for the nineteenth century police court missionaries: that social context is gone forever.
>
> (Bottoms and McWilliams 1979: 167)

With clients determining their own needs, the professional justification of knowing the best interests of the client was therefore questioned. Choice (for the client) should be maximized and probation officers should cease to believe they have the expertise to treat clients or the authority to compel their attendance.

Bottoms and McWilliams questioned the efficacy of professional distance from the client for the purposes of diagnosis. If probation officers continued to be autonomous from the employing organization, they also had the latitude to ignore diagnostic prescriptions. In this sense, the state and the managers of the service were reliant upon the judgement and discretion of probation officers for the effective implementation of rehabilitation. After all, the basis of their traditional task required a degree of autonomy to define the client needs (diagnosis) and prescribe the cure (treatment): conception and execution were synonymous. However, the questioning of the diagnostic method was not to be based simply on an occupational dimension. The rise of the 'alternatives to custody industry' and the pressures this placed on the ethos of the probation service led to other changes. Political pressure, via the Home Office, was placed on probation areas which, in turn, reacted. It seemed for the probation service's political masters that welfare had failed and punishment was demanded.

Therapy to punishment: challenging the probation consensus

Crime out of control?

The criminal statistics for England and Wales are 'grim and relentless in their ascending monotony': Radzinowicz was commenting in 1959 on the rise in reported crime from half a million to three-quarters of a million offences in the previous decade.[3] During 1988 the police recorded 3,716,000 indictable crimes.[4] The Howard League (1987a) estimate that on current trends this figure would have reached 7,400,000 by the turn of the century and the number of people found guilty in magistrates courts will have nearly doubled to 4,000,000.

Sentencing practices have responded to this increase. During 1986 magistrates committed 44,000 people to prison (including fine defaulters). Geographical variation in the courts' use of custody fluctuate between 8 per cent and 39 per cent for adult males; 4 per cent and 16 per cent for adult females and 4 per cent and 22 per cent for males between 17 and 21.[5] While the government urges the use of custody only as a last resort in 'protecting the public' and a wide range of alternatives to custody already exist, information from the Council of Europe shows the United Kingdom had a prison population of 95 per 100,000 on 1 September 1986 (Collier and Tarling 1987). Of twenty member states only Turkey and Austria had higher prison populations measured on this basis. In England and Wales on 3 July 1987, the highest prison population in history was recorded at 50,969. The National Association for the Care and Resettlement of Offenders (NACRO) calculated a new prison the size of Dartmoor would have to open every three weeks to accommodate a continuing increase on this scale.[6]

The government response

The government's response has been to increase expenditure on the prison service by 34 per cent in real terms since 1979 and nearly double the captial budget. The actual prison building programme seems to vary, but with proposed new prisons and the refurbishment of existing ones, approximately 20,000 new places will have been created by 1995. In addition, from 1979 to 1983 the expenditure on the police force increased by 5 per cent per annum – compared with overall government expenditure at 2 per cent – with, it should be added, little impact on detection rates.[7] The law and order budget increased from £3,179 million in 1980–81 to £5,388 million in 1985–86 (D. King 1987: 122). In real terms the percentage increase in expenditure from the period 1981–82 to 1987–88 was: 22.9 per cent for the police service; 30.8 per cent for the probation service and 23.0 per cent for the prison service.[8]

It is clear the government's commitment to the reduction of public expenditure does not so easily extend to law and order.[9] Willis, admitting this to be somewhat cynical, notes:

> Although there are no votes in prison, I suspect there are votes to be won by endorsing crime-control strategies which would send ever-increasing numbers there.
>
> (Willis 1986a: 23)

The evidence from a survey conducted before the polls closed in the 1979 election substantiates Willis's assertion: of those whose allegiance changed in the Tories' favour, 23 per cent had done so on their law-and-order platform (Downes 1983: 2). With a perceived breakdown in the post-war consensus on the management of the economy (through Keynesian economic principles) the economy has been given a free-market rein to find its natural level. At the same time, this has led to the exploitation of:

> popular ideologies: the moralism endemic in conservative philosophies . . . traditional and uncorrected common sense is a massively conservative force, penetrated thoroughly – as it has been – by religious notions of Good and Evil, by fixed conceptions of the unchanging and unchangeable character of human nature, and by ideas of retributive justice.
>
> (S. Hall 1980: 177–8)

What Hall (1979) calls this 'authoritarian populism' began before the Conservatives came to power in 1979. However, he argues, the government has not only rejuvenated, but also added considerably to its popularity. It combines, as he notes, 'organic Toryism', with its emphasis on nation, standards, authority and discipline, with the self-interest and anti-statism of neo-liberalism. While these elements appear contradictory, this is the very essence of authoritarian populism. People's fear of rising crime is real enough, but the answer has been to increase the law-and-order industry and sentencing practices have become more retributive. The acquisitive individualism of the market; increasing unemployment; homelessness and a social security system increasingly under strain, are seen as unconnected with rising crime. As a result a paradox arises:

That paradox is the ease with which the law can be subverted
to counterfeit justice and wrenched into the shape required by
'order'. . . . The order that results is a regimented and repressive variety, not what people have in mind when they
demand law and order.

(Downes 1983: 31)

In this process, riots become the illegitimate expression of a deviant
population, not that of politically and economically marginalized
groups. Strikes are motivated by the 'enemy within', rather than
the understandable means through which people can attempt to
exercise more control over their lives. Crime? That is directly
connected with individual responsibility: 'There is no such thing as
society. There are individual men and women and there are fam-
ilies' (Margaret Thatcher 1 November 1987, as reported in 'Sayings
of the Decade', *The Observer*, 30 April 1989). The link between
social and economic conditions and crime is thus irrelevant to a
morality which views right and wrong in terms of personal responsibility – regardless of the circumstances in which individuals find
themselves.

The above also affects the legal system:

By abstracting crime from its social context, by abstracting
individuals from their collectivities, by abstracting the administration of criminal justice from the wider field of political struggle, the justice model thus inextricably allies itself
with the use of the legal system as an important part of the
apparatuses of repression.

(Hudson 1987: 166)

However, this is *not* to excuse crime, nor celebrate it. In reviewing
nearly fifty research projects on the link between recession and
crime, Box draws two conclusions. First, that 'the relationship
between overall unemployment and crime is inconsistent', and
second, that inequality of income is 'strongly related to crime'
(1987: 96). One lesson which can be learned from this extensive
survey, is that politicians cannot afford to ignore the inequality of
income distribution, or the 'unfair burden of unemployment'
(1987: 97) in strategies to reduce crime. Criminal activity can, Box
argues, 'be altered by paying attention to the social and economic
conditions which contribute to it' (1987: 97).

Superficially it would appear that the traditional image of the
probation service aligns itself with such beliefs; although by dif-

ferent means. By concentrating on individual pathology, the 'science of diagnosis' seems to give this ideology its justification. However, not only is this a gross simplification, but also it is not mirrored in the practice of probation officers, or the ethos of the service (Raynor 1985; Willis 1986b). The philosophy emphasizes 'justice through punishment'; the tradition, 'rehabilitation through therapy'. The means and ends are incompatible and ideologically opposed. Even so, these changes in the service's environment were to lead to considerable organizational change.

Probation in a volatile climate

Probation management (assistant chief probation officers (ACPO) and above) are increasingly criticized by probation officers for the lack of any social work input into policy initiatives. It appears that they are reacting to Home Office directives which, with increasing central control and the use of probation inspectors, are difficult to resist. For example, the Treen Probation Service Annual Report (1986/7) states that a probation or community service order

> must protect the public as effectively as a prison sentence by seeking to ensure no offences are committed during the period of such an order.

The National Association of Probation Officers (NAPO), on the other hand, in a paper entitled 'The provision of alternatives to custody and the use of the probation order', noted that supervision should not be based on surveillance, containment or deterrence:

> For the probation service to attempt to impose such control on individual offenders would involve an unacceptable change in the principles and ethos of our work.
>
> (NAPO 1981: 8)

The reaction of the service to the changes in its climate, appears to have created considerable internal differences of opinion over the conception of the task. Authors refer to 'cynicism' and 'alienation' among those at the front line of the organization looking up towards management who, under pressure to create an economic organization, are considered at odds with its social work base (Boswell and Worthington 1988). Others speak of a centralization of power as an advantage in the survival of the service during the 1980s but which, at the same time, also makes it more vulnerable to Home Office dictats (Vanstone 1988). Thus, increasingly, the charge of dysfunctional bureaucracy is made, with the underlying philosophy of probation being seen as 'unclear and diffuse' (Vanstone and Seymour 1986). Organizational change results in conflict:

> management are insidiously re-defining the aims of the organisation and so further harnessing the energies of the professional to bureaucratic needs.
>
> (Hankinson and Stephens 1986: 18)

While Hankinson and Stephen's article did not question the substantive as opposed to bureaucratic aspects of accountability, it was indicative of tensions between organizational change and occupational practice. Nevertheless, these concerns were not new. For instance, the Butterworth Inquiry (Home Office 1972) – examining the work and pay of probation officers and social workers – found probation officers, who emphasized casework, were suspicious of senior officers and assistant principals, whose tasks were predominantly administrative in nature. What was new about these changes was both the form they took and the way in which they were enacted.

Accounting for organizational changes

In the 1970s organizational changes were thought by some to be necessary given the changes in the nature and tasks of the serivce. A new structure was required:

> What we had was piece-meal <u>diversification</u> without any significant changes in the organisational structure and the way it exacts its accountability. . . . How can officers get out of the trap of individual accountability for individual cases in order to be responsive organisationally.
>
> (Read 1978: 1, original underlining)

Teamwork became the means for overcoming the perceived lack of organizational effectiveness. Such change was believed to provide a liberal ground between radical left attacks and the justice model of the ascending New Right (Millard and Read 1978: iii). This resulted from three factors in particular. First, the impact of radical criminology; second, a measured decline in probation effectiveness; and third, a classic practice text which urged an examination of individuals' problems in terms of their social situation (i.e. interactionally) as opposed to individualizing the problem *per se* (see Millard and Read 1978). This change in working practices meant a

movement away from the individual probation officer/client interaction, to viewing her or him as part of a team. In so doing, the
team shared a common goal and an organizational consensus is
derived which, correspondingly, turns questions of accountability
into those of means, not ends. However, Gwyneth Boswell found
that the probation service was characterized by 'highly autonomous members' whose goals conflicted not only with each other,
but also with 'powerful sections of the criminal justice system
about means, ends and philosophy'. Even so, in her study officers
survived 'functioning quite effectively by pragmatic criteria'
(Boswell 1982: 60).

Therefore, to manage the service in the contemporary climate is,
to say the least, problematic. The Home Office *Report of the
Working Party on Management Structure in the Probation and
After-Care Service* (1980) noted six purposes of management. These
included the formulation of policy, the setting of objectives, the
motivation of staff and measurement of performance against plans
(Home Office 1980: 9). Generally at the organizational or what may
be termed the mezzo layer (Harris and Webb 1987), two problems
result for management in the execution of these tasks. First, an
historical component whereby

> the development of a hierarchy of ranks has led to reduced
> <u>organisational</u> status for the probation officer. This in turn has
> led to a reduction of the <u>perceived value of the work</u> which
> they do.
>
> (McWilliams 1980: 9, original underlining)

Second, the degree of autonomy which probation officers were
believed traditionally to possess leads to conflict over threats to
this discretion. Thus, the implementors and policy-makers may
not inhabit common consensual ground. In fact, the Home Office
Working Party (1980) alluded to this problem:

> It seems to us almost inevitable that in a service which has
> evolved from a simple and entirely individual intuitive basis of
> working to a complex sophisticated operation in a very short
> space of time, feelings will arise about the curtailment of
> initiative.
>
> (Home Office 1980: 25)

To attempt to overcome this conflict, effective leadership must be
in common with the 'occupational culture' (Schein 1985). Despite
having this in mind and noting the need for participation in

decision-making and a two-way flow of information, the Home Office Report (1980) was itself characterized by disharmony. A minority report was produced which was said to be 'nearer to NAPO activist thinking'.[10] This report dissented from nine of the twenty-two recommendations, believing line management to be 'obstructive' and 'against meaningful communication'. The answer to administrative problems lay, its authors believed, in smaller units servicing courts, with the implementation of a maingrade (career) officer grade, in opposition to the increasing hierarchy.

Central control and local autonomy in conflict

The Conservative position on punishment, ironic given its commitment to minimal state activity, leads to an increased centralization of the state's penal activities (Christie 1982). Home Office Circulars, Statute and Probation Rules have become the means for implementing the resulting alternatives to custody industry. Given the autonomy of local probation committees, which are statutory bodies in their own right, most of the directions have been aimed at full-time professional personnel, in particular, the chief probation officer (CPO). The duties of the person holding this post are not defined by Statute. However, the appointment of this person must be approved by the Secretary of State (Probation Rules 1984: r. 28) and she or he is accountable to the Probation Committee and 'responsible for the direction of the probation service in the area, for its effective operation and *the efficient use of its resources*' (Probation Rules 1984: r. 30, italics added). Therefore, it is not surprising to find CPOs in the difficult position of implementing government policy, being accountable to the local Probation Committee and balancing this against the traditional culture of members of their service.

In addition to the above considerations, the constraints within which CPOs operate, as well as the criminal justice system and social work in general, are considered to be politically bounded and politics cannot therefore be ignored (M. Day 1987). As a result

> the probation service cannot wholly escape from political controversy, debate and conflict, because its work is constantly under political review in an era when 'law and order' is a major topic of public concern.
>
> (Jordan 1984: 129)

In this position, the service has been 'at more crossroads than the average long distance lorry driver encounters in a lifetime' (Harris 1989: 57). Such rapid changes add to CPOs' difficulties in managing their staff. Staff may then identify management with their political masters. Thus, during one probation team meeting I attended, a probation officer remarked: 'The Home Office are creating Chiefs in their own image more successfully than God on Man!'

While CPOs may be hemmed in the middle, short of stricter sentencing guidelines, the probation service is also the only body in a position to influence sentencing policy and moderate what has been referred to as the most 'vindictive penal system in Western Europe' (Willis 1986a: 30). It is not without its significance, therefore, that under the Criminal Justice Act 1982 (CJA 1982) the 'Probation and After-Care Service' reverted to the 'Probation Service'. This Act also amended the provision of the Powers of Criminal Courts Act 1973 for day training centres by the introduction of day centres (1973 Sec. 2. 4A and 4B as amended by Sch. 11 of CJA 1982). This enabled courts to include in a probation order a requirement for the offender to participate in or refrain from certain activities and/or attend specified places for specified activities up to a maximum of sixty days. Under Section 4A(1)(b) it is also possible for a court to include so-called negative requirements, i.e. for offenders to refrain from certain activities. Not surprisingly, this is a contentious issue given the implied degree of control over offenders' behaviour that officers would then have to exercise.

This particular alternative to custody is, on the optimistic side, enabling offenders to comply with the conditions of their order and avoid 'breach', as well as influencing magistrates 'to impose fewer fines on those without adequate means' (A. Wright 1984: 1). On the negative side, the humanitarian traditions of the probation service were believed to be under attack by such measures (Vanstone 1985). These measures also, according to some authors, blur the distinction between prison and the community (T. Mathieson 1983; Cohen 1985).

In terms of its implementation the 1982 Act required probation committees either to provide or approve day centres before such a requirement can be part of a probation order. Thus, those probation areas with punitive courts upon whom little impression was made in their custodial disposal rates, should be offered more credible alternatives to custody. After all, what service would not provide such a facility if magistrates are reluctant to issue probation or community service orders as alternatives to custody? Such thinking has led to innovations, such as the Kent Control Unit, containing high components of control over offenders and subsequent criticism from within the service itself.[11] This 'controltalk' (Cohen 1985) of credibility to magistrates is associated with both a control and training element. As the 1982 Act (and now the Criminal Justice Act 1988) includes the criterion for a custodial disposal as the 'protection of the public', a credible alternative must, to be effective, include a control element.

The consequence of these moves is not the intended reduction in the prison population (see Bottoms 1987). Instead, requirements in probation orders have become 'alternatives to alternatives', with the result that an increasing number of people fall within the realm of the formal mechanisms of social control. At the level of practice, this has its consequences (see Walker and Beaumont 1985). If the strategy were successful, as it can be in some areas (see Raynor 1988), then this also has its effects. The types of clients that probation officers work with may change (more serious offences); the expectations of courts change (in relation to control) and these factors, in turn, have an effect on the type of work probation staff can perform, for example in their attempts to balance the elements of rehabilitation and control in working with offenders.

Organizationally this also has its consequences. Probation staff at the front line, given their traditional humanitarian predispositions, may identify with the client in the face of such a punitive climate. Indeed, some would argue that concentrating on offender needs rather than their control is in the spirit of the social work tradition (Raynor 1984). As Harris (1977) has suggested, probation officers due to their social work training could ignore conditions, externally imposed, which they perceive as damaging to the client. Therefore, to whom are probation officers and their non-CQSW counterparts (ancillaries) then accountable? The courts (who make the disposal), the organization, as identified by probation management (who are seen as colluding with the punitive climate and over-bureaucratizing the service in response to Home Office pressure to implement changes) or their occupational ethos (either exemplified by the peer group or as norms inculcated during the training period)? The result may drive a wedge between front-line staff's formal and substantive accountability to both the courts and the organization. Further, these issues are compounded by the Barclay Report (1982), which urged more use of community work to mobilize resources in the solution of social problems. Thus, this is another potential catalyst to further divisions within social work:

between those who emphasize either a community-based or traditional one-to-one casework approach to individuals' problems.

Lynch (1976) identified some of the above problems. In particular, those between the organization and front-line service deliverers. Three-quarters of those whom he interviewed said they operated outside the framework of the employing organization, finding it an 'impediment to professional service delivery'. The potential for conflict between the values of probation officers and those of the organization have also been highlighted by Millard (1977). This conflict has an organizational effect:

> Any organisation's goals are implemented by front-line staff, be they doctors, car-assembly workers or local government officials, and, in terms of organisational design, we neglect them at our peril.
>
> (D. Cooper 1982: 53)

Anomalies also result. In the face of increasing client problems, those at the front line may resort to innovative solutions. However, as bureaucratic and centralized elements of the organization increase, these may be met by the 'understandable caution of the hierarchy' (Millard 1977: 3).

These tensions seem to increase as the element of punishment in alternatives to custody has become more pronounced. Bill McWilliams (1987) identified three schools of thought within the probation service: the 'radical', 'managerial' and 'personalist', each characterized by its own beliefs. In the past, the service was characterized by a 'professional-supervisory-administrative model of organisation' (McWilliams 1987: 106). The conception and execution of the task was in the hands of the front-line worker. Yet the new managerial style, as exemplified in the Home Office Report (1980), impinges on one part of this equation: its conception. While probation officers believe they are in a process of de-skilling and their autonomy eroded, *vis-à-vis* the organization, this is not unconnected with the rise of the justice model of punishment:

> recent developments in rethinking probation have made the professionalization effort even more problematic. In particular, some view the justice model as a threat to professionalization. Inasmuch as justice model initiatives seek limitations on probation officers discretion, this suspicion is understandable.
>
> (Thomson 1987: 110)

The justice model requires more of an element of control than care. It could be argued, given that it emphasizes administration rather than diagnostic capabilities, that it could be as effectively implemented by non-probation officers. Policy changes inspired by this model also then have an effect on relations between staff in the service. For example, take the case of community service in which 47 per cent (679) of ancillaries and only 5 per cent (274) of probation officers are employed. The uneasy tension between the philosophy of community service and a traditional probation ethos has allegedly created an 'under-class of workers' within the organization. The effect has been to establish 'two Services in one' (Vass 1988: 49). In practice this is exacerbated by having to deal with day-to-day pressures which arise from dealing with offenders' needs, as well as implementing Home Office directed agency goals (Vass 1984). Ancillary workers may, therefore, feel under-valued by the agency and their front-line counterparts – the probation officers – even though it is believed that ancillaries are 'crucial to the future development of the Service' (Findlater 1982: 46).

This organizational and occupational conflict was exacerbated by the introduction of further policy changes. For the first time in its history, the Home Office (1984) issued a *Statement of National Objectives and Priorities* (SNOP) for the service.

A Statement of National Objectives

The autonomy of local probation committees from central government control was considered a strength. However, as noted, the implementation of the justice model also requires more centralized state activity. There is now an emphasis on a cost-efficient probation service for which CPOs are deemed responsible under the 1984 Probation Rules.

SNOP referred to the efficient and effective use of resources as the responsibility of both the area Probation Committees and their CPOs, allegedly because they can best assess local needs and design programmes to meet these. However, despite these allusions to local autonomy, such programmes should also 'reflect consistent principles which *cannot just be determined locally*' (Home Office 1984: para. 2, italics added).

Leaving aside the understandable retort that such criteria may more effectively be applied to the regional variations in courts' sentencing practices, three points appear to arise from SNOP. First, to provide national objectives to local services indicated a hitherto unprecedented acknowledgement of Home Office involvement in local policy initiatives. Second, the emphasis on efficiency and effectiveness (deriving from the government's Financial Management Initiative (FMI) in 1982) was thought to be applicable to agencies in the criminal justice system, which also included the police (see Horton and Smith 1988). Third, a change in how finances were to be perceived within the organization. This last point required a change in the organization's way of working which has an effect at a practice level. As Rob Mawby notes of probation officers:

> economic-type problems are more pertinent with regard to the client's experience of the social and economic system, rather than in terms of what the Probation Service can and should provide.
>
> (1980: 277)

In the past, the economics of the organization as a whole were not at the forefront of probation practice. The application of supply-side economics to the public sector was to have a considerable impact on the service. In addition, SNOP prioritized the diversion of offenders from custody. If necessary, cash-limited budgets should be diverted and allocated from important areas to the following priorities. First, the provision of alternatives to custody. Second, the preparation of social inquiry reports (to divert offenders from custody). Third – rather ambiguously – 'sufficient resources to through-care in order that minimum statutory obligations are fulfilled'. Fourth, 'appropriate and effective contributions to work in the wider community' (supporting victims; liaising with other agencies; prevention of crime and taking account of wider social influences on offending) and finally, resources to civil work should be 'consistent with local circumstances and the foregoing priorities' (Home Office 1984: para. vi). On this last point, the Statement refers to the duties of the service and yet adds: 'The Service also has duties arising from the civil jurisdiction of the courts' (1984: para. iii). Thus, the important civil work performed by probation officers – leaving aside the question of whether or not the service should be involved in this area – was, along with through-care, accorded a low priority.

Lloyd (1986) analysed forty-five probation area responses to SNOP. He uncovered a variety of local policy reactions in the form of 'Statements of Local Objectives and Priorities' (SLOP): 'the most notable feature of the local statements of objectives and priorities is their great diversity' (Lloyd 1986: 1). This he attributed to three factors. First, the nature of probation areas: whether they were rural or urban; had low or high unemployment; the degree of union influence over local policy and the identity of the authors (some were chief probation officers and two in his sample were Probation Committees). Further, of the forty-five local responses he examined, twenty-nine did not make any initial mention of SNOP. Second, the fact that the nature of SNOP itself was open to a range of interpretations. Third, some of the local statements were not 'final responses'. However, while these variations existed, Lloyd concluded that it was a difference in philosophy that was a fundamental explanatory factor:

> conflicts between Home Office/Government and Service principles seem to underly most of the disagreements between SNOP and local areas cited under different sections.
>
> (Lloyd 1986: 72)

In relation to SNOP according a low priority to civil work, he noted that the area of 'out-of-court conciliation' was cost-effective and may also considerably reduce the stress involved in legal proceedings. Nevertheless, despite SNOP, most areas in his study were still committed to developing their civil work service (Lloyd 1986: 49); although he concluded that there was pressure on local areas to cease its development (1986: 55). In addition, SNOP (Home Office 1984: para vi. (c)) appeared to ignore seconded probation work in prisons when examining through-care and, it was widely believed, after-care was 'under threat' (Lloyd 1986: ch. 3) which, in terms of the emphasis on crime prevention, seems somewhat incongruous.

The content analysis of local statements, as Lloyd himself conceded, is about 'what is said', not 'what is done'. Even so, it is another indicator of conflict which characterized the service in the 1980s. Similarly the increased attempts by the Home Office to bypass the magistracy in pursuing control of full-time probation management, were apparent by the lack of references to Probation Committees: a point not lost in the response to SNOP by the Association of Chief Officers of Probation (ACOP):

> The organisation of the service is deliberately localised. One of the major requirements of the Service is that it engages responsibly and differentially with local committees ... We believe that there is a danger that these important aspects of

the work of the Service could be damaged by the process of which the National Statement of Purpose and Objectives will be a part.

(ACOP 1983: para. 2.8)

In retrospect, the introductory letter to SNOP from the Home Office to area chief officers appeared optimistic and out of touch with the reality of conflict within the service. The document, it said, was one 'which we believe will command a large measure of support'. Despite this, the Statement did achieve an internal consideration of the aims of the service. As such, the past reliance on the discretion of front-line officers to implement varied and sometimes unstated organizational goals seemed no longer applicable in this new climate. Part of the answer to the resulting organizational problems was considered not to lie in probation management pursuing Home Office led objectives, but the advancement of leadership which expressed probation 'values' (Morrison 1984: 110).

The economics of the 'new realism'

The Financial Management Initiative, led by one of the Prime Minister's first appointments, Sir Derek (now Lord) Rayner, Chairman of Marks and Spencer, also led to organizational change. Economy, efficiency and effectiveness became important aims of the Civil Service; the high-street mentality was thought applicable to the public sector. This came to the service early in 1986 in the form of management consultants Deloitte, Haskins and Sells. They were appointed to advise and produce a Financial Management Information System for the service and their terms of reference were

to advise on the requirements of a financial management information system for the efficient, effective and economical use of their resources, and, in particular, to devise and apply a cost-effective means of getting the necessary information.

(quoted in Crawforth 1987: 58)

Information-gathering then increased. Now, most research within the probation service is concerned with the monitoring and evaluation of front-line work, with the result that probation management is often viewed with scepticism by those whose effectiveness they seek to evaluate. Further, there are criticisms of an overemphasis on the quantitative as opposed to qualitative aspects of probation work (McWilliams 1989). Workload measurement, while acknowledged to be possible, is often 'imprecise' and 'inaccurate' (Orme 1988). 'Risk of custody scales' are said to offer probation officers an addition to their professional armoury, as a means of predicting an offender's likelihood of receiving a custodial sentence and subsequently 'diverting' her or him (Bale 1988). On the other hand, some see this as an impediment to practice and that the only instrument capable of making this judgement is the individual practitioner (MacLeod 1988).

All this led to a science of management approach to the service. Questions of measurement and administration of change predominate over those of purpose and value (McWilliams 1986). Historically, probation officers were believed to possess a sense of purpose. With values increasingly undermined, administrative solutions are said to have no solid foundation upon which to justify change. Yet there has been a move towards management by objectives – again, not without disagreement (see Parry-Khan 1988; Coker 1988). However, the Criminal Justice Act 1982, SNOP and FMI were by no means the end of externally imposed changes to which probation management, in various ways, were to react. A boost to the FMI and quantitative measurement of the performance of probation work came from the Grimsey Report (Home Office 1987), which recommended 'efficiency and effectiveness' inspections. In addition, the Audit Commission (1989) recommended targeting activities 'more effectively'; the 'training of staff to meet new responsibilities'; 'the clarification of lines of accountability' and 'strengthening the management of the Service'. NAPO responded by 'rejecting the Commissons' criticisms' (*NAPO News* May/June 1989).

'Fresh Start', following Home Office research by Jepson and Elliott (1985), also encouraged greater use of prison officers in the provision of welfare within institutions, which added to the arguments within NAPO to withdraw seconded probation officers from prisons, believed to be an inappropriate role for a community service (see NAPO 1987). The Home Office Circular, *Social Inquiry Reports* (1986), was also symptomatic of the increasing trend of directing local policy from the centre. This set the nature and bounds of 'good professional practice' by discussion and recommendations which concerned the nature, purpose, structure and content of social inquiry reports. This increased the pressure on the probation service to provide 'better' information to courts, so they may consider the full range of disposals available when sentencing an offender. Subsequently, conflict developed over the preparation of reports in not-guilty pleas and 'response to supervision' reports which, NAPO claimed, would mean offenders are sentenced without a social inquiry report (*NAPO Newsletter*, December 1987). NAPO members were then balloted on industrial action, which was narrowly defeated. This prompted the Assistant Under-Secretary of State, who in the 1970s was in charge of one of the Home Office probation service divisions, to note: 'The fuss over Social Inquiry Reports in not-guilty pleas seemed to be carrying on from precisely the point I left it in 1978' (Head 1988: 2).

In the face of such rapid policy developments, groups representing the probation service also published their own policy documents. Heightening this 'politics of penality' was the publication of *Probation – The Next Five Years* (ACOP/CCPC/NAPO 1987). This was probably the first coherent statement of national policy following SNOP to come from the probation service. Published jointly by the Association of Chief Officers of Probation (ACOP), the Central Council of Probation Committees (CCPC) and NAPO, it reaffirmed priorities to those areas where SNOP had accorded a low priority: civil work and through-care. Increased community involvement and use of non-custodial options, improved service to the criminal and civil courts and to through-care were, broadly, the issues covered. Therefore, the document appeared to offer a unity of purpose in the face of Home Office and government led change:

> It is important that developments build upon the established strengths of the probation service, utilise the skills of its professionals and other fieldwork staff and work with the grain of the service. Any other approach risks disorientation, dislocation and inefficiency.
>
> (ACOP/CCPC/NAPO 1987: 3)

The document alluded to the reduced costs involved in alternatives to custody (the average cost of prison, at the time, being £246 per week, community service £12 and a probation order £14), so a 'fiscal conservative' emphasis was used in the service's favour. However, the consensus of values of the three bodies who were its authors was questioned. By not fully addressing the issue of value conflict, the document was said to add to divisions of opinion. Thus, commentators have called for an 'examination of these issues and a commitment to the furtherance of debate' (Rumgay 1988: 201). Yet the speed of change was to prevent such pro-active work and in anticipation of the government's Green Paper *Punishment, Custody and the Community* (Home Office 1988b), ACOP broke ranks and published a paper 'More demanding than prison' (ACOP 1988). In response NAPO stated:

> There had been no prior consultation with either NAPO or Central Council and no warning had been given that ACOP planned to embark on such a controversial course.
>
> (*NAPO News* July 1988: 2)

The allusion to the thinking of fiscal conservatives was also apparent in ACOP's paper. It spoke of 'substantial savings' available from its proposed measures (ACOP 1988: 2). However, its purpose was 'not primarily about costs', but to reduce the 'dependency on carceral thinking as the sentencing baseline in the Criminal Justice System' (ACOP 1988: 2). The individualization of sentencing is reaffirmed (ACOP 1988: 4, para. 7) as is the need for sentencing guidelines to reduce the net-widening effect of the new sentence suggested – the Community Restitution Order. The offenders who would be targeted for this sentence

> may be of limited intelligence, have emotional problems, poor attitudes towards authority, multiple practical problems, an inability to learn from previous mistakes, and a distinct tendency to give up and act deliquently when they feel unable to cope.
>
> (ACOP 1988: para. 23)

The trend in atheoretical criminology does little to counter such thinking, providing instead the research upon which it is based. However, one may add to ACOP's description of its targeted group: 'or have no jobs; live in poverty or are members of de-legitimated minorities' (the paper recognizing, at least, the 'meagre sources of income' of many offenders when in debt to courts: ACOP 1988: para. 26). How far our thinking has come in the last hundred years.

ACOP may reply that the speed in which proposals had to be made necessitated bypassing protracted discussions with other interested parties. The government had announced its intentions of presenting the 1988 Green Paper earlier in the year at approximately the same time that it published *National Standards for Community Service Orders* (Home Office 1988a). This document was another manifestation of increased central control and spoke of a need to increase the 'confidence of courts in the Community

Service Order'. This was to be achieved by 'ensuring that CS makes uniformly stiff demands on offenders' (Home Office 1988a: para. 3). Despite a second draft in May of the same year – following a detailed reply by NAPO to the first – NAPO still felt that the courts would be 'inundated with breaches' which would, in turn, 'weaken confidence in the scheme' and increase the use of custody (*NAPO Newsletter* July 1988: 1). It was not long after the publication of the *National Standards for Community Service* (implemented on 1 April 1989) that the Green Paper was published.

Popular penal discourse

Popular penal discourse is dominated by a belief that the increase in violent crime is due to a softening of discipline, itself symptomatic of a breakdown of traditional values. Now, efforts are to be concentrated against violent crime, whereas non-violent offenders can be dealt with in the community by an emphasis on punishment. Prisons are seen as 'colleges of crime' (Hurd 1988: 10), but its alternative should not be a soft option. The vandal, for instance, should be doing

> demanding work. Clearing up his neighbourhood. Scrubbing those graffitti off the walls, putting right the damage he has caused. That's what we want to see.
>
> (The Home Secretary Douglas Hurd addressing the Conservative Party Conference on 12 October 1988)

The Green Paper *Punishment, Custody and the Community* outlines three principles of alternatives to custody where a fine alone, given the seriousness of the offence, would be inadequate. First, restrictions on freedom, in order to punish the offender; second, action to reduce recidivism; and third, 'reparation to the community and, where possible, compensation to the victim' (Home Office 1988b: para. 1.5). The Green Paper acknowledges the 'ineffectiveness' and 'inappropriateness', in many cases, of custodial sentences in achieving these objectives. As such, they can 'often best be met by supervising and punishing the offender in the community' (para. 1.6). A 'new realism' finds its mark in its underlying philosophy:

> We must get away from the notion that the only punishment which counts is sending someone to prison. Indeed, the figures suggest that in terms of re-offending, sending young offenders

into custody earlier than really necessary may harden their tendency towards crime. For many offenders a demanding sentence, carried out in the community, may be more effective in turning them from crime. For some, punishment in the community may be better than punishment in prison.

(John Patten, Minister of State, Home Office, 28 December 1987, quoted in the NACRO Annual Report 1988: 3)

No doubt anticipating the antagonistic response from the probation service, the final part of the Green Paper mentions the possibility of a 'new organization' to administer punishment in the community (Home Office 1988b: part iv). A reference probably aimed at encouraging the probation service to align itself with this new realism. However, the basic question of how to replace existing custodial disposals with non-custodial disposals remained unexamined. In the conclusion to their response to the Green Paper, NACRO stated

It would be futile and potentially counter-productive to introduce more intensive non-custodial options without a clear and comprehensive strategy to ensure that they are used instead of custody.

(NACRO 1988: para. 57)

The Green Paper does not achieve this, instead alluding to ninety-day day centre orders as opposed to the existing sixty days (Home Office 1988b: 3.16); the restriction of offenders' liberty through 'tracking' (offenders reporting to stipulated people at regular intervals to monitor their behaviour: para 3.17); courts being empowered to order offenders to stay at home (para 3.19); the possibility of the fitting of electronic tags to offenders to monitor their movements and restrict their liberty (para. 3.22) – introduced as a pilot scheme in Nottingham, August 1989 – and a new supervision and restriction order (para. 3.27), to mention but a few of the proposals. In particular, young adults were to be targeted. This position was reiterated in the paper issued by the Home Office in August 1988: *Tackling Offending: An Action Plan* (Home Office 1988c). Existing orders were to be 'strengthened' and their implementation was to be 'effective'. It is not surprising to find NAPO then declaring a 'United opposition to punishment plans' (*NAPO News*, November 1988). This reaction culminated with a rally of Parliament (on 23 November 1988) attended by over 1,000 NAPO members.

Discussion

These policy developments have created a substantial change in the role and tasks of the probation service. The foundation upon which the organization or occupation can accommodate to new externally imposed duties is important in terms of such changes. However, with a decline in the rehabilitative ideal and a hostile political climate, the legitimacy of this foundation appears undermined. The proposals emphasizing punishment were not new. For example, the Younger Report on the Penal System (Home Office 1974) suggested strengthening probation orders.[12] While these changes were not implemented, the political, ideological and economic climate in which these discourses take place has changed. This renders the arguments of the probation service increasingly weak in an environment peculiarly hostile to its ethos.

The organizational reaction has been to centralize its structure and move towards bureaucratic elements of organization, in order to set objectives and evaluate effectiveness in the face of political pressure from the government and Home Office. These changes appear to align themselves with Mintzberg's (1979) original hypothesis that organizations will centralize in the face of hostility. The organization's response is then important: 'it must respond quickly and in an integrated fashion'. In the process it may turn 'to its leader for directions' (Mintzberg 1983: 141). Yet, as noted, probation management have been accused of attempting to control the work of front-line personnel in the pursuit of organizational effectiveness: management for control, rather than leadership for direction. It appears that there is not the necessary congruence between the beliefs of the front-line personnel and their management to follow Mintzberg's suggestions. The head, to use a popular metaphor, is considered to be separate from the heart. Intra-organizational conflict has arisen, heated by a search for a floundering purpose in a climate where public sector organizations are increasingly controlled by centralized administration.

Even the economic argument concerning alternatives to custody does not appear sufficient. Official concern is expressed over the conviction with which the element of punishment (in non-custodial disposals) would be implemented by the service. Grafting punishment on to an organization with a humanitarian tradition is not then enough:

The humanity of community corrections is thus its Achilles' heel, precisely the feature most likely to alienate (fiscal) conservations.

(Scull 1983: 158)

As this debate continues, with, it should be added, no sign of a change in policy, our prisons are overcrowded and more people are the subject of non-custodial disposals. The probation service finds itself in the position of trying to alter the sentencing patterns of courts through the use of credible alternatives. This credibility, however, must be based on an element of punishment at odds with its tradition. Tensions develop as the expectation of public policy falls on the probation service to alter such practices. Management react, but in so doing conflicts arises.

The dynamics of the changes outlined in this chapter now need to be examined in terms of Treen's responses, its subsequent policy changes and the reactions of staff to these and the process of policy-making itself.

For heuristic purposes, the changes outlined in this chapter are now summarized.

Level of Change	
	Environment
'Macro'	Changes in criminal justice system; dependent on political, economic and ideological climate which guides the perception of the 'crime problem'.
	Alternatives to custody, implemented by the Home Office, via Rules, Statute and Probation Inspections; FMI emphasizes 'economy, efficiency and effectiveness'.
	Organization
'Mezzo'	A 'new managerialism' implementing policy and objectives and monitoring, evaluating and targeting the work of front-line personnel.
	Interactive
'Micro'	Changes in the nature of personnel (more 'non-professional' staff); accountability emphasized over autonomy; types of clients alter, creating tensions between personnel and affecting working practices with clients.

PART II

Policy and practice

3

Implementing policy change

A welfare ideology which is imposed by government inevitably creates greater problems than a welfare ideology sustained by a professional group and legitimated by government.
(Adler and Asquith 1981: 29)

It cannot be too strongly emphasised that the communication of ideas is a two-way process.
(Home Office 1980: 30)

Accountability within an organization may be secured by several means. However, its success, like that of efficiency and effectiveness, is dependent on the degree of coherence between management and front-line perspectives on the goals of the organization. Further, the achievement of accountability is clearly assisted by the nature of the task performed. A highly visible, standardized task in a predictable environment is more amenable to organizational accountability, than one which is variable and dependent for its conception and execution on the discretion of organizational officials, performing differing and situationally demanding tasks. The mass production factory line is, therefore, fundamentally different from a human service organization; this point can often be forgotten when such an organization is undergoing rapid change.

This chapter is concerned with the beliefs and actions of different members of the probation service in relation to certain policy changes. It charts a major policy initiative that, in Treen, can be traced back to 1974 and eventually produced an objectives booklet in 1985; a process which then enjoyed a new lease of life during the course of this research. This is achieved by examining the ways in which changes in policy were interpreted by the service and the reactions of staff to the subsequent policy implementation process. I shall consider first how the organization reacts to Home Office policy changes, the resulting organizational changes and how they are perceived by members of the service, and in so doing move from the political world of the criminal justice system to

> the organization's ability to cope with it – to predict it, comprehend it, deal with its diversity, and respond quickly to it.
>
> (Mintzberg 1983: 137)

The changes, outlined in Chapter 2, challenge existing and possibly outdated practices. If the Home Office holds the service increasingly accountable for the effectiveness of its alternatives to custody industry, can it then afford to allow the continuation of traditional discretionary elements of practice around a series of different and sometimes, as Boswell (1982) discovered, disparate goals? But who manages such change? The history of the service has been one of probation officers having a high degree of responsibility for the formulation and implementation of programmes. 'Do their interests necessarily coincide or conflict with the nature of this change?'

The senior consultative group: towards a 'new' service

The history

In 1984 David Faulkner, the Under-Secretary of State at the Home Office, said NAPO and the government seemingly occupied 'irreconcilable positions'. Nevertheless, he did not believe that this was 'actually the case' (Faulkner 1984: 3). So he posed the question: 'Where does the service go from here?' Changes were required: in particular, he identified two stages for this process. First, the 1984 Home Office *Statement of National Objectives and Priorities* (SNOP)

> must be translated into area statements for each service, endorsed by the probation committee as the authority responsible for overall policy in its area.
>
> (Faulkner 1984: 3)

Second, there were targets, timetables, the assignment of responsibilities and the measurement of achievements, all of which should not 'be confined to probation service headquarters' (Faulkner 1984: 4), but had to go all the way to teams – locally.

Apart from SNOP, these ministerial statements also found their outlet in Home Office Circulars such as those on *Social Inquiry Reports* (1986) and more recently *Tackling Offending: An Action Plan* (1988c), which followed the Green Paper. In this latter document probation areas were called upon to 'strengthen existing orders; implement them effectively and target young adult offenders (17–20 year olds)'. Probation areas were then expected to report to the Home Office on their plans for these changes by 31 March 1989.

A new climate thus developed and organizational strategies altered. Some of these strategies, bolstered by Home Office Circulars, were the incorporation of key-workers in the new realism climate with its general emphasis on budgeting, goal-setting and procedural accountability and the setting of objectives, targets and their measurement. As part of this process, the Financial Management Initiative aimed to

> direct attention to outputs and the measurement of performance . . . to improve the effectiveness of government administration, through 'good management' of resources.
>
> (Humphrey 1987: 52)

This pursuit of performance by explicit objectives was not new to private enterprise. Over thirty years ago, Drucker wrote:

> *Objectives are needed in every area where performance and results directly and vitally affect the survival and prosperity of the business.*
>
> (Drucker 1955: 83, original italics)

However, to the service the proposed form was new.

Treen had already begun to respond to this change in climate. In its 1981 Annual Report, there was a final section on 'Objectives' under two headings: 'Diversion' and 'Diversification'. Specifically the report mentioned four aims for 1982. First, there was a need to convince the public of the value of probation work. Second, the service needed to convince employers of the value of employing offenders. Third, it aimed to increase the use of landladies and landlords in assisting offenders in the community. Finally, it

needed to convince the community that they too 'have a contribution to make to the prevention of re-offending'. By 1984, the
Annual Report aimed

> to describe how the definition of objectives for the Probation
> Service has been emerging for a review of the best aspects of
> traditional practice.

The following year, Treen published its statement of objectives,
with the one aim of the service being 'the reduction of crime
through cooperation with other criminal justice agencies and members of the wider community'. In relation to this general aim, all
aspects of probation work were to have specific objectives that
could be 'capable of achievement as well as measurement'. Staff
were encouraged to prioritize work with 15–24-year-old males who
were vulnerable to custody and to provide intensive orders for
those vulnerable to custody and avoid – except in high risk/need
situations – supervision recommendations for women or first
offenders.

While Treen had begun the response to changes in the service's
role before SNOP and *Tackling Offending*, during the course of the
research Treen management re-vitalized this process and it became
known as the Senior Consultative Group (SCG). In these policy
meetings, members of management met with senior probation
officers (SPOs) to discuss the formulation of new policies, their
implementation and the setting of objectives. They were also
intended to allow a discussion of the information systems which
would then measure subsequent organizational performance.

In the first SCG meeting twenty pages of documentation outlin-
ing the programme, with a 'Planning for Action: Priority Areas'
document, was intended to guide the proceedings. 'Planning for
Action' would, according to the Introduction:

> constitute the foundation for all our work together on this
> occasion; in effect, it is the Programme for the two days. As
> you will see, it also constitutes a management Programme:
> taking broad directional objectives on to specific targets and
> methods for achieving those targets in draft form at this stage.
>   (original underlining)

Its purpose was to address the perceived lack of co-ordination
between Treen's sub-areas in the setting of their objectives, with an
additional need for aims to be 'prioritized' and more 'precise'. Also
included was a timetable for ACPOs and their SPOs to set targets to

be consistent with the objectives outlined in 'Planning for Action'. Dates were given for the next SCG meeting, which was to consider individual team objectives, again set in relation to the Service's overall objectives.

Policy as a sailing metaphor

From 10 am to 4.30 pm over two days, discussion took place around 'Planning for Action'. The Chief Probation Officer (CPO) opened the proceedings with a summary of the last two years and a recognition of the work of senior officers. The CPO used a sailing metaphor: 'Our boat is in the harbour and we will set sail to see where we go at sea'. 'Some had been further in their objectives than others' and the CPO specifically mentioned community service (CS). The purpose of the probation service was 'to instil responsibility and self-respect in clients, as well as standing for the more abstract notion of social justice'.

An ACPO then said that objectives were to assist in a common aim. However, there existed a need for information to meet 'objectives and "service" managerial decision-making'. Despite these requirements and a set agenda, 'Planning for Action' was stressed as being a negotiable document which posed several questions. One of these was 'Will staff "own it"?'

Who has most influence over policy formulation?

SCG members and other Treen staff complained that policy change was being imposed by probation management without consultation. Historically as Chapter 2 has indicated, the destination of the service was believed to lie mainly in the hands of probation officers working at the front line. However, with the change in the service, this was believed to have altered to become the preserve of management within an increased hierarchy. Using the CPO's metaphor, probation personnel may provide the ship's power, but did they believe they had any influence over its destination? I draw on the results of my questionnaire to Treen staff to answer this question.

Table 1 shows that probation management, the Home Office, the government, ACOP (Association of Chief Officers of Probation) and the Probation Committee were considered the most influential groups in the formation of area policies. In particular, probation management was considered very influential by nearly two-thirds of respondents, whereas their employers – the Probation

Table 1   Who has most influence over policy formation?

	Very influential	Influential	Not very influential	Not influential
Probation management	63.0	34.3	2.8	0.0
Home Office	48.0	43.5	8.3	0.0
Government	28.6	41.0	24.8	5.8
ACOP	17.8	50.5	26.2	5.6
Probation Committee	9.4	54.7	34.0	1.9
SPOs	4.7	46.7	44.0	4.7
Treen magistrates	6.6	35.8	47.2	10.4
NAPO	0.0	33.6	52.3	14.0
Main-grade officers	2.8	20.4	59.2	17.6
Public opinion	0.0	19.8	57.5	22.6
Ancillaries	0.0	6.5	30.0	64.0
				(N = 109)

Committee – was considered to be very influential by relatively few and less influential than the government. Main-grade officers were believed to have little influence, only just exceeding public opinion, with ancillary workers exercising, by far, the least influence over policy.

This table indicates several important points. First, that front-line personnel and their representatives (NAPO) are thought to have little influence. Second, probation management was the most influential group in an environment where the Home Office and government were clearly considered to be very influential. Third,

Table 2   Are probation management out of touch with the realities of front-line work?

	Agree	Neither agree nor disagree	Disagree
Ancillaries	74.0	4.3	21.7
Probation officers	53.0	28.0	18.8
SPOs	66.7	11.0	22.2
Column total	60.0	20.0	20.0 (N = 105)

opinion was broadly split on whether middle-managers exercised any influence. If, therefore, probation management are believed to have such influence over policy, were they also believed to be in touch with the realities of front-line work?

Of the probation officers who agreed probation management were out of touch with the realities of 'the field' (53 per cent), just over one-third of them 'agreed strongly' (see Table 2). No statistically significant differences of opinion emerged between groups. Nevertheless, a clear majority believed probation management were out of touch with their work.

Probation management was, therefore, believed to be the most influential group in forming policies, but without a corresponding understanding of the 'everyday realities' of front-line work. However, given this, were probation management then believed to *control* the work of probation personnel? If, as K. Young (1977) argues, the outcome of policy is partly dependent upon the degree of control exercised by management over discretionary officials, then how widespread was there a belief that probation management direct the work of probation personnel?

Table 3 shows that nearly one-third were undecided and one-quarter believed that their work was controlled, not enabled, by probation management – a statistically significant finding amongst SPOs. It appears that the further one goes down the hierarchy, the less personnel feel directed by management.

In considering this feeling of control among SPOs, Minztberg (1979) lists three functions of middle-management in 'machine bureaucracies'. First, to handle 'disturbances' which occur at the front-line; second, to act as go-between between the technostructure (those who set the standards of the organization) and the

Table 3 Probation management facilitates rather than directs my work

	Agree	Neither agree nor disagree	Disagree
Ancillaries	56.5	26.1	17.4
Probation officers	35.9	40.6	23.4
SPOs	55.6	5.6	38.9
Column total	43.8	31.4	24.8 ($N = 105$)

$\chi^2 = 10.1$, $p > 0.05$

Table 4   SPOs are becoming more remote from main-grade issues?

	Agree	Neither agree nor disagree	Disagree
Ancillaries	34.8	30.4	34.8
Probation officers	42.2	23.4	34.4
SPOs	33.3	11.1	55.6
Column total	39.0	22.9	38.1 (N = 105)

operating core (those who implement those standards); and third, to support the vertical flow of information. During the SCG meeting probation management expected SPOs to fulfil all of these functions. Given this expectation and the differences in perception of directed work, did the survey then show that members of the service considered SPOs were also out of touch with front-line issues?

Opinion seems to be equally split on this issue (see Table 4). As such, there exists the possibility that as go-betweens SPOs may not fulfil the function adequately, given that a significant minority believed them to be increasingly remote from the front-line issues facing probation officers and ancillaries. To overcome these differences between SPOs and other grades, did members then feel information flowed up and down the hierarchy, or was it believed SPOs simply supported a vertical flow of information towards management? If the management of the service is then open to the flow of information on its policy initiatives from the front line, this would be important in relation to Young's other issue: the extent to

Table 5   Information flows from probation management to other grades and vice versa?

	Agree	Neither agree nor disagree	Disagree
Ancillaries	47.8	17.4	34.8
Probation officers	43.8	22.0	34.4
SPOs	89.0	11.1	0.0
Column total	52.4	19.0	28.6 (N = 105)

$\chi^2 = 12.7$, p > 0.02.

which officials and policy-makers' 'definitions of the situation' inhabit common ground.

Table 5 indicates that while no SPOs disagreed, over one-third of both ancillaries and probation officers disagreed. Therefore, SPOs believed that they participated in exchanges of information with probation management, but a significant percentage of front-line personnel did not.

Given the changes in the service, it was thought that longer-serving members may have differing beliefs from other staff. In relation to management facilitating rather than controlling work, this produced significant results with those who had served eleven years or more ($\chi^2 = 5.75$, $p > 0.05$). Therefore, changes in managerial styles were felt more strongly by the longer-serving members of the service. However, on the other questions, long service was not a determining factor (and neither was gender on any of the questions).

How can these tables be summarized? First, members of the service felt that under the government and Home Office influence, probation management exercised the most influence over the policy process. Second, the majority believed, despite this, that probation management was not in touch with probation work at the front line. Third, probation management was not then believed to control the service's work at the front line (but SPOs felt managerial control to a statistically significant greater extent than ancillaries and probation officers). Fourth, while SPOs were thought to be the link-persons in the policy process, opinion was divided when staff were asked if they were in touch with front-line work. Fifth, SPOs believed information flowed through the organization to a greater extent than front-line personnel.

The inclusion of SPOs in the policy process is then of significance in respect to their perceptions of information flow through the organization: the message of change could reach them. However, it appears that from this point – SPOs to the front line – there exists within the organization an 'implementation gap' (Dunsire 1978). For instance, probation management was not believed to be in touch with the realities of front-line work; probation management was also not believed to direct work at the front line, yet information about policy change reached SPOs but not main-grade officers and ancillaries. Looking at policy implementation from the 'top down' – that is 'what obstacles prevent policy from being implemented as planned'? (Cordell 1988: 251) – the implementation of policy to the front line was problematic given these changes in perception. Yet the incorporation of SPOs in the policy process was intended to leave the implementation of policy – from probation management to team level – in their hands. Indeed, more recently, Faulkner has written of SPOs:

> Their management role is crucial – not so much in terms of exercising authority or giving detailed direction to their teams, but in the sense of fixing priorities and arranging dispositions, so as to achieve the maximum results from a team's collective effort and a maximum contribution to the service's overall objectives.
>
> (Faulkner 1989: 625)

In the implementation of policy this places SPOs in a compressed position between management directives and front-line concerns.

With these background beliefs from the survey in mind, I now turn to the study of this process of incorporation of SPOs into the new climate via the SCG meetings. In particular, this will examine how SPOs reacted to the changes and the concerns they had about them. In addition, some aspects of policy implementation is examined, together with managerial and front-line (probation officers and ancillaries) expectations of the policy process.

The SCG continues

The first session of the SCG meeting was entitled 'County Objectives to Targets and Standards'. It was apparent a discrepancy existed in the different Treen areas' experience of custodial rates. In one of the large urban conurbations, custodial sentences were nearly twice the national average for 17–20-year-old males (22 per cent compared to a national average of 12 per cent), while Treen as a whole sentenced nearly 15 per cent of males found guilty of indictable offences to immediate custody, compared to a national average of 9 per cent. Thus, not surprisingly, one objective of the County was to 'Increase numbers of young people in the 17–20 age range placed on Probation, as an alternative to custody'.

Having set this agenda for the reduction of these rates, SPOs were split into four equal teams, termed a 'downloading session'. In these groups, divisions of opinion – between SPOs and probation management – were apparent. The major concern was the way in which the service 'improved' on magistrates' sentencing decisions to reduce custodial rates. In policy terms, as translated by probation management, it was a question of presenting 'quality' social inquiry reports

(SIRs). SPOs then translated this in terms of two other issues. First, the practical aspects of its implementation, and second, how realistic it was to assume the service could achieve a reduction in custody.

Organizational change and environmental conditions

One of the four groups spoke about how they could 'practically' achieve this aim, given most probation officers were, in the words of one SPO, 'already working hard in difficult circumstances'. The conversation then turned away from the intra-organizational issue of improving SIRs to an environmental one: the extent to which magistrates were in tune with public opinion on sentencing. 'Like the Bishop', one SPO said, maybe the job was to tell magistrates they are 'out of step with their brothers and local opinion'. The issue then became one of challenging the background assumptions of magistrates' decisions, not the improvement of SIRs.[1]

The overwhelming majority of Treen staff believed that the confidence of magistrates in the standards of the probation service was of central importance (90 per cent). They also believed that they possessed the ability to influence the courts' decisions (88 per cent). However, this was not the issue the SPOs focused upon in the group discussions. The questions raised were not of a general nature, but more specific. First, in order to perfect the type of change the SCG required, how could they motivate personnel who were already working hard, and second, how realistic was it to place the onus on probation personnel to perfect radical changes in sentencing patterns? This latter issue is very important. Constitutionally given the traditional independence of the executive from the judiciary, the onus is then placed on the probation service to change sentencing practices. However, in order to achieve this the service has to steer a fine line by not challenging the 'independence' of the courts.

This issue was discussed during the SCG meetings. For example, it was said area disparities in practice make the objective of reducing custody contingent upon the courts' culture. One of the objectives stressed the importance of intervening at the pre-hearing stage (held in custody prior to hearing). For this to be successful, good liaison with solicitors was important. However, so too was the provision of community-based bail schemes and available facilities to engage with the client in the court setting (the provision of

interview rooms in courts is a variable commodity not just re-
stricted to probation clients.[2] These provide physical restraints on
the implementation of objectives; other restraints also exist. In one
fines court, for example, the Clerk makes it difficult, it not impossible, for probation officers to be present! Despite such practices,
concerns were expressed during the SCG meetings about 'treading
in the Clerk's territory'. It was acknowledged that there was a need
to demonstrate to magistrates the effects of fining clients on small
incomes, with the resulting custodial penalties for subsequent
default. However, it was also acknowledged that Clerks may consider this an unacceptable extension of the service's traditional
role.

As the fieldwork showed (see Chapter 5), the extent to which
probation officers and magistrates interact varied. Further, as noted
by participants during the SCG meetings, if, to improve effectiveness, a team internally reorganizes to specialize in supervision and
report writing, the officer writing the report was not then necessarily in a position to answer certain questions regarding the
offender's conduct during any present or past supervision. Thus,
magistrates deferring informally (as on several occasions during
observation in the courtroom) about a client's behaviour on supervision, apparently found the reply wanting. Officers, the SCG
noted, may then earn reputations by anticipating the information a
court may require. Yet, as following chapters indicate, this is
dependent not only on physical restraints, but also on the extent to
which an officer is part of the 'culture of the court'. This is an
environmental condition which organizational solutions cannot
on their own provide.

Pro-active work – necessary for impact – was therefore seen
by SPOs as problematic. For example, a Department of Social
Security clampdown on claimants (as happened on several occasions during the research) meant officers had to react to these
circumstances. Indeed, when members of the service were asked
about the worst aspects of their work, replies related to these
environmental constraints:

Helplessness in the wake of Government policy . . . an unen-
lightened court.

Campaigning against sensational media coverage of crime and
punishment, so influential on public opinion and, in turn,
magistrates.

Staff morale can therefore be affected by the unrealistic expectations of the policy process. If policy initiatives are not in tune with the daily demands of probation personnel's environment, then discontent occurs. As Hugman has remarked, as effectiveness of the organization is questioned, so too is its credibility and the result is considerable demoralization' (1980: 128). This is the case in Treen – a disjuncture in explicit policy expectations with differing environments for their implementation. To express this in terms of the sailing metaphor, for some the seas are choppy; to others, rough and inhospitable! I shall now turn to an example of how environmental conditions can inhibit the implementation of policy.

A case study: a Probation Liaison Committee in action

In sentencing decisions, the Clerk's role is intended to be clear. As one text on decision-making in magistrates courts notes:

> It is clearly understood that the clerk of the court must not be a party to the final decision as to sentence but at various stages of the sentencing decision he [sic] should have been able to advise on such matters as the options provided by the law, guidance relevant to choice of penalty, and the decisions of superior courts and other authorities.
>
> (Barker and Sturges 1986: 18)

This implies – as many descriptions of 'professionals' do – a *neutral* individual who takes no sides and disseminates information to *interested* parties. Formally, the definition is impressive.

The SCG process assumed improvements could be made in communicating with magistrates. As Bottomley has written, this tactic is not without foundation:

> the most fundamental influences upon sentencing behaviour are the penal philosophies and attitudes of individual magistrates.
>
> (Bottomley 1973: 169)

Admitting this, in a later work, to be a somewhat 'simplistic interpretation', he also notes how persistent the 'human factor "theme"' (Bottomley 1979: 86) is in relation to decisions in the penal process. One of the methods through which Treen then attempted to inform magistrates of alternatives to custody was the Probation Liaison Committees (PLCs) – magistrates meeting with the service to discuss innovations and practices of common interest.

On one such occasion in which I was an invited observer, thirteen magistrates and two members of probation management were in attendance. The agenda covered improving the work of PLCs, suspended sentences and juvenile justice. During the discussion on juvenile offenders Essex – a county adopting an inter-agency policy – was mentioned, as was the zero custodial rate for Basingstoke. Asked to comment on the reasons for these successes, one of the service representatives replied: 'Some of the impetus for this has come from the juvenile panel', and added, 'the magistrates' Clerk'. The Chair of the Committee then asked about Section 4A and 4B requirements in probation orders and what the service was providing in the area. They were told that 'much was happening' but the Clerk and magistrates were 'out of the process'. This prompted an immediate reply from a magistrate: 'The impetus must come from the service'.

A probation manager continued, noting the value to be gained in the Juvenile Panel and PLC having a meeting with the police, social services and probation to increase information about the alternatives available to magistrates. For instance, Essex included a 'Supervised Activity Order' enabling courts, under a Supervision Order, to include requirements with which the person must comply. A magistrate responded: 'We can only make Supervision Orders and can't make a Supervised Activity Order'. One officer replied: 'Oh yes you can' (CJA 1982, s. 20(1)). This comment brought the meeting to a critical issue facing the service and the reduction of custody through its policy initiatives.

A magistrate noted that the Clerks in the court had not informed him that 4A and 4B requirements were available in the area which, he added, 'makes me very angry'. Another magistrate, also acknowledging this lack of information, suggested it could be prevented 'in the retiring-room'. It transpired, as other members of the committee confirmed, Clerks had not provided the necessary information upon which to base an informed decision. Indeed, a magistrate commented that one of the Benches had repeatedly asked a Clerk to inform them what disposals were available, thus illustrating not only the lack of knowledge magistrates had regarding options in the sentencing process, but also the extent to which the withholding of information – deliberately or otherwise – affected decisions which had a direct bearing on the effectiveness of the service.

Organizational solutions to altering court practice

This problem of court impact within the SCG was a question, as a member of probation management put it, of professional assertion. The SCG document stated that a reduction in custody and increase in probation and community service orders would 'become effective [only] if we have the confidence of the Courts in terms of credibility'. The methods for achieving this aim included the following: monitoring proposals for measuring the effectiveness of SIRs; the development of guidelines for a criteria of excellence in report writing; probation management issuing advice in not-guilty pleas; a staff development officer to develop staff skills for 'relevant staff'; area management to plan a programme for liaison with magistrates' associations and PLCs, plus the Research and Information Committee to mount a consumer survey of magistrates to assess the extent to which their expectations were being met.

In a staff circular – issued as an Instruction – dated 20 May 1986, staff were told of a system of monitoring, designed to

> measure, evaluate, estimate, appraise your results in some form, in any terms that rest on anything beyond faith, assertion and the 'illustrative' case.

Such monitoring – by services in general – is designed to pursue a credibility increasingly dependent on the ability of services to offer a 'control in the community element', for those who might otherwise be sentenced to custody. Nevertheless, as the 'Planning for Action' document filtered through the Treen Probation Service to teams, its problem of implementation became more apparent.

Front-line personnel, as well as SPOs, were critical of the SCG's suggestions. During one team's consideration of 'Planning for Action', members felt they were more in tune with clients' needs than management and asked the senior officer when they were going to 'stop the nonsense of reacting to pieces of paper'. Thus, in the process of implementation the 'client' had then changed from the court (at the SCG level), to the offender (at team level). Further, conflict also manifested itself between the punitive credibility sought by the SCG and the provision of social work at the front line. As one officer noted, 'Nowhere in the paper does it mention the word social work', and then questioned how it was possible to divert people from custody by social work means.

These same criticisms also manifested themselves at other levels of policy implementation. At a Research and Information

Committee meeting, it was noted how, implicit in 'Planning for Action', a 'conventional' probation order was an alternative to custody. Yet this was a low risk/high need provision and magistrates and the Probation Committee saw community service as *the* alternative to custody. However, the Committee had an administrative remit – the devising of means for monitoring and evaluating programmes – so the discussion mainly focused on the technical aspects of measuring programmes of work, as opposed to their feasibility and desirability.

Back to SCG

SPOs also raised issues concerning administrative presuppositions within the SCG itself. In one of four 'down-loading' groups, the discussion centred on through-care/post-custody. The 'Planning for Action' aim was 'Successful resettlement of those released from custody'. The Home Office perspective was:

> Sufficient resources should be allocated to through-care to enable the Service's statutory obligations to be discharged . . . Beyond that, social work for offenders released from custody, though important in itself, can only command the priority which is consistent with the *main objective* of implementing non-custodial measures for offenders who might otherwise receive custodial stentences.
>
>   (Home Office 1984: part VI, para. C, italics added)

This is considered to be an attempt to redefine the role of the probation service *vis-à-vis* the criminal justice system, 'rather than in relation to the needs of individual offenders' (Raynor 1984: 43). Given this implicit questioning of the service's traditional role, the Home Office agenda had some bearing on the group's discussions.

One member of the group considered that anyone, given the limitations on resources, who was 'not eligible for parole would not be engaged with'. Team resources would be prioritized in other areas of work (in line with SNOP) and that would mean withdrawing staff from lower priority areas. Offenders would then be seen only 'if they were in trouble and actually stated they wanted help'. As a result one suggestion was 'to put all parolees on reporting unless they cry help and then put resources at the other end'. However, as group members noted, this solution would have problems in relation to crime prevention – some clients would not then be regularly supervised.

Members then discussed using community resources to alleviate this situation. Nevertheless, it was generally believed that a fine line was to be drawn between helping clients in the community by using its available resources – for example, voluntary groups – and competing with other groups in the community for resources which were known to be already limited.

The end of the first 'voyage'

After two days of extensive discussions, SPOs expressed a feeling of exhaustion. In a feedback session at the end of the second day, the limits on time and lack of consultation involved in the policy process were singled out for criticism. In reply, the CPO made it clear that consultation could take place at team level around the formulation of local targets, implying that the onus was on SPOs to 'sell' the document to team members. The completion date for team objectives was October (six months hence). One senior officer said it sounded as if they had no option and the document was not 'consultative', but a 'tablet of stone'. The CPO simply replied that 'Planning for Action' was 'a *management document*' (original emphasis).

Phase two of the SCG: setting sail again

Six months after the first SCG meetings, team objectives were to be received and considered, together with the implications they had for resources, priorities and their information and measurement needs. Tasks had been set by the first SCG meeting and team responses were to be analysed. For this purpose, SPOs were asked to bring the 'Planning for Action' document, a Research and Information Committee document relating to 'information and measurement' and six copies of their team objectives. A detailed examination of team objectives was to ensure, in the words of the Introduction to the meeting, their 'congruence and viability (measurable, achievable, time-limited)'.

The CPO alluded to the conflict which had evolved around the SCG process and its implementation to teams:

> our service is about tending to people whose lives are somewhat chaotic and disorganized . . . this whole objectives thing poses problems not just for people like me, but people like you.

This prompted replies to the CPO. It was noted how one area within Treen – with nearly twice the national average of custodial sentences – 'was tantamount, almost, to a corrupt system in the criminal justice system'. What, therefore, it was asked, could the service realistically be expected to achieve in this area? Another senior officer, also critical of the underlying logic of the policy process, added: 'We must recognize the powerful social factors leading to criminalization' and continued:

> It is like typhoid; you can treat those who come to you, but you will use your resources more effectively by going to the water and drainage.

An ACPO agreed, adding that management had argued with the Home Office over their 'mechanistic view of objectives' and expectations made on the service. He also noted the consequences of making unrealistic demands on staff in the policy process: 'If we don't address this issue we are going to get a very demoralised staff'. Discussion was then curtailed by the set administrative agenda. ACPOs were then invited to present their 'area perspectives' to the meeting, which resulted from reactions to 'Planning for Action'.

Different environments and standardized policy

The first ACPO spoke about the peculiarities of the area. It worked to one court, which had a very high custody rate and inner city problems which were 'not recognized by the Home Office' (even though the Department of the Environment had the city listed as a 'targeted area'). Each year '120 men over 21 go into custody'. These men were 'the classic picture of the petty, persistent offender'. In order to alleviate this situation, as required by the SCG and Home Office, a co-ordinating group of agencies had been suggested. However, the Clerk to the magistrates had indicated an opposition to this proposal. Resistance in the environment had, therefore, rendered the implementation of change highly problematic. This area was seen by some officers as Treen's 'Bermuda triangle'.

The second area in Treen was more rural in its composition and was considered to be 'uneconomic' which, as its ACPO noted, was a contentious issue among probation staff. Fines (and hence default) were very high and it was important to focus on these individuals by targeting and debt counselling. The fact that many of these individuals had little money when the fine was imposed was a political question, so the service's strategy was to focus on individual offenders. Indeed, following this second SCG meeting an internal Treen memo addressed the issue of fine-default in two ways. First, by setting-up a working party on day-fines, and second, the core of the issue, which could not be publicly declared:

> We need to discuss with sentencers the way the sentence works against their intentions not only in reducing their scope but also punishing people socially.

The answer was in targeting, monitoring and working parties, not directly confronting the issue.

The ACPO continued with sub-area problems and policy responses. Of the forty who were likely to receive Section 4A or 4B requirements in that year, it was important to ensure that it was those who were 'most vulnerable to custody'. In addition, it was necessary to 'focus on statutory clients' – in line with policy change – which meant less contact with voluntary clients; this, while contentious, was dictated by budgetary considerations. A senior officer interjected: this was 'in conflict with the targeting of vulnerable groups' as an aim of crime prevention. One town within her area could justify a probation officer only three times a week, not because there was less crime but because 'fewer go into court'. Therefore, in crime prevention terms to target statutory clients would be a 'short-sighted policy'. However, the number of individuals who became statutory clients was not only dictated by local courts, but also an organizational criteria for additional staffing. Thus, there was a clear conflict between crime prevention work and the emphasis on focusing on statutory clients: one was the aim, but the other secured an increased number of staff.

The third area in Treen was the most geographically dispersed; its first objective was 'to make this more manageable'. The local prison needed an 'improvement in its resources' and a day centre needed to attract more clients: the custodial rate for the main city was just under twice the national average. As with the other Treen areas, unrealistic fines and imprisonment for default were particularly problematic. Yet the satellite team in the area seemed to be successful in diverting people from custody, with a custodial rate just below the national average. However, this generated some discussion when the ACPO alluded to the overall aim of reducing re-offending. One senior officer wished to distance himself from the service's ability to prevent recidivism as this 'was not within our power'. He continued: 'The service did not, nor could not, work in this way'. Its purpose, he contended, was the provision of 'a social work service to offenders'.

Comments such as these characterized the first two SCG meetings. First, SPOs referred to the *purpose* of probation and how realistic it was to assume they could achieve those ends which the policy process implied. In other words, the purpose of probation – traditionally the rehabilitation of offenders – became in the SCG process the diversion from custody by the provision of tougher alternatives with no apparent purpose, except pursuing a court-led search for credibility based on demanding and punishing regimes. Second, however, the climate of policy-making modified the principle into what can be loosely termed pragmatism. Thus, while some SPOs agreed that the purpose of probation was a social work service to offenders, it was still important to 'keep hold of the person' if they do re-offend, 'in order to continue social work with them'. It was pointed out that to keep hold of the individual offender, the price would have to be a higher component of control in order to satisfy the magistracy. Nevertheless, these justifications followed from the general feeling that it was only the service – apart from defence solicitors – who seemed to be 'bothered about them [the offenders] and offer a helping hand'! (The service dealt with only a minority of offenders; it being noted that the majority of crime was undetected.) Admitted to be in a 'Catch 22' situation – social work service and a court-led credibility – members as a whole were still concerned that their effectiveness was 'to be judged by the rate of re-offending'.

Measurement, information, budgets and effectiveness

Following the ACPO's presentations, the agenda continued with two other major components of the policy process: budgeting and information systems to measure organizational performance. The CPO spoke about Financial Management Initiative (FMI), which had three systems. First, there was 'information for operational control'. Second, there was the system of 'Resource management – called "outputs" – which the probation service calls social inquiry reports, plus numbers on community service and supervision'. Third, there was a system for developing 'effectiveness management'. It was the latter, in particular, where the FMI had become, in the CPO's words, 'very unstuck'.

Objectives, monitoring and resources

The CPO continued on the subject of measures which would examine offending behaviour and the 'improvement of SIRs'. While serious offences had been uncovered in the monitoring process – which explained the sentences individuals received – occupational practice could still be at fault. Further, because information on offenders from other agencies could be unreliable, the CPO suggested an improvement in the filling of Home Office forms to gain information on sentences, offences and offenders.[3]

The comment of one ACPO that the resultant figures would be simplistic acted as a catalyst for an exchange of views on the expectations of the policy process. One officer noted it was not magistrates courts in their area that 'sent people down', but the Crown Court. The SCG was solely concentrating on sentencing practices in magistrates courts. On the other hand, in one magistrates court, which was very punitive, 'young and committed solicitors are trying to get away from the magistrates to Crown Court', which was less punitive. This obviously had implications for motivating staff. Nevertheless, while sympathetic to these environmental issues, SCG members were told by a member of probation management that 'the HMIs [Probation Inspectorate] are not into this'. Members then dispersed into their allotted groups.

In each group, SPOs were to present their team objectives. In the first presentation, the conversation soon picked up where the open forum had left off. Members wished to detach themselves from the belief that they could reduce re-offending. Also, 'Planning for Action' had mentioned appropriateness and client need, but never quality. In one team's area the influence on sentencing came 'not from objectives, targets and information', but 'chatting to the Clerk and getting local newspaper articles'. In reflecting on this situation, a senior officer added that objectives appeared to be 'your own hangman's noose'!

Members within the group also spoke of the uncritical acceptance of SNOP by management and its translation into SLOP (Statements of Local Objectives and Priorities). As one senior officer noted: 'A good point seems to be we don't learn from history. New ideas come into the landscape and the old is entirely forgotten'. Others agreed, also questioning the nature of the process: 'Are the goal posts shifted too frequently?' However, a senior officer retorted, 'You don't have to shift the goal posts to justify your existence'. This was the crux of the issue. From the Home Office and government standpoint, the probation service do.

Returning to the open forum these same points were raised by other groups. Each reported on the progress of presenting their team objectives. However, questions were again asked of management. In order to improve effectiveness, one SPO asked: 'Are we about encouraging clients to appeal against unfair sentences?' 'This', came the management reply, 'was not a question of aims and objectives, but professioanl practice'. In the view of management, objectives were to enhance, not debilitate, front-line practice.

The second day began with team SPOs writing their objectives on large sheets of paper, which were posted at each corner of the room for general discussion. In examining one team's objectives, the SPO told me that of the team's 142 SIRs, 22 were from outside courts, 'many of which are from London, who are issuing 240-hour CSOs, which is out of my control, but shows up on my figures'. As such, they felt the policy process was not addressing these 'real' issues.

After lunch, the agenda moved on to resources and priorities. The CPO noted the difficulties of bidding for resources at both local government and Home Office level and felt that a pragmatic style in such a situation was required. Bids for additional resources had to anticipate those areas of probation work that the Home Office wanted to develop. ACPOs and their area SPOs then met to consider area resourcing in relation to objectives.

It was immediately pointed out that diversions from prosecution had resource implications. One SPO said they would need an additional sessional probation officer so 'Why not go for it!' This proposal agitated another senior officer who felt that resourcing should not be reduced to such bidding, believing that it depended on client need. 'But', said another member, 'we live in a pragmatic world . . . as the Chief said, funding is about politics'.

Returning to the open forum, the first area indicated that if they get the orders they asked for – 'requiring a change in the way the court works' – then resources 'would collapse': if they succeeded in being more effective they would not be in a financial position to provide the increased services necessary. An additional probation officer, some improved liaison between teams, the flexible use of ancillaries and better monitoring were all suggested to alleviate this possibility. Another area split their requirements into 'essential', 'necessary' and 'desirable' in order to strengthen their arguments in the politics of resourcing. Heated exchanges ensued. Some of their arguments could be generally justified by all the areas and perhaps, therefore, it should all 'go into a pool and everybody bid against each other'.

These exchanges were designed to get SPOs not only to see resourcing issues more globally, but also to take more responsibility for resourcing in the new organizational culture. Senior officers, I was told, tend to see the organization 'end at team level'. These issues were new to them and as SPOs themselves confirmed, it was the first time resources were discussed in such a competitive way at this level.

Finance, budgeting and research

This was a key issue in the politics of change. It was important to management to co-opt SPOs otherwise further differences of opinion could develop between administration and practice. This might then introduce further intra-organizational conflict around FMI concepts of economy, efficiency and effectiveness. The third SCG meeting therefore covered finance, budgeting, team managers' roles and responsibilities, court impact and research and information. The Introduction stated:

> It is proposed to use SCG to look at budget work on both a macro – County Probation Committee Treasurer – and micro – Team Manager – level.

The Introduction also drew attention to the volume of information that SPOs were expected to digest – ninety pages – and looked forward 'to a highly participatory event'.

Following a paper, 'Planning for Action: The budgets and structures for court impact', the CPO spoke about Treen's budget. Its implementation began with the CPO and the County Treasurer getting together to interpret important statements – for instance, the Chancellor's autumn statement – and draft a budget which the local authority was unlikely to challenge and would be approved by the Probation Committee. If the local authority did challenge the budget, it was important that the Home Office then determined in favour of the Committee. Anticipating the politics of the situation was, therefore, part of the method of budgetary approval. However, the Home Office had (according to the CPO) 'called in all budgets for 1988/89, by 31 January 1988' and 'there was a feeling among CPOs of staffing control by the Home Office'. The Home Office could then, continued the CPO, take the current year 'as a baseline and stop all capital expenditure' (for instance, the possibility of a new probation office). The future was worrying: the Home Office might take indicators through the Probation Inspectorate and then 'tell us what they think our budget should be'.

The CPO felt that court impact needed to be increased to gain the necessary credibility for the Home Office to approve its budgets, which required a greater 'officer presence' in the courts. This would be determined by locally identified targets which meant that SPOs would have to spend more time in the courts. The CPO noted that the new CS standards would also be more expensive: ACOP had indicated this to the Home Office. The 'punishment in the community' proposals could not be implemented without additional resources.

A senior officer interrupted the CPO. She felt that 'all this talk of time allocation and court impact' was fine at a macro level but what specific things would be done to improve the situation? To increase the presence of SPOs in court – to improve impact and anticipate Home Office budgetary criteria – could, in practice, 'undermine the authority of the probation officer's role in the court'. Another member agreed, adding that he wanted to get back to being the SPO he was 'six or seven years ago' and be more pro-active in his work:

> You monitor SIRs after the bloke has gone down and the ACPO comes along and says the figures are too high. This is all retrospective.

The CPO believed this was a case of officers' 'assertiveness training' in the court and closed the dissent by considering the next agenda item: the new Research Officer appointment.

The post was designed to provide officers with information in relation to professional practice. SPOs were concerned about who the officer worked for – management or the front line? In some probation services research and information was provided for management but not POs: 'We don't want anyone who is going to sit in Head Office'. The CPO replied that the appointee needed 'to be on one of those dog leads which lets itself out', indicating a degree of autonomy circumscribed by managerial authority.

Groups were again allocated to feedback and members shared common concerns, not least about the appointment of a Research Officer. Who was this appointment for? Two SPOs who had worked in other probation areas, both agreed that their research officers 'made constant demands and that is the last you heard of it'. This increased those suspicions probation officers already had about research. Senior officers believed that a priority role of these appointments was the measurement of performance indicators in order to justify resourcing to the Home Office, as the CPO's discussion of budgets had indicated. Research then becomes relevant not to practice *per se*, but to the gathering of information for management and 'politics of resourcing' purposes.

Talking about finances

In the afternoon session, a representative of the County Council (also the Probation Committee's Treasurer) stressed that his department was not a 'police force' which 'takes away the underspends, disciplines for overspends and locks people up for discrepancies. Without you we wouldn't have a job . . . we are here to help you'. The budget was defined as 'an attempt at predicting, in advance, the cost of service delivery taking into account all known variables and policies'.

Statements of accountability also featured in his speech. The service was spending taxpayers' money and the budget was 'very strongly controlled from the centre'. Key phrases of budgetary responsibility also featured, for example overspending was 'like taking away from your next-door neighbour', while 'at the end of the day the pot is only so big'. SPOs were also told that for every £1 overspent, £3 comes off the Rate Support Grant as a central government sanction. While the Treasurer is there to support and not control, 'we would show the overspenders that they have a responsibility for their budgets'.

At this point a senior officer interrupted: 'What if you feel you have a good cause?' 'Then', came the reply, 'increased resources is a decision of Probation Committee members and it is our duty to inform them of its resource implications'.

The ensuing discussion – opened to the floor – was one of the most charged I had witnessed. The movement from the traditional to cost-centre approach of budgeting was clearly something – contrary to the Treasury representative's assertion – that the SPOs were not going to relish. During fieldwork, two probation officers told me that their experiences with a pilot of this method split the team and became divisive. I was told they 'just inherited it' and despite complaints to NAPO, there was 'nothing we could do about it'. These concerns were also reflected in the SCG forum. One senior officer, experienced in this area, was emphatic:

I don't want anybody to be under the illusion it is a problem-free process. Probation officers do not think easily in terms of the budgeting process.

This SPO, as part of a budgetary pilot programme, had previously had control over marginal savings: allowing phone calls only in the afternoon, only second-class post, and 'doubling up' to save travel costs. However, this was offset by the 'increased SPO time in managing this'. All of which, he said, saved only '10 per cent of 10 per cent'. A member of management interjected: SPOs' new role, like that of senior secretaries, was as resource managers and these were 'focusing roles', integrating the efforts of senior secretaries, area management, SPOs and ultimately, teams. 'Yet', replied another senior officer 'if we only have control over 10 per cent of 10 per cent what use is this?' This heated discussion was brought to a close by a member of probation management, not with an appeal to reason, but fatalism: 'If we are going to be in it, so are you!'

Discussion

In this chapter I have described a new 'environment' at odds with the traditional nature and function of the probation service. In the process of interpretation and implementation of Home Office policy – an understanding of which has been the purpose of this chapter – it was clear that an implementation gap exists between probation management and front-line staff. SPOs translated management policy in terms of how it could be practically implemented and its effects on staff morale, as well as the environmental impediments which existed to its effective implementation. Front-line staff translated the purpose of policy change from being the court as the client, to the offender. In addition, the focus of policy change itself appeared, at times, to be contradictory. For example, policy demanded a focus on statutory clients, which would also gain the service additional staffing in terms of increased client/staff ratios. However, in concentrating on statutory clients, other clients could be neglected which had implications for the probation service's general aim of crime prevention. This created a tension which SPOs perceived as one between clients' needs and the politics of the service gaining additional resources using performance indicators.

Senior officers' reactions were, in the main, suppressed, but still found their outlet in the SCG process itself. Outside of the SCG meetings beliefs were expressed in the questionnaire and during fieldwork, which demonstrated divisions of opinion occurring within the organization, in particular, between probation management and the front line. As one person said:

> It's like living in a one-party State. We should get back to our core task: the supervision of offenders, and buy in professionals for other tasks and not try to do them ourselves.

Change undoubtedly affects the 'dynamic conservatism' (Schon 1971) of some organizations – the old is understood and anything new is viewed with suspicion. Nevertheless, in top-down implementation terms it was possible to see how probation management were under increased pressure to alter the nature of the operation and practice of the service. These changes revolved around not only ends, but also means. In the public sector, one change which causes particular conflict is the drive to economize and rationalize organizations. I have suggested (in Chapter 2) that probation officers were familiar with budgeting in terms of assisting their clients, but not with that of the organization as a whole. Whether this perspective is right or wrong is not the case at this level of policy-making in the organization. What is clear was that change in this direction is all too readily subsumed by management under the general guise of a new realism and responsibility on the part of *all* staff.

These changes are politically charged and inspired, requiring change by persuasion and ultimately, if necessary, an allusion to fatalism. This occurred during discussions on budgeting. Senior officers, clearly unhappy with the nature of SCG discussions, were finally told by a member of probation management: 'This is the way it is and we have no choice'.

As objectives and targets were set, dissent arose not only within the SCG and teams – as discussed – but also at other meetings. The result was that the political logic and underlying values of the process were, albeit temporarily, exposed. Thus, during one Research and Information Committee meeting the discussion centred on a particular target. The ACPO was asked: 'Where did you get this 15 per cent from?' The ACPO gestured to signify it was plucked from the sky. The questioner asked if it was then 'open to negotiation'. However, the Chair of the meeting intervened to bring the agenda back to the issue of the target's measurement, not its rationale.

These tensions, between the technical (measurement) and political (desirability/feasibility), cause a sense of frustration among those subjected to such changes. When asked 'What are the worst aspects of your work?' answer to the survey were divided. First, there was the inability to help some clients and the stress this causes (occupational and task related), such as 'Stress management and balancing the identification with the client and society he has offended against'. Second, there was considerable dissatisfaction over administrative issues. For some, administration was 'necessary but boring'. However, most were negative: 'We are drowning in irrelevant paper', with an 'emphasis on recording everything, including trivial details'. Themes in the replies also concentrated on measurement in relation to objectives, noting it is 'very hard for good quality social work to be measured; official methods of evaluation don't tell the whole story'. One person felt frustrated 'because R and I is seldom directly relevant to work pressures and needs, and one can see the potential for a closer working relationship'.

Some spoke of the organization 'upholding common processes, not standards'. The HQ of Treen had also been nicknamed 'The Ark', removed from the realities of probation work: 'A result of this is that one feels HQ is an incestuous unit that could function nicely if we did not in fact exist!' These replies expressed tensions between the justifications for administrative action on the one hand and those of occupational practice on the other. As Etzioni has noted, the justification for a professional's action 'is that it is, to the best of the professional's knowledge, the right act' (1969: x). On the other hand, the

> ultimate justification for an administrative act is that it is in line with the organisation's rules and regulations, and that it has been approved, directly or by implication – by a superior rank.
>
> (Etzioni 1969: xi)

The divisions, of which these replies are symptomatic, were also beginning to show between SPOs and main-grade and ancillary staff. Even within the SCG there was a clear feeling, found among all ranks, that it was 'going in the wrong direction'. This was further substantiated by the comments members made in relation to the changes the service had faced in the 1980s: 'the industrial model of objectives and targets' had 'only limited application' for the service. Performance measures, as an indicator of this trend, also led to dysfunctions. One member spoke of 'a bit more of watching one's back'. This rapid organizational change resulted in a

blur of activity as a means of obscuring diminished effectiveness . . . unrealistic aims and too much publicity that cannot
be lived up to.

Further, staff wanted to know whether the 'emphasis on practice
consistency' was for them 'or management'.

For a few, these changes provided a means to challenge existing
and outdated practices. For instance, SNOP provided opportunities:

SNOP has not been popular in terms of its philosophical
tenets, but has had the benefit of concentrating the mind on
the Service and the rest of us on what we are about.

Although the opinion of a small number, it infuses change with
increased political potential within the organization.

Probation management, as a study of the SCG has suggested,
responded to Home Office changes and enacted 'mezzo' policy
changes. However, the reactions of staff were mainly negative,
which can be expressed in terms of the efficiency/effectiveness
debate. One senior member of the service told me that 'efficiency is
doing things right' and effectiveness 'doing the right things'. He saw
his job as the reconciliation of 'different tunes' in the organization:
the Home Office on one side and the practitioner and their clients
on the other. Yet perspectives varied on the potential for such
reconciliation; even more so as policy becomes the preserve of
management, despite the fact over half (56 per cent) of respondents
felt the setting of new county-wide objectives was part of their role.

Senior officers and probation management also found themselves
expressing different beliefs concerning the expectations of policy.
For SPOs it was how to motivate front-line staff who, they argued,
were already working hard in difficult circumstances. Within the
SCG this translated itself as the question: 'For whom and how are
standards derived?'

Summary

This chapter has examined policy changes enacted by probation
management and the reactions of other grades to these. However,
no analysis would be complete without understanding the 'environment' in which such policies are supposed to be implemented
and the perspectives of probation personnel in relation to the
organization and their work. This provides an alternative view to

this chapter: not from the point of view of seeing policy from the top-down, but from the bottom-up. Situational constraints within the environment may exist which prevent the implementation of policy. If policy is not in tune with the environment, it will be at best ineffective and at worst obstructive. (This is the subject of Chapters 4, 5 and 6.) While the implementation gap shows a discrepancy between probation management and the front line, the understanding of this should

> be searched for not in the breakdown of the compliance system, but in the structure of the work situation from which the workers 'antagonistic' interests arise.
>
> (Lipsky 1980: 17)

This moves away from the top-down implementation perspective – which assumes a compliance on the part of those who enact policy and an understanding of their environment on the part of those who make policy – towards a greater understanding of the environment in which probation work is enacted and the problems faced by front-line personnel on an everyday basis. It is to this 'micro' world that I now turn.

4

Accountability, autonomy and changing roles

If qualitative aspects of service delivery are neglected, cost reductions and volume receive more attention as workers and managers accommodate their behaviour to agency signals of priorities. This contributes to the self-fulfilling prophecy of the ineffectiveness and ultimate irrelevance of social services.

(Lipsky 1980: 179)

In describing the community brief of the probation officer we are highlighting an essential task of the Service – namely, to reduce the isolation of those men and women who have become involved with the criminal justice process.

(Harding 1987: 8)

Chapter 3 examined policy change and the conflict that surrounded it. This chapter and Chapters 5 and 6 will examine the issues which surround probation work in an everyday (interactional) context. They are about the 'nuts and bolts' of probation: working with offenders in a variety of settings and with the courts in different areas – at the front line. In Lipsky's (1980) terms, they are about people's work situation and beliefs. I shall examine the discretionary nature of probation work, adding to an understanding of the implementation gap.

Background and issues

Within these broader aims this chapter examines the perspectives of probation staff on certain key issues and on their changing roles. My questionnaire posed several questions, for example 'What is it that people find most satisfying about probation work?' 'What are their beliefs concerning the degree of accountability and autonomy they have within the service?' 'How accountable do they feel towards different groups, such as the courts, Home Office and clients?' 'What are the changes in role of staff which have been and are taking place within the service?' Finally, how do probation personnel feel about these and what are their effects on working practice? First, the question is asked: 'What is it that provides service members with the impetus to undertake probation work?'

The 'binding ethos'

Space precludes venturing into the 'staggering current literature' (A. Abbott 1981: 820) on professions. Some authors have operationalized the concept on the basis of a list of characteristics and the extent to which occupations approximate to these, determines the level of their professional status. Thus, Toren stated after listing occupational characteristics:

> An occupation will be classified as a semi-profession if it lacks one or more of the professional qualities pointed out above.
>
> (Toren 1969: 141)

However, the focus of the study of professions then switched from what a profession is, to the process whereby occupations attempt to become professions (Becker 1962; Hughes 1971) and from there to one of the relationship of professions to the economic and political system (Johnson 1972, 1980; Larson 1977).

While these variations in approach exist, it is possible to discern within occupations certain beliefs which provide an impetus to join their ranks and continue the work. That is, not just why people join certain occupations, but what beliefs do they share, if any? Thus, probation personnel were asked: 'If a person was seeking work like yours and asked you to briefly tell them what personal satisfaction you gained from it, what would you tell them?'

Integrity, creativity and variety all featured in detailed replies: 'I still believe our intervention can change people's lives for the better'. For some, probation work gave an opportunity to satisfy deep-rooted needs:

> These are generally associated with the common humane spiritual need within everybody to feel at one with one's fellow man, and to share what one has with those who don't have it.

The work was even described as 'a little like painting a picture with people instead of colour'. To one ancillary it was 'the most reward-ing job I have done', thereby giving to others a 'sense of achieve-ment in empowering people and helping them towards personal solutions'. Another person linked this belief with the latitude the job gave her for its execution: 'it caters for my personal philosophy'.

Others explicitly mentioned the social and political aspects of the work, as well as helping individuals *per se*:

> The ability to occasionally make a positive contribution to someone else's life and to minimize the potential damage done by the authority of the state.

Enjoying 'helping the underprivileged and misunderstood' and giving pleasure to come 'between bureaucracy and a distressed person', were also mentioned. The majority would have agreed with these sentiments:

> We should always attempt to reflect the acceptable and caring face of a system designed to grind down those at the lower levels of society.

The answers to this question reflected two dominant themes. First, the ability to help people, and second, having the latitude to do so. The former is the binding ethos of probation work. It combines elements of altruism with a view of an agency which allows elements of discretion to assist in this aim. This ethos has, in part, been identified in other research undertaken on the service (Keynon and Rhodes undated; Boswell 1982; Davies and Wright 1989). Within the service, this core belief is strong. With this in mind, the remainder of this chapter is devoted to examining the perceptions of staff on autonomy, accountability and the changing role of staff.

Autonomy and accountability

A set of questions in the survey asked probation personnel about their affiliations to both the organization and its clients. Chapter 3 indicated a change in perspective as policy was implemented; to front-line staff the client was not the court as the SCG intended. I also asked about the degree of accountability staff felt towards various groups, and whether they wished this to 'remain the same', 'increase' or 'decrease'.

First, how has autonomy been defined? Hall has stated autonomy is

> the feeling that the practitioner ought to be allowed to make decisions without external pressure from clients, from others who are not members of his [sic] profession, or from his employing organisation.
>
> (R. Hall 1969: 82)

Autonomy, according to Forsyth and Danisiewicz, may be measured on two dimensions: first, from the client, and second, from the employing organization. They also note that

> the levels of attitudinal autonomy among occupational members might well provide a means to index the professionalization of occupations.
>
> (Forsyth and Danisiewicz 1985: 61)

The resulting beliefs form a picture of the 'assumptive worlds' (K. Young 1977) of probation personnel.

When asked 'In cases of doubt over occupational practice, should the criteria for its resolution be in the interests of the reputation of the service?', half the survey (52 per cent) believed that if such doubt existed, the deciding criteria should *not* be what seems best for the reputation of the service, and just under one-quarter (23 per cent) believed it should be in the interests of its reputation. However, when asked if probation officers should be allowed to violate an organizational rule if they believed it to be in the best interest of the client, the results were more striking. One-half disagreed, but one-third agreed with this proposition. This latter group comprised a quarter of the SPOs and over a third of the POs and ancillaries, indicating a strong allegiance with the interests of the client against those of the organization.

As the findings of Chapter 3 indicated, front-line staff believed that administrative procedures were being emphasized over front-line discretion. Questions were then raised concerning the form practice should then take – administrative or occupational – as well as parallel issues about loyalty to the organization and the effects on discretion. Four questions covered these topics. When asked if occupational practice should be 'adjusted to the administration's point of view', an interesting difference between groups emerged. Less than one-fifth agreed (16 per cent), while a clear majority (62 per cent) disagreed, with nearly as many disagreeing strongly as those who agreed (14 per cent). Opinion was evenly split among SPOs, but a significant majority of both probation officers and ancillaries (both nearly 70 per cent) disagreed ($\chi^2 = 12.8$, p > 0.02). Also a substantial majority (80 per cent) believed that open criticism of the probation service by its members should be encouraged. Given this open dissent, did members then believe the service should *not* be given their wholehearted loyalty and support? Results were less skewed. About half (48 per cent) disagreed, although a significant minority agreed (38 per cent). Those who disagreed comprised a majority of both probation management and SPOs, whereas opinion was split in both the ancillary and PO groups. Thus, affiliation to occupational criteria was emphasized by front-line personnel over administrative criteria.

As a result of these beliefs did probation personnel then consider that there is enough discretion within the service to work on their own initiative? Nearly four-fifths (78 per cent) agreed that there was, which included both ancillary grades (70 per cent) and POs (80 per cent). This and the above indicate a strong belief in autonomy from the organization, but what of the client? Is independence from the client a hallmark of expert service – as per contentions regarding the traits of 'elite' professionals, such as doctors and lawyers. A clear majority disagreed (71 per cent), with over one-quarter disagreeing strongly (27 per cent). If members did not then feel a professional distance from the client was about expert service did they then believe their colleagues ought to be more flexible in allowing clients to participate in the decisions which they make on their behalf? To put it another way – more client democracy. A majority agreed (71 per cent), with a small minority disagreeing (10 per cent). However, this broad consensus on client participation fell slightly when it came to questioning the knowledge base upon which these decisions are made. Only a minority (17 per cent) agreed that because they knew their work clients should then respect their decisions. Introducing effectiveness into the PO/client decision-making process alters these beliefs. That is clients should trust their probation officer's judgements if they are to serve them effectively. Just under half agreed (44 per cent) and one-third (33 per cent) disagreed. Again, as with the above, there were no statistically significant differences between grades of staff.

The results indicate a stress on front-line discretionary decision-making in providing a service to the client, which a majority believed there was sufficient scope for within the organization. As one person noted: 'Management are attempting to define the job more . . . but it doesn't impinge that much'. Within this sphere of discretion, should any doubt arise as to the best criteria regarding occupational practice, answers to the questionnaire indicated that its resolution should not necessarily be in the interests of the service's reputation. In fact, one-third believed that they should be allowed to violate an organizational rule if it was in the best interest of the client. While half disagreed with this proposition, the majority did not then think that they should adjust their practice to the administration's point of view; a significant difference being found to exist between SPOs and probation management, who tended to agree, compounding the implementation gap between SPOs, management and front-line workers. Further, a majority (80%) felt open criticism of administrative practice should be permitted. At the same time, nearly half felt that the organization should have some loyalty and support, although a substantial minority (37%) disagreed with this (controls by length of service and gender failed to uncover statistically significant differences in the results).

In relation to clients, the majority believed colleagues ought to allow more client participation in decisions. Also, that independence from the client was not a hallmark of expert service. In addition, simply because they knew their work it did not follow clients should then trust and respect their judgements. However, some differences emerged when alluding to the knowledge base of probation work. Just under half (44 per cent) felt that if they were to serve clients effectively, then clients should trust their judgements. Therefore, while further sharing in decisions was possible, challenges to the knowledge base upon which these are made was less desirable.

Overall, the survey revealed a stress on discretion in judgements, not to aid any administrative procedures, but principally for the client's welfare. This was particularly pertinent when one considers the earlier discussion on helping clients as the prime satisfaction gained from probation work, together with the autonomy permitted in its execution. However, while probation personnel aligned themselves with helping clients, whom did they then feel accountable to for the work they performed? Was it to the client, to probation management, their employers (the Probation Committee), the courts (as implied by the SCG) or colleagues?

Some of my questions concerned the degree to which members of

Table 6   Accountability to groups and organizations

	Accountable	Not accountable
Probation clients	82.0	16.0
Probation Committee	82.0	18.0
SPOs	94.0	3.0
Colleagues	86.0	14.0
Probation management	95.0	6.0
Home Office	76.0	24.0
Courts	86.0	14.0

(*N* = 112)

the service considered themselves accountable to different groups and organizations for the work they performed.

Treen staff felt accountable to all groups, in particular to SPOs and probation management (see Table 6). However, nearly one-quarter of staff did not feel accountable to the Home Office and within the organization, nearly one-fifth did not feel accountable to their employers – the Probation Committee. Of that one-fifth, all grades – SPOs and above – felt accountable. Those who did not were POs and ancillaries. This was the case throughout, with the majority of SPOs and probation management expressing accountability to the above and any minority dissent coming from ancillaries and POs. Once again, differences in perception emerged between SPOs, management and front-line staff. How, therefore, did probation staff evaluate this accountability?

As with the questions on autonomy there was a strong identification with clients. Just over one-fifth of respondents felt that accountability should increase to the client (21 per cent), some believing this was the only check on their decisions: 'My actions could be interpreted as arbitrary and the only safeguard is my personal integrity'. Most of those who thought that they should be more accountable to clients would have agreed with these sentiments: 'I cannot make a decision affecting people's lives without being accountable'. Some went further, speaking of the 'client's right to know' about decisions which affected their lives. Nevertheless, the majority felt client accountability was 'about right'. Despite this a conflict was noted:

> I recognize the conflict in being accountable to clients (for the service to them) and to those whose prime interest is in control (e.g. over parolees). But accountability to clients ensures service is good and principled.

To many this is the check on the 'probation sandwich': that between the expectations of the court disposal and the client. This is the Janus quality of probation work that officers have sometimes mentioned (see Boswell 1989). Its resolution was found by a small minority to lie in their judgement: 'that which I perceive to be the best course for the client is not always what they would desire'. As such, any conflict between the expressed needs of the client and the judged needs of probation personnel was resolved in terms of the probation respresentative 'knowing better'. However, for the majority its resolution lay in identification with the client.

Results on accountability to the Probation Committee were less spread. A majority (86 per cent) felt that it should remain the same, simply because, as many of this group noted, they were the employers. Yet, in everyday practice terms, accountability to the Committee was a distant consideration:

> My accountability is via 'line' management and so more direct accountability would (in my opinion) be impracticable, for both me and the Committee.

Thus, the Committee were considered too remote from probation work (for a historical parallel see Chapter 1). Over one-quarter of replies explicitly referred to this, where not only their isolation from everyday work was considered, but also their ability to assess it: 'The more professional the service becomes, the less able magistrates will be to assess accountability'. In addition,

> They appear to have little concern with our methods of working with clients, more so with management roles, image-making, etc.

The Committee were seen as remote and members felt accountable to it via line management. How then did staff assess the level of accountability to SPOs, who are increasingly being pulled towards an administrative point of view?

A majority (83 per cent) believed the level of accountability to SPOs should remain the same. 'Professional support' (48 per cent discussed work with their supervisor rather than colleagues, family or friends) or a 'need to maintain standards' and the fact they were 'middle management', were reasons given. However, while acknowledging a need to be accountable to the SPO, several officers also stipulated that their autonomy should remain intact. SPOs should 'allow some main-grade autonomy' but this should not be total: 'I would not expect my decisions to be overridden by them'.

This would lead, as one officer put it, to a removal of 'all autonomy from working with clients'.

A minority (12 per cent) considered accountability to SPOs should increase, believing that professional support decreased the longer one is in the service. One person, who had noted a change in the relationship towards more monitoring and targeting, felt this was not a relevant criterion. These organizational considerations, she argued, needed to relate to individual officers in terms of their professional development. Indeed, Michael Davies refers to this problem in his study of staff supervision:

> The senior that reviews his [*sic*] objectives and needs solely with his assistant chief probation officer without reference to the team does so at his peril.
>
> (Davies 1988: 143)

One person even felt the SPO should be accountable to them as this officer had often wondered 'what the SPO does'.

The focus of replies to the question on accountability to colleagues moved away from organizational considerations to those of practice and the team. This should, perhaps, be considered an indicator of where members felt the administration starts. That is, to identify with an SPO is to see her or him as part of the overall administration and to identify with colleagues is to do so based upon practice criteria. Support for this is found in the statements of members such as 'If I let them down I would feel bad'. Also 'because they are my colleagues and we work as a team. If there were not some accountability we could not function as a team'. Staff felt a responsibility to other team members for the work they performed. To feel accountable to colleagues gave them an opportunity to share work and keep a check on each other: 'I don't think we share enough and if we don't share we can't support. Also what we do reflects on colleagues'.

Accountability to colleagues was invoked by the concept of shared experiences. The justification for accountability thus moves according to the reference group; although this is also related to the *type* of task performed. For instance, one person was part of a multi-disciplinary team and involved in Divorce Court work. In a note on her questionnaire, she said she did not feel accountable to her colleagues for how she performed the task, but did feel accountable for her overall work performance.

Management were the body members felt most accountable to and the majority (86 per cent) felt it should remain the same. What were the reasons for this? Replies referred to a 'need to maintain organizational standards' or that management 'represent the employers'. Others felt it was the 'SPO who carries the can' and in the words of another: 'management should have overall oversight not direct accountability'. These answers can therefore be considered in relation to the distance that members felt probation management were from the reality of probation practice. This conflict also emerged in replies concerning accountability to the Home Office. This is the body which most regard as having too great an input into the determination of area policies as the voice of government. Here, as with all questions, the vast majority wished the level of accountability to remain the same. However, the tendency to answer in this way is not problematic given the elaboration of replies in the second part of the question.

The Home Office were, according to probation staff, exerting too much control with too little understanding of probation work. The belief that they, like the Probation Committee, were 'too distant' from everyday practice and were a 'faceless bureaucracy', were the main criticisms: 'I do not see the Home Office as participating in a very professionally relevant way to my work'. Replies also indicated that it was probation management and not the front line who were accountable to the Home Office: 'They are not a local level body, therefore as a team, the management will account to our overall controllers'.

An increase in central control by the Home Office was viewed as a reason to reduce accountability. It was probation management and not practitioners who were 'more influenced by them'. This extended to a 'control of resources and funding' which should 'be devolved to more local responsibility'. Political economy was also mentioned simply as 'He who pays the piper calls the tune'.

The policy emphasis on probation service credibility in the courts, make replies to court accountability an important topic. A minority (14 per cent) felt accountability to the courts should increase. The requirement to 'maintain credibility', to work within the 'framework of the law' and 'carrying out their sentences' were key phrases. At the same time as recognizing these factors, there was also a stress on a 'need for professional distance'. Despite these direct replies, few were as matter-of-fact and alluded to a conflict:

If we are accountable to Courts and clients we can only sometimes be accountable to either one and then only in certain aspects of our work.

Answers made a distinction between the court's disposal (legislative) and its administration (by members of the service). This is, of course, compounded by an increased use of punitive sanctions in the community and Home Office standards – such as the Community Service National Standards – which diminish the degree of discretion available in the administration of a disposal by a more precise specification of breach proceedings (see Eadie and Willis 1989). This, it seems, further exacerbates conflicts between the court's motive for the disposal and the probation ethos which guides its execution. Thus, Martin Davies notes:

> It is probably safe to assert that most courts would deny that their primary aim was to provide a social service for offenders no matter what their identified needs.
>
> (Davies 1978: 205)

Probation staff referred to this dual accountability: 'We do not *just* serve the courts'. What this means is that tensions occur between occupational belief and expectations of the court. This can be compounded by the change in who the client is during the implementation of policy: from the court to the offender. As Walker and Beaumont note:

> Many probation officers now argue that they are not 'officers of the court' and prefer to explain their actions and decisions in terms of professional judgement or autonomy.
>
> (1981: 30)

In addition, probation officers 'are trained as social workers and not as correctional agents'. Therefore, if a reduction in recidivism does result from supervision, as is required by policy, 'it is as a by-product of their primary task of serving the client' (Davies 1978: 205–6). This point was highlighted by one probation officer, who commented:

> My actions are according to team policy and not local court requests, although I do bend to the whims of the local courts, especially when the Chairman of the Probation Committee puts pressure on me via the Chief Probation Officer. I resent this.

One answer took this a step further in referring to the political dynamics of the central/local relationship. The officer wrote at the top of the questionnaire that there was 'Big trouble brewing here!' and answered:

I don't honestly understand the politics of the situation very well. Up to now <u>Home Office</u> has led <u>us</u> (notably with SNOP) whereas we should be far more professionally progressive and not allow ourselves to become mere civil servants.

(original underlining)

In summary, the replies on autonomy and accountability tended to focus on two levels of justification: those which referred to the formal structures of the service and its relations to outside bodies and those which referred to elements of practice which did not take their justification from these structures but from beliefs concerning occupational practice. It was the latter which front-line staff alluded to in their rationalizations on accountability to different groups. Thus, as the groups to whom officers feel accountable become more remote from this core activity, so the nature of justifications alters. For example, the Probation Committee was recognized as the employer but considered too remote from everyday practice. Similarly, probation management were acknowledged to represent the employers and to whom a line accountability was also acknowledged to exist. However, they too were considered remote from front-line work. Further, the Home Office are not a local-level body and exist only as a faceless bureaucracy to which probation management are accountable as representatives of the service, not front-line personnel.

Within the sphere of discretion in which probation staff operate – noted in the previous questions on occupational autonomy – accountability to the client features as a check on arbitrary decisions made within this sphere. It is the client who forms the backbone of probation work. Even so, a conflict between service to the client – the ethos of probation work – and control for the court was also recognized. Therefore, while being accountable to the court, if the court disposal impinges on this sphere of discretion, it was seen as a bad thing in that it undermined the client/officer relationship. Yet within this sphere it is recognized that accountability to colleagues was an important consideration: probation work is a team enterprise towards a collective end, but it is the end for which staff feel accountable to colleagues and not always the means. Thus, members felt accountable to the team for their overall work performance, but not necessarily for the mechanics of how they perform the task. Goffman once summarized this position:

it would seem that while a team-performance is in progress, any member of the team has the power to give the show away or to disrupt it by inappropriate conduct.

(Goffman 1969: 88)

In this sense and in relation to SPOs, they are there to maintain overall standards – the team performance – but not directly to affect the sphere of discretion that determines how the work is performed – the individual performance. What emerges, therefore, is a recognition of a formal accountability through line management, but a substantive accountability to clients and colleagues. Where one impinges on the other – administrative procedures perceived as threatening this sphere of responsibility which is informed by the binding ethos – conflict ensues, for instance in targets and monitoring affecting supervision and support in the SPO/PO relationship.

Accountability can be defined as the 'obligation to explain and justify actions' (McWilliams 1980: 6). Formally accountability is exerted through procedural means for the purposes of 'organizational preservation and infallibility'. Substantively, particularly in interacting with clients in a human service organization, it is reliant on the decisions and actions of its representatives and that, in turn, on their conceptions of good and bad practice. This may be expressed in another way as the difference between official and operative goals (Perrow 1967). A conflict then ensues around the notion of boundary maintenance, which Morgan defines as 'the interface between different elements of an organisation' (1986: 169). In the case of the probation service this would be between different teams, groups or between the organization and its environment. At this point, the distinct concepts of occupational and bureaucratic control may be employed, with the former referring to occupational socialization, based upon a series of values and beliefs to which members broadly adhere. Given the types of judgements – relating to clients – which the service is involved in, some would argue that this then necessitates the adoption of a core set of beliefs to justify their activities. However, this also carries with it the risk that these beliefs 'will be contested by various groups' (Sarri and Hasenfeld 1978: 3). The nature of the current contest as it affects front-line staff is mediated by organizational policy as a result of government – via the Home Office – ideology.

From this discussion, the answer to the question on management accountability then becomes, albeit crudely expressed, 'Yes, we may be accountable to management for what we ultimately do, but not how we achieve it': front-line personnel clearly believe that the tasks they perform are not amenable to bureaucratic control. This involves a question of means within the organization. But the political dimension enters in an environmental conflict around ends: are clients to be punished, as the justice model implies, or helped, as the probation ethos suggests? These issues are further developed in the final chapter, which discusses the interaction of the three dimensions identified in Chapter 2.

There still exists a consideration which requires further illumination. I have alluded to the importance of understanding probation work in *context*. The above accounts require examination in terms of the work situations which give rise to these conflicts. As Mills has argued:

> There is no explanatory value in subsuming various vocabularies of motive under some terminology or list. . . . What is needed is to take all these *terminologies* of motive and locate them as *vocabularies* of motive in historic epochs and specified situations.
>
> (1940: 913, original italics)

That is, we should seek to understand these conflicts not as organizational 'inconveniences', but as potentially emerging from the everyday contingencies and difficulties of probation work at the front-line. The purpose of Chapters 5 and 6 is to achieve this aim. First, in order to add some further understanding to this analysis, I wish to examine changes in the roles of key personnel in the service, in particular ancillary staff and probation staff's perspectives on these changes and their consequences for working practice.

Changes in the roles

There are several limitations to seeing the performance of a task simply as the extension of an individual's characteristics, in particular the importance of a performance being part of a 'projection that is fostered and sustained by the intimate cooperation of more than one participant' (Goffman 1969: 83–5). This is applicable in relation to the probation team. As discussed in Chapters 2 and 3, specialization, an increased number of different tasks, plus a change in the organization and its hierarchy, are often considered the disruptive elements to a past consensus around a team's working practice. For example, not only have ancillaries numerically increased, but also the type of work they undertake has altered. Therefore, the roles and tasks of team members have changed. What, then, do staff feel about these changes? First, I consider ancillaries, whose duties and numbers, especially in relation to community service and day centres, have increased alongside change in the service's tasks. What are probation staff's beliefs about their contribution to the work of the service and their role in relation to its duties?

Ancillary staff

Two-thirds (67 per cent) of service personnel felt that the employment of non-professional staff increased the service's ability to communicate with more clients (about one-fifth disagreed: 18 per cent). Given that no ancillaries disagreed, statistically significant differences emerged between the groups ($\chi^2 = 12.6$, $p > 0.01$). However, when asked about ancillaries widening the levels of skill the service has at its disposal, members were more favourable, with a substantial majority agreeing (87.5 per cent). A majority (69 per cent) agreed that, apart from the necessary experience, all probation officers should have a professional qualification, although significant differences emerged between ancillaries and POs and SPOs on this question ($\chi^2 = 23.6$, $p > 0.001$). Thus, while a majority agreed that communication with clients was increased by employing ancillaries, differences emerged between the groups when considering the qualifications each group possesses. This could be due to seeing ancillaries in a role which should be circumscribed and does not impinge upon a role which involves working with clients, for which probation officers have been trained. In order to examine this possibility, I turn to an examination of other beliefs.

Nearly four-fifths of replies from probation officers were favourably predisposed to the increased employment of ancillary staff (78 per cent), with under one-fifth (19 per cent) indifferent or unfavourable. Of these, some were in favour of the employment of other professionals and specifically mentioned researchers, accountants and psychologists. The increase in the number of ancillaries and its consequences was also mentioned:

> Eventually it will be found that you do not need probation officers to run the Probation Service. Therefore, a decline in standards, quality, status and career prospects.

While social work training was often seen as 'mickey mouse', the service's enthusiasm for untrained staff, according to one PO, 'is pure cheapskating and shouldn't be seen as anything else. Others referred to ancillaries having 'perspectives and values which undermine the ethos of the service', with probation officers being the 'personnel carrying the social work ethos into the service'. One officer mentioned how helpful ancillaries were, but added:

> If placed at HQ or elsewhere, they tend to generate work so that time is taken servicing them rather than the client.

The majority of probation officers were favourable concerning the employment of ancillaries, but also felt that it was important to define their roles clearly: 'role boundaries must be clearly established and job substitution must be guarded against'. Ancillaries should 'not be used as a substitute for a qualified PO but as an extension to the service we can offer'. Officers commented: 'It's OK as long as they stay within their area of expertise and do not get used as cheap unqualified POs' and 'There are areas of work which do not require a CQSW qualification'. Others focused not on role boundaries, but on the types of skills which ancillaries bring to the service:

> In many tasks the basic requirements are for common sense, social skills in the wider sense and perhaps an aptitude for a particular role.

This officer suggested the increased employment of ancillary staff in areas of unemployment, housing, workshops and projects. One person, while maintaining a distinction between tasks, also acknowledged that

> The use of people with other skills adds considerably to the wide range of services the probation service can offer.

This increase in the scope of the service's work and its requirement for other specialisms featured in several replies.

Ancillary staff also felt their employment increased the skills the service can offer to clients and provided a 'more down-to-earth approach'. Several also felt the emphasis on the possession of a CQSW unwarranted:

> I do not believe that a basic CQSW qualification is always the best qualification: other outside qualifications I feel can be just as helpful to the service.

Just because staff don't have a CQSW does that make them non-professional in decision-making and working practice? Are other specialist qualifications not also relevant?

More and more emphasis is being put on possessing a CQSW with little or no credit being given for one's life experience.

These arguments were substantiated by a category of probation officers who felt ancillaries actually brought new and fresh ideas into the service and challenged the idea of professionalism:

We must learn to recognize that clients' needs must come first, not protective so-called 'Professionalism'. Clients live in the community and often the most effective help comes from those living within the same community who often have a variety of skills to offer.

During fieldwork this was emphasized to me by one ancillary, who felt better able to relate to the clients: 'They come into the office all polite and say "Thank you", but outside it's a different matter'. As a result of this association with clients – he knew them outside the office – 'Perhaps', he said, 'that is why I am not professional'. Those probation officers who saw the ancillary as bringing new skills to offer clients were also challenging the concept of professionalism as distance from the client.

The accounts concerning the employment of non-professionals were reflected in experiences during fieldwork. One ancillary told me she was thinking of applying for a job in another team, but discovered it was just an 'office gofer'. Another ancillary frequently found himself in charge of the unit where he worked and being part of the decision-making process within the unit (his supervisor was very favourably predisposed to the employment of non-professionals). However, he did not often attend team meetings due to the response of other team members towards his role. In the same team, two other ancillaries spoke to me of the difficulty of fitting in; some members of the team had such a 'fixed idea of professional expertise'. They had been told in their criticisms of the officers' attitudes: 'You have a choice, either leave or get professionally qualified'. A fine line can therefore exist for ancillaries between what is often termed an officer's professional attitude and a professional arrogance towards their non-CQSW colleagues. Yet, despite this potential and the assertions of some probation officers, this work has shown that the vast majority of ancillaries also adhere to the same binding ethos of the service as probation officers. In other words, they are also interested in the well-being of the client.

Katan (1973) distinguishes three broad types of role for non-professionals. First the 'conformists', who do not cast doubt on the knowledge base of the professional. Ancillaries told me they were not professional because they identified with the clients; probation officers in turn were happy with the role of ancillaries as long as they did not challenge their working practice. Second, a 'mediator', who will not question the professional knowledge, but will be able to communicate with sectors of the client population and offer supplementary skills which would not undermine the officers' practices. Some ancillaries taught clients practical skills, leaving the counselling to the probation officers. Third, there are the 'innovators', who cast doubt on the professional knowledge base and who will point to their powers of empathy with the client group and bring 'the client perspective into the delivery system' (Katan 1973: 129). They (like police recruits) will use 'local knowledge' in relating to clients (see Fielding 1988). Innovators may even reject the officer's knowledge base as the only means to help clients. Some ancillaries said the CQSW was 'useless' and pointed to other essential skills which the possession of a professional qualification did not guarantee and questioned the emphasis on the acquiring of a CQSW.

Clearly the extent to which certain POs are favourably predisposed to ancillaries will have an effect on their role and status within the team. This internal dynamic (Klegon 1978) is linked to the nature of the task the ancillary engages in and the ability of probation officers, as a group, to mobilize power resources to maintain their roles. These resources derive from the social and historical milieux in which officers operate: the external dynamic. For example, community service and day centres are mainly staffed by ancillaries and to many officers represented an aspect of the service which was at odds with its traditional ways of working. In effect, this may result in both these aspects of probation work operating outside of the team concept. Thus, within one team I was told and indeed witnessed that 'some of the officers "duck"' when they went through the day centre. In another team, the attempt to move away from a day centre to probation centre was met with opposition from other team members who were suspicious of day centre probation orders and the use of groupwork – it lacked a professional input. Community service also experienced its problems as officers viewed CS workers with suspicion. As one officer remarked: 'It is not because they are not social work trained, but that they do not possess the social work ethos.' While one may refer to officers' conservatism and resistance to change, this is a manifestation of a wider issue: the rise of aspects of probation work which are not so reliant on 'trained' staff.

This internal conflict also manifests itself in the suspicion of officers that ancillaries are being used as cheap labour: an issue not without substance, which is also challenged by officers who see it as an ideological mask which puts the needs of the occupation, in maintaining its prestige, before the needs of clients. This results in a 'self-perpetuation of professional privileges, status and self-interest' (Katan 1973: 238). Day centre sessional supervisors do not normally receive holiday or sick pay, despite the fact that as officers increasingly serve administrative requirements – meetings, filling in forms, etc. – ancillaries are left in charge of the day-to-day running of day centres and community service. Further, while this has occupational ramifications, it may also be part of the drive to economize the organization. During a Joint Staff Consultative and Negotiation Committee (when management meet the union representatives), the subject of ancillary pay was discussed. The Chair of the meeting said of ancillaries: 'We think they are excellent and very good value for money'. Despite the resistance of some probation officers to ancillary recruitment, their representatives on this committee said: 'Almost the word ancillary is wrong now . . . day centres put ancillaries much more in the front line with clients'. Therefore, ancillaries have advantages not only to employers in terms of their cost but also to staff in their practice skills.

Secretaries

The place of secretaries in an organization is often underplayed in its significance. They are frequently the first person that someone visiting the probation service meets and with increasing demands on their skills, particularly with the introduction of new technology, their tasks and workload are rapidly changing. Within the service these issues are compounded by a continued increase in paperwork, much of which is produced at Head Office and filtered through secretaries to the teams. Indeed, the role of senior secretaries in the process of change was considered important enough by probation management to include them in parts of the SCG meetings.

The issues of new technology and training were raised in a Joint

Staff Consultative and Negotiating Committee meeting. Representatives of the secretarial staff were mentioning their lack of training, as well as the increase in their duties which resulted from new budgeting arrangements and statistical monitoring. Probation management replied that senior secretaries were also to be managers of their teams. More paperwork, new information technology, plus the drive to computerize the profiles of clients meant, as with all grades of staff, a fundamental reappraisal of the roles and tasks of secretaries.

With an increasing emphasis on the accountability of officers via form-filling, it is the secretaries who can bear the brunt of these changes. Ringing a secretary for the minutes of a meeting I had attended, she replied that she was 'absolutely snowed under here'. I asked another secretary for some papers she was preparing for an officer. She said she would look for me, but there was 'so much of it':

> I don't know where it's coming from . . . I was sitting in bed last night reading the manual for the word processor; I had no training for it. I'm supposed to be an assistant, but I need an assistant!

Secretaries are also being co-opted into the new regime. They remind members of the team of their duties to fill in forms and questionnaires, and are expected by some officers to sort through their paperwork. One officer said:

> I get so much paperwork it piles up and my secretary goes through it and then asks me if I've done anything about them.

Some officers also expected secretaries to fill in their travel claims, while the organization of officers' diaries was part of the job description of secretaries in Treen. The secretaries were acknowledged by some officers to be indispensable. Looking for some papers when the secretary was absent in one team, the SPO turned to me: 'I don't know what I would do without her ... she possesses a computer mind'. Without the secretary in one day centre, I was told, 'everything would come to a halt'. In another team the relocation of secretaries, away from the main office of probation personnel, caused conflict between the team and the SPO and ACPO, being finally resolved by the prison authorities, who relocated them.

Secretaries also provide the front line to a visitor to teams, providing initial impressions and as G. Smith (1981) has noted, making decisions which affect services to clients. Secretaries are also vulnerable to potentially violent clients. (There was an alarm button on the floor of one Treen area office which, if necessary, the secretary could activate with her foot.) Secretarial staff may filter information selectively to unfavoured officers or use local knowledge to the advantage of the team. For instance, one secretary used to drive past the court registry in the mornings and because she knew the other office staff, borrowed files on clients, photocopied them for the Divorce Court welfare officer and returned them at lunch-time.

Senior probation officers

Like senior secretaries, SPOs are supposed to be the managers which the new climate requires. Management argue that there is not necessarily a conflict within their role between administrative and occupational concerns. Yet the results of my research clearly question this. SPOs and probation management tend to believe the organization should have loyalty and support and POs and ancillaries tend not to. Similar differences emerged when considering the adjustment of practice to the administration's point of view. Even those who felt they should be more accountable to SPOs mentioned how the relationship was changing with an emphasis on general organizational objectives – to the detriment of support for the front-line worker. An indicator of this trend is also given by the result of research on supervision by Davies (1988). Although he was more concerned with the administrative nature of supervision – tending not to enter the realm of organizational and environmental change – he notes a shift in the service's organization from the consultative to the benevolent authoritative:

> in the area of decision-making and the extent to which subordinates feel they influence goals, methods and activity in the service, and more locally, teams.
>
> (Davies 1988: 98)

At the same time, the functions of supervision and support by line managers, in the face of increasing task specialization, has 'become questionable' (Davies 1988: 103).

These points were reinforced during fieldwork. One SPO lamented the days of generic work with her ability to keep in touch with main-grade issues by having a caseload of her own. In discussion with two SPOs on the subjects of professional autonomy and decision-making they simply said that 'there is no autonomy and little decision-making now'. They told me their jobs were very different from when they joined the service. This prompted another, who overheard our conversation, to add that they try to do court work and SIRs to 'keep in touch' with front-line issues. However, in doing so they got 'rapped over the knuckles' by management. During a meeting of SPOs, one said she was supposed to 'supervise thirteen people while attending six to seven meetings at HQ a month'. She had a choice given this workload. It was either to 'skate over the surface' or 'work 8 am to midnight and drop dead in six months'! This, as she added, 'makes me accountable, but not responsible'.

The differences that emerge between SPOs, probation management and others in the organization – including how distant they are from main-grade issues – may be explicable using Gouldner's (1970) analysis. He refers to two latent organizational identities: cosmopolitan and local. Cosmopolitan describes those who are not very loyal to the organization and are 'high on commitment to specialized role skills, and likely to use an outer reference group orientation'. Locals, on the other hand, are loyal to the organization, 'low on commitment to specialized role skills and likely to use an inner reference group orientation' (Gouldner 1970: 481). While SPOs and probation management, on autonomy and accountability dimensions, possessed characteristics of cosmopolitans in terms of a degree of professional commitment, this was relatively weak when compared to POs. Similarly POs and ancillaries are not entirely without loyalty to the organization. What did appear to emerge when comparing these two groups (SPOs and probation management) with POs and ancillaries in the process of change, is an increasing *tendency* towards the administrative frame of reference, which emerges as a significant difference when *compared* to other grades. In respect to SPOs, this would appear to substantiate the findings of Kakabadse and Worrall that

> the expectation of bosses are more important in determining the work related behaviour of supervisors than the expectations of subordinates.
>
> (Kakabadse and Worrall 1978: 66)

As an SPO told me: 'We feel we are management servicing up rather than down as it should be'.

In terms of the actual process of incorporation into the administrative mode, we must turn to a consideration of the position of

SPOs within the organization. SPOs are increasingly seen as being part of the process of formulating policy and setting objectives, which was considered by probation staff to be the preserve of probation management under the influence of the Home Office and government. Some SPOs found this administrative frame of reference non-problematic. However, in so doing, they became unpopular with their team, for example one SPO was not popular because his sights were firmly focused on upward mobility. For others, not so favourably predisposed to administration, it had become an increasing part of their role as their position in the organization makes them more susceptible to change. They now furnished the needs of the policy process: the setting of team objectives, the control of specified budgets and attending a larger number of meetings. All of these met with complaints from SPOs. Therefore, the traditional and professional component of their work – having a caseload and working at the front line – had diminished. This affects their attempts to control a domain of activity as their role was increasingly prescribed by administrative ends.

The above changes also have an effect on the relationship between an SPO and her or his team. Thus, in one team, because the SPO was often away at meetings, POs and ancillaries sought the advice of a long-serving PO. Even when he was discussing these changes with me, he was interrupted by a PO and an ancillary seeking advice on their respective cases. SPOs are also expected to be go-betweens in the new climate – filtering information from the front line to probation management; this gives them a role in identifying with each. Thus they are expected to be both the specialist, who maintains the team's performance, as well as the individual who collects information on that performance. A dilemma in their role then arises:

> the individual who helps collect and formulate the array of facts used in a team's verbal show may also be employed in the distinctly different task of presenting or conveying this front in person to the audience.
>
> (Goffman 1969: 157, fn.)

The dilemma in these roles is that the audience has changed. It is not the team, but the Home Office via probation management. Divisions may then occur between the team's needs and the organization's administrative criteria represented, increasingly, by the SPO.

Probation officers

For the probation officer, the very process of individualization, as evinced by the logic of the SIR process, means considering two entities: the court and the client. This is the logic of the situation in which members of the service routinely find themselves. In the very administration of our criminal justice system, an adversarial nature gives rise to the exclusion of the victim in the prosecution/defence equation (see Mawby and Gill 1988). A similar conflict may exist between a concern with the needs of the client and the court's function, particularly in a more retributive climate that often demands justice (in this case punishment). The balance between the two, it is contended, has in the past been possible. One manual on practice in the courts stated:

> the close communication which grew between them (the Justices and probation officers), and the evident success of the system, led to the courts placing great confidence in the recommendations of the probation officer.
>
> (Wright 1979: 92)

The scales have now tilted and with it the conflict between the court and client. If members hold to the binding ethos, can this balance now be thought of as a feasible juggling act or the 'skill of autonomy management' (Boswell 1989: 73)? The ethos which informs autonomy management is under question in this environment. The ethos is a belief, but how does that belief manifest itself in the environment in which it is enacted?

These questions about changing roles, autonomy and accountability make it necessary to observe the routine pressures of probation work in different environments. The values which have been expressed by probation staff in this chapter would not be complete without examining the everyday work which probation officers undertake. These settings may either enable or constrain the execution of probation tasks and the realization of its values.

5

At the front line

*All occupational groups seek to reduce uncertainty; that is
they attempt to increase control over their environment.
Uncertainty might lie in the obduracy, complexity or
volatility of the material or people being considered. It might
also lie in the efficacy of the techniques available to handle
such objects and people.*

(Howe 1986: 98)

*I have got more impatient with the analysis of why people com-
mit crime. Five years ago we were told it was the Tories in
power and it was unemployment, now the Tories are in power
and it's affluence that causes crime. All these things are
absurd. In the end people commit crime because they are bad.*
(John Patten, interviewed by Nigel Stone in the Probation
Journal, *September 1988)*

Chapters 1 and 2 charted the formation of the probation service and
the traditional belief that probation officers exercised a degree of
discretion in deciding the *way* in which a probation or Community
Service Order was to be performed by the client. However, as
Chapter 2 indicated this is changing. The aim of this chapter (and
Chapter 6 on prisons) is, therefore, to examine this sphere of
discretion in relation to the daily demands made upon front-line
personnel in the execution of their duties. In so doing it assists in an
understanding of the implementation gap discussed in Chapter 3 by
concentrating on everyday work in several areas: the courts, day
centres, one-to-one interviews with probationers, Divorce Court
welfare, community service and a probation hostel.

Order in court: variations in the settings

Getting the 'impact' right

The impact of the service – in terms of diverting offenders from custodial disposals – must begin in the courts. It is they who provide the service with their customers. This involves influencing their decisions. However,

> the primary decision of whether or not an offender is to be sentenced on the basis of the tariff should not in theory be influenced by the social inquiry report.
>
> (Davies 1978: 203)

As indicated in Chapters 2 and 3, this process is undergoing considerable change. Indeed, following the Home Office Circular (1986) on *Social Inquiry Reports* (SIRs), Treen sent out an instruction on their preparation. The primary purpose of an SIR was to assist

> a Court to decided the most suitable way of dealing with the case when a person has been convicted of a particular offence or set of offences.

In organizational terms the impact on court decisions involves influencing the way an officer constructs a social inquiry report. The means that the organization uses are staff training, 'risk of custody scales' and targeting offenders. To these considerations are added those of cost: the Audit Commission puts the cost of an SIR at an estimated £150 (1989: para 71). In practice, however, while an 'understanding of sentencing theory' is 'vital for probation practice' (Rawson 1982: 41), so too is the officer's relations with the local court. It is here that organizational impact is determined. As such, the decision-making process in courts should be analysed not in terms of outcome – as monitoring implies – but 'in the context of the relationship between each officer and court' (Davies 1978: 207). My interest, therefore, is in the mediation of SIRs in terms of the actions of members of the service and other parties in the court-room setting.

Following observations in several different courts, the courts themselves are divided into two broad categories. This does not so much carry connotations regarding the form of justice which takes place within these different settings, but provides a means for indicating the extent to which representatives of the service may be a recognized part of court proceedings – both formally and informally. This, in turn, has an effect on court impact.

'Open' to probation

The relationship between the service and the courts is clearly important in the alternatives to custody industry. The better the links, the better the communications and understanding that then exists between the two agencies.

In the town which I shall call 'Steeple', some of the officers were known to the magistrates; in particular those who have been in the district for some years or who service small local courts. Returning to one of these courts one day, a PO told me that she met the local magistrates. One of them asked her opinion on a case heard during the morning session. She was 'deliberately deferential' and agreed with their decision. This was, as she later acknowledged, because 'few go down in the area'. Even in the main court in the team's area, magistrates are, noted another team member, 'reluctant to use prison' and 'rarely go against the decision of an SIR'. As a result of these assertions concerning the consensus which existed between the courts's decisions and the values of probation officers, together with statistical analysis of the court's sentencing patterns, I decided to study the nature of the relations which exists within the main court. As Carlen notes:

> A court of law, like the theatre, is an arena where the social values and the devices employed to choose between them can be studied.
>
> (Carlen 1976: 37)

With this in mind, the quality of the interactions can also be gauged when the magistrates retire. An informality may then emerge where the 'ritual organization of social encounters' (Goffman 1972: 45) is temporarily suspended; there is potential for an acknowledgement of the presence of a probation officer by others in the court.

On one occasion magistrates had, at the Clerk's suggestion, retired for five minutes. The defence solicitor was handed the times of her client's appearances in the downstairs court. She threw it back to the Clerk and requested that the case be 'heard in this court'. The PO interjected: 'Who is the Clerk here?' The solicitor joked that she was going to call a witness on a 'CSO breach'. The PO replied: 'You must be joking, he hasn't turned up on several occasions'. At this point one of the other solicitors in the court took the opportunity of asking the PO if there were any bail hostel places for his client? The PO said she would phone the bail hostel to assist the solicitor in his plea (by the time the defendant appeared, all the bail places had been filled).

This familiarity between the groups has advantages; for example it assists defence solicitors. However, it also has its problems. One PO 'deliberately sits at the side of the court' to give her a vantage point, but this also ensures that she does not become 'too involved' in the talk about 'skiing holidays and buying new cars' and 'past defendants' which takes place among solicitors when the magistrates have retired. This she felt was 'wrong' for the client when they were 'in the dock awaiting a decision'. Therefore, she tried not to be 'too familiar' with the solicitors in her concern for the clients' welfare. In addition, sitting where she did enabled her to be visible to the magistrates. Tactically space is an important part of courtroom procedure and visibility in the eyes of magistrates is central.

One case in this court involved a breach of a 180-hour Community Service Order after completion of only 18 hours. The PO lifted his hand slightly, raised his head and looked towards the magistrates. They acknowledged his gesture and asked for his comments on the case. There were three 'failures to attend' and one 'illness'. This, the PO added, was 'really not acceptable within the guidelines of the order'. The Clerk then asked the PO what his views were of the client continuing the order. While he acknowledged the poor attendance, if the court wanted the service 'to persevere with him', then he would. However, 'at the end of the day it is up to the individual to attend'.

The defence said that the defendant was a musician and 'Frankly sir [to the Chair of the Bench] he hasn't a cat in hell's chance of fulfilling the conditions of the order'. In mitigation, the accused had organized a charity concern and had a 'steady job' as a musician in the evenings. 'You have every right to impose a custodial sentence', the solicitor acknowledged. Nevertheless, he asked for a deferred sentence 'to keep his employment and organize the concert as a real service to the community'. To substantiate the plea, the solicitor alluded to an 'independent report'. This was written by an officer 'who your worships know has considerable experience'. The result was that the magistrates deferred a decision for six months.

As we left the court, the PO said he felt guilty about breaching people on CS 'but it's got to be done'. He had once breached someone whose son was waiting for him outside the court and the client was sent down; he then had to tell the client's wife and son of the result. That evening when playing with his own son, his sense of guilt was compounded. He then noted how the new National Guidelines for CS will mean more breaches and provide no latitude in decisions which can 'take account of individual's circumstances' which the court had just done.

In this court and the Crown Court, the PO in attendance was given the opportunity to speak to an SIR. The magistrates retired while a PO phoned a colleague who had written an SIR because the magistrates were considering a disposal which his colleague had not recommended. As the report writer was known to the magistrates, they were concerned enough to seek his opinion before making a contrary recommendation. They had considered a 4B order, but the defence noted that the day centre was based on group-work and the SIR spoke of the client's 'inability to relate to groups'. While they had retired awaiting the reply, the Crown Prosecution Service representative turned to me: 'The Clerk keeps the smelling salts for me in case they pass a custodial sentence!' The PO returned having been told by his colleague that group-work would not necessarily be a problem for the client. The magistrates then made a 4B day centre order with a two-year probation order, plus psychiatric treatment conditons.[1]

'Closed' to probation

Cover for the six magistrates courts was being provided by two POs and an ancillary. It used to be just one PO, but a pilot scheme was being introduced on Thursdays and Fridays each week. Nevertheless, in this court:

> It is a Catch 22 situation. If you are not here, they say probation doesn't care and if here . . . nothing!

In one case, after a lengthy summing up, the defence solicitor finished by saying: 'may I respectfully remind your worships' and noted the 'protection of the public criteria' as a precondition of incarceration (CJA 1988, s. 123). He was referring to two of his clients with no previous convictions who were charged, along with three others, with vehicle theft, theft of property from the car, no insurance and failure to stop. As the magistrates retired, one of the POs turned to me in hushed tones. It was, she said, significant that the defence solicitor had mentioned the 'protection of the public' criteria.

The magistrates returned. The two POs were sitting behind the clients in this courtroom which, they said, did not help their image of being identified with clients and known as 'the enemy' to court officials. The Chair of the Bench then announced forty-two days in a detention centre for the vehicle theft and theft of property and £140 fine on the other charges to both the lads with no previous convictions. The atmosphere in the court changed as relatives in the gallery let out a gasp of disbelief. As the lads were escorted away by police, the POs gathered their papers and told me to follow hurriedly.

We went down to the cells and one of the POs turned to me, referring to the decision: 'I can't believe it!' As we entered, four police officers and the custody sergeant were escorting the lads into the temporary cells. 'Who do you want to see first?', the sergeant asked one of the POs. He gave him the names of those he wished to interview. However, the solicitor was allowed to see them first because 'it's part of the pecking order'. Then, one at a time, the lads were searched and told they were allowed one phone call. One of them could not remember a phone number, so was told to go back to the cells until he could.

The solicitor came out of the cell and one of the POs asked if he was going to appeal against the sentence. He said the lad would 'only be inside for three weeks' so there was no point. A police officer said that the POs could interview the lads in the same room. In response, one of the POs stopped at the threshold of the cell: 'No, I want to interview him alone'. We sat in a small cell (3 feet by 5 feet) and the PO asked the lad if he was going to appeal. He said that the solicitor told him 'not to bother'. However, the discussion was curtailed by a third glance from a police officer through the cell door. When the PO stood up the police officer unlocked the door and handcuffed the lad, saying as he did so: 'You'll think twice about nicking cars again', adding that he would have to call everybody 'sir' in prison. The PO could not contain himself any longer: 'Next time he'll say, "sir" do you mind if I steal your car?' Another police officer said it would stop him committing further offences. The probation officer made a reference to recidivism rates and we left the cells in silence.

Back at the team office, a PO asked how her 'lad got on this morning'. She was shocked to learn he got three months: 'But three of them scored 0 on the risk of custody scale!' She had even told him to go to the motor project that evening as she did not believe the court was 'being like that'. As a result of their sense of injustice, three members of the team insisted that she ring the solicitor to appeal against the sentences.

When the SPO rang the solicitor, she was told that the police had overheard the POs discussing with their clients whether they were going to appeal. They had relayed this information to the magistrates who, apparently, were 'displeased' with the POs. The solicitor added that it was not probation's job to inform clients of their right to appeal. When the SPO told the officers of the phone call, they retorted that they had a right to do so on the client's behalf.

In this court events were usually less dramatic. For two hours one morning remand after remand appeared. Despite this, the PO I was with noted that 'you have to have your wits about you'. He had tried to get the attention of the usher to ask about court appearances (who, unlike the other courts I attended, was in uniform). The usher was important to members of the service in letting them know where and when a case was to be heard. However, in this court, ceremony was heightened and the air of formality maintained by the court-workers. As Carlen has observed:

> Throughout the court hearing, usher ensures that the magistrate is granted deference, interposing himself between those who, without further intermediary, would try to hand documents or letters directly into the magistrate's hands.
>
> (Carlen 1976: 31)

Thus, unlike the more open courts the usher could be observed to rush up the stairs to open the door to the retiring-room for the magistrates and intervene when notes or SIRs were passed to the magistrates.

The maintenance of this formality by the court-workers worked against the service. The PO could not get the usher's attention, although he clearly turned round when he heard his voice. The magistrates retired and the usher went over to the lawyers. The PO, being at the side of the court, was partly obscured by the high partitions that separated the rows of seats from the Clerk's table and the dock. I asked him if he ever got consulted in this process. 'Never' was the one-word reply. The usher then came over and standing only four feet away, announced the changes. The PO started to sort through the cases and confirmed my observations that the opportunities to 'speak to a report' were 'very few' in the magistrates court. 'You get stand-downs which I don't like. But, if I go back to the court and say I need a full SIR they just make the order anyway!'[2]

Summary

When an SIR is considered by the court, a PO may be called upon to elaborate upon their recommendations. The Clerk may be pivotal in directing the magistrates, or the magistrates themselves may wish to hear a representative of the service. Whoever decides, the decision will rest on the extent to which the service is considered to be part of the routine of the court and this, in turn, rests on the values which magistrates and Clerks bestow on the service.

Only when breaching or revoking an order was the PO pro-active in the court, otherwise the extent of the PO's participation was dependent on other participants. Even the behaviour of ushers in the courts differed. Their unwillingness to give a PO information on appearance times in the more 'closed' court must be considered alongside a willingness to see probation as part of court procedure in the 'open' court. Thus, a PO could not easily gain information on client appearances on the one hand. On the other hand, an usher handed a PO a note she had written concerning information on a client because the PO had temporarily left the court and she thought it would be of use to him. Not only can such information be of importance to the PO in her or his case, but also the willingness to disclose it makes work in the court setting more pleasant for service representatives.

The 'dramaturgical discipline' (Carlen 1976) of the different types of courts requires a certain deference on the part of those who are party to the performance. Here the requirements of courtroom deportment leave any organizational requirements on personnel to play second fiddle to the enactment of probation practice in that setting. Here also lies the officers' latitude in the execution of their tasks. However, that latitude and the degree of participation is bounded by the different courts' cultures.

A court which appears more in line with officers' values in terms of its decisions may have ramifications at levels other than the interactional. As a PO in Steeple said in comparing the area with a previous one she had worked in, 'there was a price'. While the 'criminals' in Steeple were 'nicer', if she had 'had such low-tariff offenders on probation' in her old area, she would 'have been reprimanded'. Thus, probation service activities and their members' actions within the courtroom in pursual of these, can have unintended consequences: up-tariffing offenders and spreading the formal net of social control even further.[3]

Day centres

Day centres are not without controversy, particularly due to one part of a section (4A) of the Criminal Justice Act 1982. This required offenders to present themselves at a place and 'participate in or refrain from certain activities. The latter – negative requirements – have caused conflict due to the overt nature of the controlling function in the order. In *Jarvis's Probation Officers' Manual*, Weston speaks of the importance of being satisfied 'that compliance is feasible' or 'likely' and if 'unrealistic requirements' would lead to impairing 'the probation officer/probationer relationship' (Weston 1987: 40). Therefore, authors have spoken of a challenge to the service in day centres. That is

> to use the provisions of the Act and its day centre resources to continue to provide a human and caring dimension to the penal system and for the benefit of a wide range of offenders.
>
> (A. Wright 1984: 31)

The 'daily' demands

In one day centre (of three that I attended) several clients were signing in for the day (which counted towards their sixty days). Two members of staff were engaged in this process, one talking to a client in the kitchen and the other distributing forms to three new clients to fill in (these concerned the practical and social skills which they would like to improve in themselves). The staff said they were 'starting the day off . . . by keeping the clients busy'. One client was sent off to the hospital to have a check-up. It was a traumatic time for him; it was nearly one year since his wife had drowned while 'injecting' in the bath.

An ancillary was unlocking a filing cabinet which contained money so that two clients could go and buy the day's lunch. She stopped, closed the door and commented: 'We are always on constant demand here'. 'Something', she continued, 'is always going on'. It varied from clients wanting 'small things' to dealing with 'personal tragedies'.

The problems I noted were variable. During the day, clients came in frustrated at the level of social security benefit allocated to them and demanded the immediate attention of the staff. Another client, suffering from symptoms of heroin withdrawal, needed a prescription for methadone (not helped by an allegation that the Home

Office had contacted GPs to stop them seeing registered addicts and prescribing methadone). One client had bought a stereo on hire purchase – at, it transpired, an extortionate rate of interest – and now owed more to the hire-purchase company than when she bought it a year ago; she was understandably upset. From these everyday occurrences even a closed office door was not always a refuge from these demands. Clients would still, in the words of one ancillary, 'just come in'.

Voluntary drop-in clients also attended in one day centre, in addition to the statutory clients. They would enter the office wanting playing cards and games or, in one case, to be shown how to knit. To add to this staff said it was always important to 'keep an eye on some of them'. This point was reinforced when a previous client had pulled a knife on a member of staff. As staff recognized, the control of this setting can sometimes rest on a tenuous basis.

During one of my visits I was asked if I wanted to join a group. Seven of us sat in a circle with a probation officer. He turned to one of the group who was sitting outside the circle and pointed to a chair: 'Come on, Tony, I put it there especially for you'. Reluctantly Tony sat down. Having told the group to tell the person next to us 'about ourselves', the officer left to see another client. Tony, who I was talking to, lit a fag and offered them round. Two minutes later the officer returned. 'No smoking in here Tony'. Tony looked at his cigarette and around the room at the others, who were also smoking. The officer, noting his reaction, pointed to one of the others in the group, who had painted the room and 'didn't want it ruined by cigarette smoke'. The painter looked away, not answering. Tony then looked down and played with his fingernails. 'Why not put it to the vote?' he asked. The officer then changed tactics and said he and the other 'day centre workers' found the smoke 'offensive'. Tony eventually put his cigarette out.

This simple example provides a backdrop against which one can see an exercise of power within interactions between staff and clients in these settings. For example, an officer experienced difficulty when she told a group in the day centre to stop playing cards for money. It took a few minutes for them to stop, during which time a series of resistances took place around justifications such as 'We're not doing any harm'; this was compounded by the culprits' withdrawing eye contact and turning his back on the PO. In the end, staff achieved the desired outcome. However, clients can also exercise their own power in frustration against what was to many of them a demanding regime.

In one group on road safety, a member of staff had mentioned the importance of obeying traffic laws; her authority was questioned by one of the group, who noted that the officer had driven 'over the speed limit' and therefore also 'broke the law'. Others in the group also agreed. The subject was then changed by the officer, for the credibility upon which the questioning was based – legal driving by the PO – had been collectively undermined by the group.

Making the setting work

While the power to breach a client who is on an alternative to custody order should not be underestimated, this was bounded in day centres by a desire *and* need to take account of individual circumstances. This, in turn, had a pragmatic payoff given the degree of situational uncertainty in these settings, owing to both the clients' problems and a need for the smooth running of the day centre, which necessitated the overlooking of some transgressions.

A client was late into the day centre and the staff asked the other clients where he was. His dog had been run over and he had taken it to the vet. Apparently the dog was a real friend to him. It was therefore decided not to record his lack of attendance until lunchtime. Staff did this for two reasons: first, because he wasn't usually late and second, on compassionate grounds. He turned up later and the staff decided he could make up his hours on another occasion given they understood the circumstances. Another client wished to visit his estranged wife and child. He was feeling very upset given the tenuous state of their relationship. He asked staff if a friend, also at the day centre, could accompany him just to 'keep an eye' on him in case he did anything he 'might regret'. The staff were well aware of the situation and given the emotional circumstances surrounding the relationship, granted him leave of absence (to be made up on another occasion). For the staff it was important that they should enable him to sort these personal problems out. Simply commanding his attendance at the day centre on that occasion was counter-productive.

Summary

The routine in the day centres varied not only with the type of work that members of the service undertook with clients, but also with the demands that were placed upon both parties. As a result, there was a high degree of uncertainty in these settings. They were busy places where staff tried to be pro-active in their counselling work with clients, but were mostly reactive to the constant problems which clients experienced on a day-to-day or longer-term basis. A visibility to clients also had implications for the authority which staff could exert over clients: it is more difficult to control several dissenters than just one; at the same time, a group can be used to control one dissenter.

While some staff had their own offices – a potential retreat from the demands of clients – others found themselves on display and constantly in demand. Clients would ask personal questions of some staff leaving, as I was told, some more traditionally minded officers 'feeling awkward'. This can be compounded by working in a rural setting and meeting clients out of hours. One officer told me she experienced this when 'doing the Saturday shopping'. On the other hand, the *degree* of client deprivation in inner cities also creates problems: clients addicted to alcohol and drugs and those with financial difficulties, simply because they have little money upon which to live. As an officer remarked, changes in social security legislation will exacerbate these problems: 'I don't know how some of them are going to cope'. This also has a knock-on effect in the courts, summed up by a member of the Crown Prosecution Service who told me that she was 'getting so many now with these changes in the DSS regulations'.

Holding on to 'tradition': the one-to-one

The preferred method of working with clients still seems to remain the one-to-one situation (Boswell 1985; Davies and Wright 1989). The use of this method within the probation order is based upon the potential for the individual's rehabilitation. The court selects suitable individuals for probation orders and the probation officer then has a responsibility to 'advise, assist and befriend' and supervise them. Traditionally this was achieved by regular meetings with the client based upon the casework method. This has been defined as 'an approach which emphasised some understanding of individual psychology and pathology' (Rees 1978: 52). However, with the changes outlined in Chapter 2, the nature of this task has altered and as the following accounts show, the potential for its realization is both variable and dependent on environmental factors.

The traditional approach

'George' said he was a conservative officer – 'large and small *c'* – and felt authority was important 'for people to feel it and test the barriers', but not for him to represent it as a 'threat to them'; the balance was important. For those on community programmes he waited until early evening to see them. If clients were late that was 'O.K.' as long as they turn up and let him know. He sometimes wanted to see clients in their home and get to know 'their home circumstances and meet girlfriends and wives', but would not push this if the client was reluctant. One probationer he wanted to see at home, but he was hesitant so George did not pursue it, later telling me he would gain the probationer's confidence first. Despite this temporary setback, at the end of this twenty-minute meeting he had established that the client brewed his own beer, liked drinking, but felt he had, in his own words, 'no real friends'.

George said he was from the 'method of casework school' and in the business of offering help on budgeting and social skills. I suggested this sounded like practical help, but he said it was also 'diagnostic appraisal'. However, he stopped short of seeing his role as finding 'causes for behaviour'. If this was necessary he would suggest a psychiatric report.

George saw clients once a week at first and fortnightly thereafter: 'You can do something with people who are polite, well mannered and thoughtful'. These qualities ultimately determined whether he would breach them or not, although he rarely breached. He also went to the court with clients' money and paid their fines. Professionalism for George was about confidentiality. Clients 'know it [the relationship between PO and client] stops at the door'. While he recognized a conflict between the demands of the court and the needs of the client, he worked in a rural area where he knew the magistrates – whose sentencing practices rarely included imprisonment – and could balance the competing demands. George acknowledged it 'would be different in other areas'.

Working for change

The client's name was Paul. He was a drug addict who had been hooked on heroin for over four years. In order to pay for his expensive habit he committed crime. That was the officer's view and she wanted to help him. He had been breached for not keeping his appointments and on the day of his court appearance he turned up late after a warrant had been issued for his arrest. Fortunately it was revoked by the local court (a more open one). The sentence was then referred so several other charges could be heard at the same time. The officer regarded these as petty offences – confirmed by an examination of the court's charge sheet. However, this time she believed Paul 'would get a prison sentence'.

The next day Paul turned up to be interviewed by the officer and was asked to check through the list of offences for which he was appearing. The PO then asked him, 'What do you think you will get?' 'Well, I'll go down . . . won't I?', Paul replied. The officer then began to question him about his life-style. Paul looked awkward, picked up a paper clip and began to bend it between his fingers, looking away from the officer as he did so. He said he regretted what he had done and wanted to come off drugs.

Despite Paul's awkwardness he was pressed. The PO spoke of the futility of drugs and that she was not convinced he was genuine about his wish to come off. If he wanted to do something he must 'help himself' and then she could tell the magistrates he was willing to go to a drug rehabilitation centre.

Speaking about the bounds within which the PO had to work in this case she had wanted to help Paul, but the question of credibility had arisen. She could not go into court and recommend probation after Paul had been breached for it. Therefore, the provision of help to the client, which she said came first, was circumscribed by two factors in particular. First, the anticipated reaction of the court and second, by Paul's addictive habit and subsequent criminal acts to sustain that habit.

Good will and identifying with the client

This concept of helping clients extended beyond those with drug problems. The exercise of good will – conceived of as being beyond the normal course of duties – in the service was often unrecognized and was infused, as I have suggested, in the daily routines of probation work. As Willis notes:

> Probation is primarily concerned with bringing relief and service to clients whose circumstances might have otherwise appeared to them intolerable.
>
> (Willis 1986b: 177)

Thus, one probation officer derived her work satisfaction from helping clients and ameliorating the worst excesses of injustice, which was a frequent occurrence in the local court. On occasion and if appropriate, the officer would go for a drink with clients, one of whom phoned after an argument with his girlfriend. The officer told him not 'to get drunk' and would see him in a couple of days. As she put the phone down she turned to me saying what a 'lovely person' the client was and how, from a professional point of view, 'it was a serious case of over-involvement'.

So too was the case of one member of the service who took a client home one evening because he 'was in such a state'. The officer admitted that this may be seen as 'unprofessional', but he did not see any source for regret in his actions. In fact he disparaged 'professional distance' from the client, telling me of one SPO who considered it 'unprofessional to have coffee with their team'. A similar attitude was held by those who offered clients lifts in their cars out-of-hours; arranged sporting activities; used their knowledge of local resources to gain clients opportunities in employment (albeit in many cases part-time or poorly paid) and used their knowledge of local social security procedures to assist clients, or gain them money from other sources (probation funds, charities, etc).

Summary

Those officers observed in the one-to-one situation saw the clients either once a week or once a fortnight. The length of the interviews varied and the nature of the interaction was mediated by the ethos of the officer and the circumstances of the offender.

Nevertheless, there are limits to this 'negotiated order' (Strauss 1978). Consider the *type* of relationship entered into by the two parties. It is the result of a court decision. In this George was enabled by his close relationship with a local court which rarely sent people down – his traditional methods of working were enabled by the environment. However, in the case of Paul the officer felt not only that he needed specialized rehabilitative treatment, but also that the service's credibility was at stake in the eyes of the court. It was with this in mind that she had to act. In her response to the court there was also an organizational dimension. Substantive accountability rests with the probation officer. Organizational accountability was exacted by records of client contact and other means (already discussed) of monitoring workloads. This has a time component: administrative work demanded more of her time and she believed detracted from her core task of helping the client.

The hostel environment

Probation Committees were empowered to set up and run probation hostels under the Powers of Criminal Courts Act 1972. This arose

> not only as a response to the accommodation problems of offenders, but also out of recognition of the fact that they can often be adequately helped in small institutions which enabled them to remain in employment, to have freedom of movement in the community, and to avoid the dependency and institutionalisation which can come from frequent imprisonment.
>
> (Haxby 1978: 244)

The probation hostel environment

Thursday was 'giro day'. This could be a problem for staff if the 'lads' go drinking. It was 10.15 am on a Thursday and there was much activity. One of the lads came in and blew the smoke from his cigarette into the office (in which the secretary objected to smoking) and walked out, glancing at the staff in the room as he did so. Another lad entered. He wanted help filling in his job application form, but the staff were busy and he was told to come back later. Two minutes later he returned, asking to use the phone. Having tried the number several times it was still engaged. He slammed the phone down in frustration. One of the staff looked up from her desk and told him that some consideration for others would help. He replied that she 'could do with some' and left the room. Another member of staff turned to me: 'Make a note in your book that you can't do any work in here – nowhere is sacred!'

Three members of staff then discussed a lad who was owed some money by his landord; he wanted them to pay his train fare to return home for the day and collect his money. They were unsure about his real intentions. He then entered the office: 'Can I make a phone call? It must be private'. He was told to use the phone in the bedroom behind the office which staff use when sleeping in. Another member of staff immediately retorted: 'No he can't – staff only!' However, he could make his phone call in the 'quiet room'. As he left, the member of staff who had stopped him using the bedroom telephone turned to the other: 'That was a bright idea'. She then replied that using the phone in the bedroom would have been 'all right'. 'Rules are rules', she was told. At this point the lad returned: 'I can't get through, it just keeps going "beep", "beep".' 'It's engaged', came the reply, so he could use the mobile phone. 'It's O.K., I can ring from here' he said and everybody groaned. He was worried that his dole would be stopped if he didn't contact his landlord, which confirmed the suspicions of staff regarding his initial motivation to make the call. It was now 10.45 am and I have described only a few of the events.

That was my first half-hour – apart from team meetings and short visits – spent in systematic observation in a probation hostel. The same frenetic activity characterized the whole hostel environment. Mostly it was demands for practical help, such as filling in DSS claim forms, reading and helping write letters, or residents wanting access to their money, which was kept in a locked drawer in the office. In response to this, one of the staff members told me that when he first started working in the hostel, he coped with the demand by saying 'No to everything' and then 'people had to convince me'. Now, he 'invariably says yes'.

These demands were compounded by particular residents. One lad, I noted, took great delight in 'winding up' the other residents, something he admitted on one occasion. This came to one of several peaks when he was knocking on the door of another resident and running away. He was pursued down the stairs and retreated into the office. The other resident followed, extended his arm and pointed a finger at him: 'I'll give you a smack'. 'We'll have none of that in here', said a member of staff. The aggrieved resident left and the lad stayed in the office, fearing a reprisal. He then started to play with the papers and pens on an officer's desk. He was told he was being irritating, which he denied. 'Well you're irritating me', the officer told him. He took offence: 'Get on to Martyn Williams [his 'home PO'] and tell him you don't want me then'. Having been told this was not what was meant, he left the office.

This same resident had driven one member of staff to the thought of hitting him, a feeling not previously experienced. However, there was another side to the story. 'Eric' had once admitted to his key worker – later to deny it – that he had been sexually abused as a child. Another member of staff also believed that he had been a male prostitute. Eric's problems did not end there. A system of rewards had been established for him if his bed was dry in the morning – something which had to be kept from the other residents for fear of ridicule – and he was also frustrated at his inability to read. Eric needed intensive help, which in the busy environment of the hostel it was not always possible to provide. Therefore, constantly checking him and protecting him from the other residents formed more immediate considerations in the minds of the staff.

It was early evening and a new arrival had come in. He was on bail with a 6 pm curfew, the provision of which, a member of staff noted, had 'enhanced the credibility of the hostel with local magistrates'. A few of the lads were signing out for the evening. As one lad left, another resident turned to the new one and commented: 'Be careful what you say to him, he's green grass'. They started talking about their exploits and exchanging information. I left the dining-room for the office, where one member of staff, like the others, frequently found himself doing overtime. It was not his turn for sleeping in, but paperwork needed completing and the residents' concepts of night-time did not 'necessarily include sleep'. There was also the possibility of 'trouble' – it was Thursday (giro day) night.

It was now 11.15 pm and the front door was about to be locked. The rule about this, one of several which all the residents sign, read:

> Residents to return no later than 11.00 p.m. and remain on the hostel premises until 7.00 a.m. the following day. Late passes may be granted by the Duty Warden, but this should be seen as a privilege not as a right.

A late arrival came in and after we exchanged greetings the Duty Warden asked him: 'Do you want a word?' 'Yes' he replied. Another resident was asked to leave the office to allow some privacy. 'I'm not being funny, but I would like a private word'. O.K., we'll go up to the quiet room'. They left to talk in the only room which was not used as a bedroom which, according to Home Office criteria, should be a bedroom, but it was the only place in the hostel where clients could speak to each other and to staff in privacy. We sat downstairs for another hour and they still had not reappeared. The lad who had wanted a chat had attempted suicide the week before and being giro night 'things did not', in the words of the other warden, 'feel right'.

Summary

The very fact that up to twenty lads are accommodated in the hostel created peculiar pressures on the staff. There was a constant dilemma between the smooth running of the hostel and the aims of residential orders in rehabilitating offenders. This possibly underlies the comment of a member of staff, who reflected 'Perhaps probation is nothing more than a first-aid placebo'. However, there was temporary respite for the staff from the demands of this regime, for instance in seeing one of the lads moving from stage one, which begins the process of assisting them in understanding offending behaviour and on to stage two, which involved greater independence by moving into adjacent bed-sit accommodation.

There were also circumstances which militated against this. Home Office rules stipulate the number of beds which should be in use and hence question occupancy rates. Hostel effectiveness was therefore measured on a head count. As one officer remarked, 'It is no good having the right philosophy without Home Office back-up'. Further, these criteria dictated the number of staff who can be employed. There were twenty beds in the hostel; if they had had twenty-three, another member of staff could have been employed.

These criteria directly affected the type and amount of work which can be achieved in this environment. They also do not consider the additional demands that residential work requires:

> Such a ratio is confusing, because at any one time a worker on duty may be responsible for all the residents in a hostel, but have continuing responsibility for a few of them.
>
> (Glastonbury, Bradley and Orme 1987: 148)

They take no account of the suicidal resident mentioned above and the fact that a 'sleep-in' – despite that, officially, there is no twenty-four-hour cover – often becomes a 'night duty'. Also, the need to liaise with local residents, who feel uneasy about the location of the hostel – an important public relations exercise – and offer an open-door policy to them. In addition, those residents who, like Eric, have been severely affected by their earlier experiences and required help with their lives and not just the simple containment which a quantitative count inevitably implies.

To add to these restraints, the local magistrates were, according to the warden, increasingly seeing the hostel 'as an alternative to custody'. This placed additional responsibilities on the staff to keep an eye on residents. With this background of expectations made of the hostel, the balance of help and control can so easily tilt. Fisher and Wilson found this to be the case in their study of one hostel in which the staff attempted to act in a more liberal manner:

> Ironically, the staff were obliged to take on the burden of patently exercising authority, sometimes in an authoritarian manner.
>
> (Fisher and Wilson 1982: 197)

In contrast, the other hostel in their study which pursued a more authoritarian regime had, they declared, a high rate of absconding. All these criteria, and the attempts to balance one against another, circumscribe the type of work which can be undertaken in the hostel environment.

Divorce Court welfare

This study has concentrated on the probation service's work with adult offenders. However, there remains an area of work the public may not always associate with probation: Divorce Court welfare. The tasks of probation officers as Divorce Court welfare officers (DCWOs) include adoption, custody, conciliation, consent to marriage and acting as guardians *ad litem*. The officers' primary concern is with the welfare of children and they act as conciliators between parties who are in dispute over access or custody of their children. They also prepare welfare reports for the court in the case of parties failing to agree and in some circumstances undertake the supervision of a ward of court. For the purpose of comparison with other areas of work, I shall concentrate on in-court conciliation only.[4]

Divorce Court welfare officers in action

A DCWO was working with two clients in a particularly acrimonious divorce with allegations of child abuse being made against the father. The father visited the DCWO with articles about how the effect of false allegations can ruin someone's life. This kind of pressure of the work, remarked a DCWO, 'worries me, it really does'. On the other hand, another officer felt Divorce Court work was a 'cathartic experience'. She considered work with offenders was desensitizing. Continuing to see offenders who were guilty of various crimes meant that she was no longer shocked by what she saw. For example, she would sit in her office and a client would enter and she would think to herself, 'Oh! Another rapist. Come in and sit down'. The job then became 'too administrative'. Working as a DCWO was 'psychologically demanding. . . . It's a fascinating job, it really is fascinating. No two cases are the same'.

On Monday the cases are allocated and I joined three officers who were going to discuss them with the Registrar. He, unlike another Registrar, tested the officers less because he did not read all the reports thoroughly, but deferred to them on specific cases. Later, a

DCWO made contact with two parties outside the courtroom to attempt a conciliation at the Registrar's request. However, following an unsuccessful conciliation she returned to the Registrar requesting a report.

In all the conciliations attended the officers were at pains to stress their independence: a point which was reinforced by the explicit mention of their position to both parties by the Registrar and their solicitors. In practice, officers used various methods to focus the parents on their children's welfare. In one case, a father was speaking to his ex-partner through the officer. The officer leant forward, looked at him and gestured to his partner: 'They're your children' and told him to speak directly to his ex-partner. Therefore, the professional rhetoric of impartiality was sustained by DCWOs and their clients which, in turn, was empowered by the courts. This was a very different position from their counterparts in the rest of the service.

These powers, while enabling, also have a price. The preparation of a welfare report – following the attempt at conciliation prior to a court's order – means all avenues concerning the parties' circumstances and allegations must be explored (usually by an officer other than the one who conducted the conciliation). This places investigative powers in the hands of the officer, particularly in cases of contested custody where both parties attempt to present themselves in the best possible light. In court, the presentation of the welfare report may open DCWOs up to cross-examination by the parties' barristers. During one case the judge spoke to the officer about the report: 'It's not your job to make decisions Mr *X*, it's mine. But now I'm going to throw you to the lions'. Whereupon, he was cross-examined by the two barristers in a case where he had recommended the splitting of two children (something which officers are reluctant to recommend and rarely do). For this, as the officer noted, there is no training for divorce work or for facing barristers in court.

In respect to the actual exercise of investigative powers, I joined an officer who was visiting the house of a woman whose ex-husband was seeking custody of the children. He had alleged that she never did any housework and the house was always messy. The officer, while apologetic, told the woman that he had to investigate these claims because if he was 'put up in front of the barristers it was important to know all the facts'. The woman showed him round the house, later feeling it necessary to show us her cultivated garden, new furniture and 'clean' kitchen. In circumstances such as these, the discourses which surround the notion of an ideal family and its division of labour align themselves in the perspectives of the officers and assumptions and practices of the court.[5] Again, this was a very different story from criminal court-based officers.

Summary

The officers I observed and interviewed believed Divorce Court welfare work to be a two-sided affair: demanding and yet enjoyable. This can be attributed to two factors in comparison with work with offenders. First, the role of DCWOs is clearly circumscribed in law and they work with the interests of the child paramount in their task. Second, this offers an alignment:

> the clearest possible statement of precisely those moral and humanitarian motives that underpin his [*sic*] career, and reflects backwards in time to the early concerns of the police court missionary.
>
> (E. Cooper 1987: 38)

The binding ethos therefore finds its outlet in this work and is also enabled, in comparison with probation work, by the structure of the environment in which it is enacted. In this respect DCWOs also believed they had the autonomy to work towards this end. For example, the SPO allocated the cases and 'by and large' the DCWOs could 'do what we like'. Substantively the officer was accountable for the interests of the child and operationally 'I am only accountable to the judge, not the probation service as such'. As a result of these factors, ideological conflicts, say between courts and the officers' perspectives, tend to arise much less.

I am not suggesting conflicts did not arise in this task. Problems did exist in getting the magistrates courts to limit supervision orders and in the tendency for the Clerks to favour adversarial approaches as against the team's attempts to see conciliation as the norm. These considerations therefore limited the extent to which objectives and targets could be met. However, I am suggesting that when conflicts did arise, they were not so intense on an ideological and operational basis as those in criminal work. However, on an organizational basis the story changes. Competition for resources, despite the commitment of the service, inevitably resulted in DCWOs experiencing a shortfall. This had the effect of leaving personnel potentially confused about the direction of policy towards this area of work as managers attempted to maintain it, while economic considerations further negated the possibility of its development. This adds to the debate where

> Opinions vary about the propriety of allowing a Service which has become increasingly identified, in the eyes of many, with the penal system, to have total responsibility for the provision of the Divorce Court Welfare Service.
>
> (E. Cooper 1979: 95)

Community Service

With its mixture of penalty, reparation, rehabilitation and the offender agreeing to undertake unpaid work for the community, Community Service 'is often regarded as the most imaginative and valuable penal sanction introduced this century' (Eadie and Willis 1989: 412). Despite this, and while accepted by the service,

> its day-to-day practical tasks, organisation, process of administration and its ideological parameters, as well as operation, fell outside the traditional boundaries or expectations of qualified probation officers.
>
> (Vass 1988: 49)

Organizationally the effect of this was to marginalize its administration from the mainstream of service provision. Nevertheless, it was a pragmatic consideration to make the service administratively responsible for CS due to its geographical spread. Therefore, it was 'little more than an organization to put work-providing agencies and offenders in contact with each other' (Pease 1981: 11). Even so, the very implementation of CS was mediated by the values of probation officers. This gave rise to a distinction between a tough and a soft approach to offenders (Vass 1984). This appears to have been resolved by official policy in the shape of the *National Standards for Community Service* (Home Office 1988a), which came into force on 1 April 1989. Listed are the 'only acceptable reasons for a failure to attend' (para 3.2.3) and instructions for when breach proceedings 'must be started' (para 3.4). I shall now consider the effects of these changes.

The 'reality' of National Standards

The National Standards (NS) were referred to by one officer as unrealistic to implement: 'An idea in the Home Office takes off and they don't think of the implications, it's all just impression management'. Another CS officer also regarded the guidelines as 'unworkable'. In reflecting on three months' experience with them he said: 'I'm not trained as a prosecutor'. He estimated that breach rates had increased by nearly one-third. CS was 'demanding enough'. As a result, offenders were now 'just sticking two fingers up'. The new standards had tilted the balance towards control: offenders 'should be given a chance . . . to make decisions and not be subject to mechanical enforcement of their behaviour'.

The changes had altered relations not only with clients, but also with the courts. Those whom the government had attempted to appease with these changes were now asking why it was not working because of an increase in the breach rate. As a high tariff alternative to custody, failure was likely to result in imprisonment which adds to a self-fulfilling prophecy that Community Service was ineffective. As a CS officer had experienced, this had further compounded the problems of both the probation service and the offender.

Treen guidelines referred to CS as being inappropriate for those with personal problems, but it was clear that this could not be fully anticipated. There was an inevitability of either allowing some offenders through the screening process or of problems emerging for the client when on the order. For example, an offender did not turn up on a Saturday work party and the discussion among CS staff came round to the domestic dispute which the client gave as the reason he could not attend. His wife had just gone out and apparently dumped the baby on him.

The guidelines refer to 'tough demands' which are also 'constructive and reparative' (para. 1) and that 'community service orders should not be performed at the convenience of the offender' (para. 2). To these ends, oral warnings should be issued if less than half-an-hour late (para. 3.1.2) and a 'failure to attend' if more than half-an-hour late (para. 3.2). Explanations of a failure to attend must be recorded and open to inspection by a senior manager (para. 3.2.2). According to two CS sessional supervisors they could then take account of individual circumstances which was then 'constructive' in terms of the aims of CS. However, the above example (and others) are intended to be altered by two factors. First, a more 'mechanical application of a rigid breach policy' (Eadie and Willis 1989: 416) with CS credibility being at the forefront of probation practice. Second, while some latitude did exist the threat of breach was intended to be invoked at an earlier stage than current practice allowed for.

The 'two fingers' the officer mentioned was a client's reaction to an inflexibility in the administration of the CSO which resulted from the new standards. It is often forgotten, as a PO noted, that the demands of a community disposal require a self-discipline which is removed from an offender by an institutionalized regime. Thus, if offenders

> feel the burden of the community service approaches the pains of imprisonment, they may well prefer the mindless anaesthetic of incarceration to the socially useful efforts of community service.
>
> (Eadie and Willis 1989: 417)

Summary

The method of overcoming the simply punitive towards the offender, without any apparent constructive rationale, was a compromise which, in part, takes account of the 'trade-off between discipline and compliance' (Eadie and Willis 1989: 417). This is part of the skill of autonomy management which permits a balance between an account of individual circumstances and the administration of a punitive community disposal. This then allows some form of reparation and perhaps the by-product of rehabilitation. Operationally it necessitates a sphere of discretion. However, the guidelines limit this in their move towards contemporary discourses on punishment. The intention of the document was to raise the credibility of this disposal. However, its consequence was to limit the discretionary decisions of its administrators – as noted above – and render visible work demeaning. Further, it will widen the formal net of social control even further. Staff are also beginning to react to the circumstances which have resulted in further discretionary limitations and Vass's prediction may emerge more forcefully:

> Agents of administration and enforcement would be more concerned in covering up their activities than showing any real regard for a proper and just application of justice.
>
> (Vass 1984: 180)

Discussion

The areas of work examined in this chapter form spheres of organizational discretion which are informed by the binding

ethos of probation work. Therefore, within these spheres of discretion choices are being made by front-line personnel whose
outcomes will be 'attributed to the organisation' (Manning 1979:
52). However, this is one assumption of the policy process. There is
an assumed connection between the perspectives of probation
personnel and their practice. For two reasons in particular this is an
inadequate analysis. First, the historical condition of the organizationally autonomous front-line worker has changed. As one PO
commented, 'The problem is that administrative directives become political edicts'. Thus, Home Office criteria governed the
number of staff who could be employed in the hostel and the
National Standards for Community Service further limited
officers' discretion in decisions to breach. The quantitative count of
occupancy and numbers on schemes directly affect the qualitative
dimension of work with clients, resulting in a significant tension
between quantity and quality. There is also an indirect effect of
time: officers found themselves servicing administrative requirements to the detriment of time they could spend with clients.
Second, the environment in which probation staff work also varies
and either enables or constrains the realization of the binding ethos
and probation tasks. Within day centres, hostels and community
service work, a concern with control of the setting routinely
impinges on daily interactions with clients. In examining this
question, we come round to the conceptual maze of the care/
control issue on which much writing has centred.

Some authors have spoken of a collapsed dichotomy whereby
'Caring becomes the officer's overall stance, control a technique
forming an element in it' (Fielding 1984: 109). Others have
described the probation officer as being a

> Translator, negotiator, supervisor, educator, controller – all
> these roles exist within the domain of the social, all of them are
> at some time and to varying degrees played by the experts.
> (Harris and Webb 1987: 86)

Nevertheless, Rodger's comment is pertinent to the debate: there is
a 'crudeness of understanding' in many approaches in their failure
to deal with 'multifarious phenomena involved in social control'
and to analyse 'negotiations between superordinates and sub-
ordinates' (Rodgers 1988: 566). It is clear that as environmental
expectations change – for instance, of the courts and as a result the
clients – the nature of the task can also change with it. Therefore,
the above accounts uncover an 'anticipatory action' on the part of

staff. In the process, they either become concerned with the probation service's credibility in the court, or they know that a
stand-down report will have to suffice, otherwise the court will
make the sentence anyway.

The concept of a collapsed dichotomy becomes increasingly
tenuous when the daily routines in hostels, community service and
the supervision of serious offenders and parolees involves controlling a setting in order to make it manageable. For instance, the
changes in community service while retaining a degree of discretion, in practice create a form of control which appears to serve
no obvious end, apart from quenching the thirst of retributive
courts and the government. Community service is still argued to
represent a constructive alternative to custody. Nevertheless, by
the very nature of its history and operation, it is peculiarly vulnerable to change. At a policy level, officers attempt to offer this
disposal as an alternative to custody and when not successful, in
terms of targeting high-tariff offenders, are held to account for the
court's decision by the organization. The resulting control which
may then be imposed on clients could prove counter-productive:

> We take it as axiomatic that human beings will tolerate a
> culturally unusual degree of social control only if they ac-
> quiesce in or support the declared end of excessive authority, or
> because they have no other course open to them.
>
> (Fisher and Wilson 1982: 197)

Raynor (1988) has, with reservations, concluded that the alternatives to custody industry can be successful in its aims. However,
the new climate of limiting those discretionary elements in such
programmes which make them effective, may conspire to prevent
this. For example, a PO (not in Treen) reported that she had invited
magistrates to their service's day centres in order to sell the concept
as an alternative to custody. The potential purchasers of the service
were so impressed that they promptly flooded them with a variety
of customers – from first offenders to those with eight or more
previous offences – all disparate individuals with a variety of
expectations and problems. With sentencing variations of this sort –
and no sign of *directly* limiting its discretionary components – no
amount of administrative rationale can create a predictable and
manageable environment.

It is not surprising, therefore, that the idea of diverting people
from custody by social work means is questioned by practitioners,
given both the contemporary climate in sentencing trends and their

rationale. To consider this tension resolvable in a 1960s and 1970s style of practice management – still common among probation officers – ignores these changes and those which have taken place in the organization. The negotiated order analysis implied by this perspective – which draws on the binding ethos without considering the environment in which it is enacted – has to be considered alongside organizational and environmental conditions. Indeed, a split may be taking place within the service around front-line staff's attitudes to further control. In the survey, just under half (48 per cent) believed the imposition of more control on offenders would not involve an unacceptable change in the principles and ethos of probation work. However, a sizeable minority (38 per cent) felt it would.

Other implications can also be considered in relation to the above areas of work. Day centres, probation hostels and community service, by virtue of the tasks and constant demands within these settings, necessitate the use of skills which are not the sole province of the probation officer. In these environments ancillaries contributed as much to the day-to-day running as probation officers, who can hold so dearly to their professional self-conception. As Harris has written: 'probation officers spend a considerable proportion of their time doing tasks which do not necessitate the use of social work skills' (1977: 440). While he advocated the separation of treatment and punishment as a solution to this problem, I have argued that the environment has changed. Punishment is now being seen as the service's province in the Green Paper (Home Office 1988b) and the similarities of this and Harris's suggestions are not lost on the author in reflecting upon the contemporary relevance of his article (Harris 1989).

To add to these changes – increased use of ancillaries, the demands for punishment – comes another component to the equation: the everyday contingencies of clients' lives, the majority of whom face considerable practical difficulties in monetary terms: witness 'giro day' at the hostel, requests of help with DSS forms in all settings and the effects of changes in social security legislation. Officially, as one of the opening quotes of this chapter indicates, this is as an irrelevance to the causation of crime. However, the daily probation routine was one of responding to clients' immediate needs. As the courts continue to process those who are socially deprived, this problem can only be compounded. An unemployment survey of Treen's caseloads in 1987 revealed, 50 per cent were registered unemployed with only 13 per cent in paid work. Help with such everyday problems highlighted in these different areas takes up most of the time of probation staff. In these settings there is an understandable response to clients' needs which has a pragmatic payoff of making the settings more manageable. Here, there is staff latitude which is mediated through a binding ethos to assist clients. The implication is that the 'demands for casework and overt forms of social control have been ousted by the dynamics of need' (Willis 1986b: 177).

To meet the dynamics of need is, in turn, either enabled or constrained by the organization and environment. In comparing the types of work I have discussed, it is clear that George, who held on to tradition, was enabled by his rural setting and the practices of the court. In other words, he was empowered by these conditions. This does not suggest that *vis-à-vis* the client he does not possess power, but that the nature of this power changes as a result of the context of the interaction and the expectations that each party brings to it. In this sense, no internal policy can specify uniform actions in variable environments.

In Divorce Court welfare work, I have argued that the ethos was enabled to find an outlet by the environmental conditions in which it was enacted. However, organizationally this was problematic in terms of service resources. Indeed, this may be further compounded by legislative changes. Looking to the future and the proposed Children's Bill there are implications for the service. With a proposed increased workload for guardians *ad litem* will this be matched by increased resources? Further, with the possibility 'that a number of factors . . . may reduce the request for reports from welfare officers (Wells 1989: 235) will, under resource pressure, the managers of the service permit an increase in DCWO's guardian work? As Monro notes:

> it is conceded that extra legal staff and guardians *ad litem* will be required, but nowhere in the memorandum is detailed consideration given to the likely number of additional court hours which will be required as a result of these changes.
>
> (Monro 1989: 28)

Divorce Court work in the service may then find itself substantially reduced. This will then add to the debate about continuing civil work in the service.

In the day centre and hostel, negotiations took place around an allowance made for individual circumstances, but this was also dependent. Take the case of Eric. He required help, but because of the practical problems in running a hostel containing seventeen lads (whom he 'wound up'), the staff could not always provide this. On one occasion the staff considered that he was being so irritating that his inability to read was used as a means to provide a very broad interpretation of hostel rules. He insisted on seeing the rules, but was in no position to dispute what he couldn't read! While the staff felt guilty about using such means to gain his compliance, given the demands made of them by the setting in general and Eric's behaviour in particular, it may be understood, if not condoned.

Within these settings also emerge a pragmatic criterion which acts as a trade-off: that is an allowance of clients' transgressions for the purpose of eliciting more general co-operation to make the setting work. Without this possibility, community-based disposals will appear too authoritarian to the clients to be constructive and also for the staff be impossible to run. After all, a hostel is not a prison. Therefore, when new windows with locks were installed in the hostel, the residents obtained keys for them on the grounds that if they were locked in and there was a fire, they could not escape. This would appear to be a valid reason. However, their possession of the window keys constituted a security problem. This is not irrelevant; it is a major question when security and control become daily considerations in community-based disposals.

At the same time, there are offenders whom the service deals with where the issues may be less operationally problematic. In this instance, bail hostels may deal with 'heavy-end' clients and take responsibility for their behaviour – caught as they are in the credibility stakes. Further, there are parolees who may reach head-line news if found guilty of a serious crime when on parole. In respect to serious offenders, it is clear the service reacts to what may be a moral panic: the ability of the public antennae to amplify an isolated case. While these constitute a minority of cases, organizations and individuals anticipate a reaction and protect themselves from possible charges of neglect and irresponsibility. There are also those whom the service can refer only when all else had been tried, Paul being a case in point. All this appears manage-able to the traditionally minded, ignoring the fact that their work is bounded in the ways discussed.

The environment and the organization therefore affect work at the practice level which simply cannot be seen in isolation. In times of such rapid changes and when provided with the oppor-tunity for reflection, these conflicts manifest themselves in the utterances of front-line personnel – sometimes with great intensity. On the back of the questionnaire one person mentioned organizational change and added: 'This exercise has been cathartic in helping me express many pent up feelings, and I'm grateful for the opportunity'. Another person, while noting it was hard to find the time to complete the questionnaire, said: 'The desire to discuss and debate with colleagues was almost overpowering, but I guess that can wait until your findings are published'. One person simply said: 'Nicely thought provoking!'

The demands and constant problems of these settings may also manifest themselves in another way. The phenomenon of 'burnout' is now a more commonly discussed topic in the service. Three aspects to this have been identified: first, a feeling of 'emotional exhaustion'; second, a 'depersonalization of clients'; and third, a 'negative self-image' (Brown 1987: 17). The depersonalization of the client has already been mentioned by one officer and I have discussed the criticisms that staff had of the increase in administration and the effect of this on their relationship with the clients. This negative self-image derives from the first-aid nature of probation: the belief that one is doing the best one can in adverse conditions.

There still remains another area of probation work which I have not examined in detail – prisons. Therefore, before discussing the overall findings of my study, Chapter 6 is devoted to an understanding of the daily pressures of probation work in prisons.

6

In prisons

> The welfare role is firmly defined and constrained by the
> discipline and control function of the prison.
>
> *(Walker and Beaumont 1981: 46)*
>
> It's like a military machine; if you get in the way you'll go
> under the wheels.
>
> *(Probation officer)*

During the 1960s the incorporation of a community-based probation service into the sharpest end of the penal ladder was not
without its critics. The introduction of parole in 1967 added to the
'prison-based' functions of the service and has always invoked
reactions from those of luke-warm to the unequivocally hostile. In
the 1980s the Carlisle Report on parole (Home Office 1988d) was
greeted as 'An Opportunity Missed' (*NAPO News* February 1989)
following its recommendations of a minimum term sentence for
parole, as opposed to the current minimum qualifying period.
NAPO, it seems, was the only organization to submit evidence to
the Review who were 'resolutely abolitionist' (Stone 1988b) in their
stance. This is at a time when the media routinely refer to the crisis
of overcrowding in our prison system while a growing body of
literature adds to its condemnation (see Stern 1987; Blom-Cooper
1988).

This chapter analyses the work of probation officers in prisons,
taking as its starting-point the day-to-day issues of working in this
setting.[1] I shall consider the front-line contingencies of implementing a welfare-based service within the prison environment.

I shall also examine the degree of coherence between the daily realities of probation work and the rhetoric of official policy.

The observational period upon which this chapter is based was spent in three prisons. One of these I took to be a 'critical case' due to its size, population and reputation. I shall argue that to neglect the environment in which probation work takes place is to ignore a feature which is variable and either enables or constrains the execution of probation policy. The extent to which the current nature of official policy can effect change, is thereby limited.

'Shared working'

In 1967 a Home Office Circular on the *Roles and Functions of Seconded Probation Officers* identified four aspects to their role:

> as social caseworker; as the focal point of social work; as the normal channel of communication on social problems with the outside world; and as the planner of after-care.
>
> (Weston 1987: 184)

There then followed the 1974 *Social Work in Prisons* initiative and a later Home Office study by Jepson and Elliott (1985), which focused on 'shared working' – between probation and prison staff – in prisons. Governors and chief probation officers were encouraged to see through-care of prisoners in terms of a joint responsibility. The focus was on a series of objectives towards the general aim of enhancing prisoners' welfare. As Jepson and Elliott note, the objective in relation to prison staff was to enable them 'to participate more fully in work within the establishment in the field of inmate care' (1985: 66). This was, in turn, to assist seconded probation officers:

> to concentrate on arrangements for release and other aspects of social work, for which the Probation Service has particular responsibility.
>
> (Jepson and Elliott 1985: 68)

In theory, probation staff would be able to perform their tasks free from the day-to-day welfare issues which arise in the prison setting.

In relation to this general aim and the work of the service, SNOP did not specifically mention the work of seconded officers (mainly because their salaries are paid by the prison service). However, the

Home Office *Report of the Working Group on the Review of the Role of the Probation Service in Adult Penal Establishments* (1985) did suggest both services should

> develop effective partnerships for the provision of through-care as an integral part of the total regime and influencing the nature of the regime, in all establishments.
>
> (Weston 1987: 182)

Therefore, welfare functions should become a joint endeavour between the two services within the institutional setting.

Jepson and Elliott's research on shared working in prisons relied heavily on survey material. This, as they recognized, ignored a political dimension which can profoundly alter the success of shared working:

> There are clearly many factors related to the introduction/ survival of S.W.I.P. (social work in prison) that should have received greater attention. There are the political factors associated with the influence which key individuals and 'power' groups can exercise.
>
> (Jepson and Elliott 1985: 33)

Indeed, they uncovered a clear variability in its implementation. This chapter examines some of these political dimensions from the point of view of the probation officer who is charged with a rehabilitative function within an institutional environment. It examines those aspects of the environment which may either inhibit or conflict with the implementation of shared working and alternative methods to those of simple containment and control of prisoners.

An inhospitable environment

'Victoriana'

'Victoriana' prison was originally built in a geographically isolated position, but in the days of helicopters and high-speed cars its location is no longer the deterrent to potential escapees it was once thought to be. However, contrary to the reputation it still seems to possess, it is not a maximum security establishment and houses approximately 630 category 'B' and 'C' prisoners.

The probation team at Victoriana consists of an SPO and five probation officers (normally six, but part of one wing was closed for refurbishment). Each officer is attached to a wing and like the SPO is accountable to the governor, who is responsible for welfare services in the prison. Seconded officers also have a professional accountability, through probation line-management, to the chief probation officer.

Control and welfare: a source of tension

The probation office in Victoriana is situated within the outer gates, but outside the two inner gates. The office is small, housing the SPO, with another office for the secretaries. If all the officers are in at the same time, it can be cramped.

On one occasion, the SPO had three visitors – one from the locality and an officer from another area with the mother of an inmate. The SPO offered to escort them to the wings. The log of their arrival was checked with security and we went through the inner gate, which was unlocked by a member of staff who was constantly on duty. The SPO then unlocked a small gate within a large wire one, through which it was possible to see an open area of flower beds, grass and pathways leading between the wings.

Having escorted the visitors, we returned to the probation office. Shortly afterwards a prison officer entered: the mother in the visiting party had not been searched. The SPO apologized even though the visit had been checked with the office. The prison officer smiled and noted how this episode would be used by some members of security as a scapegoat; despite being their duty to perform security tasks. The SPO thanked the prison officer and turned to me, mentioning how this officer had 'helped the probation service on many occasions'.

This aspect of compatability and mutual accommodation between the welfare and control functions of the prison is clearly important in relation to policy implementation. With larger numbers in the prison system and the arguments of the government that a substantial expansion of prison places is merely designed to alleviate overcrowding, increasing questions are posed concerning the difficulty of having welfare and control functions within the same institution. The following accounts illustrate the daily realities of this tension.

A hostel near the prison is specifically designed for prison visitors. Although it is not part of the probation service, the SPO acts as a supervisor to the Project Manager who, in turn, attends team meetings at the prison. One weekend a group of visitors from Northern Ireland had come to the hostel to visit a member of their family. On the Saturday morning they went to the prison, but were refused entry. Upon returning to the hostel they decided to 'give up' and return home that day. However, the next morning the prison phoned the hostel saying the family could visit. According to the manager and SPO this incident reflected the lack of credibility the hostel has in the beliefs of prison staff (the Constitution prevents the presence of prison staff in the hostel for reasons which 'were historical'). Yet the esteem of this welfare provision could be raised when the prison staff considered it to have performed a security function. A member of staff saw a woman putting 'white powder' in cling film and reported this to a probation officer who, in turn, contacted security. This enhanced the credibility of the hostel with prison staff. As increasingly with other areas of the service's work, their credibility is measured according to the (often incompatible) criteria of others.

In practice the relationship between welfare and control is often a fragile one. At times the welfare function does not support but challenge the security function: a function which is interpreted and mediated, as Finkelstein (1989) suggests, by the philosophies of the prison staff. In this process, he suggests, prison rules are often subverted by a higher loyalty to colleagues:

> I was warned that some members of staff would attempt to sabotage our efforts and/or actively seek ways to discredit us. Although these officers constituted a small minority of the staff they none the less were considered influential.
>
> (Finkelstein 1989: 5)

These tensions relate to the different criteria which the two groups of staff apply to inmates. On the one hand, the probation service is looking towards the successful rehabilitation of the prisoner. On the other, prison officers may consider their ability to keep a low profile, do their time quietly and obey the rules as criteria of success. For instance, on one occasion a probation officer asked to see an inmate (who was in for armed robbery and had served six years of a twelve-year sentence). He entered the office and just as he was sitting down, the officer stated he was eligible for parole. He immediately stood up to leave the room, only stopping to turn and say 'Don't bother luv'. After he had left, the probation officer turned to me to explain the situation. Being part of a London gang, he believed they would see him 'all right' when he got out. While given the nature of the offence, his attitude may have been realistic, he was doing his time by the book and the prison officers liked inmates who towed the line.[2] Nevertheless, the PO felt that he 'would be vulnerable' when he was eventually discharged; the considerations of probation were orientated to his future, but the prison staff were concerned with the present.

Despite these differences, probation officers may still find themselves unwittingly co-operating with the prison authorities. During one visit to his office, a probation officer refused to allow an inmate (a drug dealer) to phone his wife. The officer was subsequently told by the prison authorities to allow him to use the phone. Then shortly afterwards, he was told to stop the prisoner using it. It transpired that the calls were being monitored by the police – without the officer's knowledge – and a number of arrests had then been made.

While some cases may be more clear than others, this inevitable collusion of probation officers with the control and containment functions of the prison has clear implications for the trust which is necessary in building a relationship with and thereby helping a prisoner overcome any personal or practical difficulties. This arises from the competing demands of the institution which ethical dilemmas can further exacerbate.

Having been told in confidence by a prisoner that a 'contract' was out on him in the prison, an officer then discussed the matter with a colleague. They both believed the wing staff would recommend Rule 43 (vulnerable prisoner). At the same time, it was acknowledged it may be a 'dodge' on the prisoner's part to get himself back to a London prison. Even so, there were obvious security risks involved: an incident might have occurred in which staff and other inmates were injured and if it had been reported, it could have been prevented. However, by reporting the incident it would signify a breach of the prisoner's confidence – an essential ingredient in the welfare relationship. The ultimate decision attempted to bridge these demands. The officer saw the prisoner and refused him help unless he agreed to tell a member of the uniformed prison staff about the contract.

These issues require careful consideration if probation officers are to perform their duties effectively. Constant dilemmas arose during research between a concern for the client and the smooth running of the prison. These were by no means always compatible. In attempting to 'do' social work in prisons, probation officers develop techniques of survival and methods for its achievement with, more or less, varying degrees of success.

Two dimensions: the influences on prison probation work

One morning I entered a wing with an officer. I was introduced to one of the prison officers who was described as a 'friend of the probation service'. In a somewhat exaggerated fashion he frowned, apparently not entirely happy with the description. We went into the probation office: a converted cell approximately 6 feet by 10 feet with a two-drawer filing cabinet, a desk and three chairs. There was a small sliding barred window about 6 feet from the floor and pin boards on each side wall. It was 11.15 am and the first prisoner for a welfare appointment was due to come in. He was, in probation terms, a 'moaner' or, as one officer said, 'He goes on a lot to no avail'.

The librarian had called at his cell a few days before to help him write a letter (he had some reading glasses which were not satisfactory), but he had been out exercising at the time. Given his resulting frustration, he wished to bypass the medical officer (MO) and see the senior medical officer (SMO) about the glasses and then he would be able to write his own letters. Despite the prisoner's insistence the officer said that such a request was not 'within the welfare's province' and he should see the wing manager. At this point, he started to speak about another topic. The officer ceased eye-contact and began to fold a piece of paper with the CPO's address on (which the prisoner had earlier requested). The officer then started to rise out of his seat and hand the prisoner the piece of paper, which served as an effective interview termination device and he left.

The agenda of such interviews is not just based upon the situational methods people use in everyday interaction. Probation interviews are affected by the wider environment of the prison and therefore so is the rehabilitative role probation officers are intended to perform. For instance, in the above case the inmate had brought to the probation officer a set of problems about which he was aggrieved. However, it transpired that the man was locked-up twenty-three hours a day because he was deemed 'not well' by the medical services. The officer thought the librarian had called while he was about to have his daily one-hour exercise period. Understandably the prisoner had asked the librarian to call back, which the librarian had not done, hence his frustration. Thus, probation interviews must be also understood as a reaction by both parties to the wider context of the prison setting and its operational priorities.

The decisions of other staff therefore affects probation work. In addition, probation tasks are frequently subordinate to other considerations. An officer had asked the prison officers to hold back a prisoner from afternoon working so that she could interview him. She could not find the prisoner that afternoon and turned to me in frustration: 'You have to put yourself forward. After all, you are only doing these things because the prison wants them done.'

As a result of this situation, probation officers use a set of strategies in the execution of their tasks which may draw upon various resources within the institution. These can include prerogatives underwritten by the formal and informal rules of the prison, for instance, the power to determine the end of an interview due to the demands of seeing other prisoners. A ringing phone, answered during an interview, can be used to terminate the interview – 'This is an important phone call, please could I see you later?' – or the caller can be asked to phone back. These choices depend on officers' intentions or the circumstances in which they find themselves. As such a *modus vivendi* emerges within the interview setting, the outcome of which becomes a

> definition of the situation which involves not so much a real agreement as to what exists but rather a real agreement as to whose claims concerning what issues will be temporarily honoured.
>
> (Goffman 1969: 21)

Two issues become important in this process: first, the operational mode by which prison probation officers try to perform their tasks, and second, the extent to which the nature of the institution does or does not permit its realization. These criteria may of course vary between prisons on an occupational practice – institutional continuum. The greater power base of the latter will override the former, as is the case in Victoriana. In addition, in relation to occupational practice, day-to-day welfare issues and the willingness of inmates to co-operate constantly militate against pro-active work. This is compounded by the institutional necessity to contain individuals.

The remainder of this chapter is devoted to the further examination, along these dimensions, of the work of probation officers in Victoriana and finishes with comparative material from two other prisons.

On the wings: 'visible and in demand'

The prison staff

The actions of prison staff can, quite simply, prevent the execution of the probation officer's task. While the prison had a set routine for eating times, working times and 'patrol state', the enforcement of this routine has a discretionary element to it which provides for what Giddens calls a 'dialectic of control' (1984: 16).

Each probation office on the wings has a blackboard outside. On this the officer can write the name of an inmate if the officer wants to see him, or if the inmate has made a request for an interview. In this way their names are visible when the prisoners come in from work duties at 11.30 am and 4.00 pm. It would be possible to leave the names with the prison officers, but there is a reluctance to do that in case 'the message does not get through'. Further, probation officers argue that while each wing has a through-care officer, 'some do not take to the task, but the wing manager tells them they have to do it'. This failure of messages to reach prisoners may possibly signify a lapse of memory, but may be a conscious effort on the part of some prison officers to undermine the work of the service, as the following examples suggest.

Four inmates were waiting outside the probation office after their names had been put on the blackboard. Inside the office, an interview was taking place. According to the prisoner who saw the incident, a prison officer came over, rubbed two names off the board and told them to collect their lunch and return to their cells. Having been told about this the probation officer decided to confront the prison officer, who denied the accusation. As the officer said to me, what more could be done apart from accusing the prison officer of lying?

On another occasion, a probation officer was covering for two absent members of staff so was in effect dealing with applications from three wings. We spent the Friday morning moving between each one, to see if there were any urgent requests. She did this on the basis of what appeared as problems requiring immediate attention: those featuring emotional difficulties which could not wait until the following Monday. These requests are filtered through the prison staff who may, on behalf of the inmate, write down the reason for the requested interview. On one of the wings a form simply read 'family problems'. Not knowing the inmate, a judgement could not be made about the seriousness of the request, so the officer decided to return it to the wing prison officers requesting further information. We then waited to see other inmates when they came in from work.

The first inmate wanted an application for pre-parole leave. The officer told him to get a form from a prison officer who should then help him to fill it in. He returned a few minutes later saying that the prison officer told him it was not his job. After he left and having helped him to fill in the application, the probation officer turned to me:

> There's an example of prison staff throwing it back at us; it's nothing to do with us at all!

In Victoriana shared working is not always in practice what it appears in principle. In this environment probation officers can experience 'role strain' when they attempt to balance the demands of inmates and those of the institution. As a result, even the smallest comment can cause frustration. One probation officer who wanted to see a prisoner asked a prison officer if the man was working. 'No inmates work', came the short and gruff reply. In jest, but also to indicate his frustration, the officer started to bang his head on the desk, shaking it at the same time!

'Giving them stick'

A sense of humour is important in the prison setting. It is not just inmates, in the words of Cohen and Taylor (1972), who fight back. One evening several of us were leaving and some prison officers were assembled at the gate. 'Twenty hours a week and on flexitime as well . . . call yourselves "welfare"!' a prison officer said, much to the amusement of his colleagues. One of the probation team turned to us, deliberately looking away from the prison officers: 'Lovely place to work this, isn't it?' Afterwards, a team member told me their tactic of survival:

> It's all down to the Cheshire Cat syndrome; lose everything, but don't lose your smile.

Other officers also followed this advice.

One probation officer, the others noted, would be the 'tobacco man' in the prison culture. He was able to get cups of tea *and* chocolate biscuits (as I discovered) on the wing without any problem. While by his own admission something of a loner, he still used humour to 'get by'. We entered a wing one day and two prison officers were walking towards the gate arm-in-arm. 'They'll talk about you two', the officer said. They did not reply and he smiled and turned to me: 'You've got to give them stick Tim!' Even so, the institution can wear this humour thin. Tactics such as smiling at the prison officers and thinking, in the words of one officer, 'Good morning, you bastard' are a way of fighting back, but disaffection still occurs.

I was returning from a wing with one probation officer. Another officer, who normally enjoyed a laugh, was in the office. The officer I was with turned to me: 'Wasn't it awful what that prison officer said about him?' I agreed, maintaining the joke, but it fell flat. Later, over a cup of tea, the subject of the joke told me why. He does his parole applications on Tuesdays and Thursdays, but today a prison officer came up to him and 'started having a go' about getting the inmates locked up for 'patrol state'. Being 'pissed off' about this he told the prison officer that this was his normal routine. The exchange then became more heated and eventually the prison officer, in the probation officer's own words, 'stormed off' saying 'We'll fucking see about this'. As a result, he had decided to come to the upper office to let him 'cool off' and to give himself a 'breather' from the demands of the wing.

This incident had an historical element to it. This probation officer's wing is the largest and also the reception wing for inmates. Together with the hostel manager he interviews two people at a time. This causes problems if one person is in for a sex offence and another inmate is present. In these cases he tries to interview them alone. However, it is not always possible to check on this before the interview. Therefore, any anticipation of forthcoming difficulties (pro-active work) is hampered by the prison routine, which includes new inmates being taken off for baths and other institutional-based demands even when the receptions are not completed.

Two practical solutions to the above problem were suggested by the team. First, the SPO would help with the backlog of parole applications, even though this might raise other difficulties in respect to his normal duties. Second, the SPO suggested to the officer he could come in on Saturdays. However, as the officer said to me in referring to the prison staff: 'Imagine how that would go down!' As such, a difference in experiences of prison officers between the SPO and the wing probation officers was apparent. Further, it could be argued that this solution would have exacerbated among prison officers 'the resentful fantasy that only probation officers are capable of helping prisoners' (D. Smith 1979: 43).

A further solution was suggested to me by an ex-Victoriana probation officer who had experience of working in this wing. She suggested probation officers should be based outside the prison and go in on a daily basis, thus alleviating the problems of institutionalization. If the prison officers took over small day-to-day matters – including phone calls for and by inmates – it would be possible to see, in their words, 'five people a day'. 'Allowing for those who did not want to see you, I could do all those in the wing in four to five weeks'. While a constructive suggestion, it opens up a heated debate within the service and is a radical departure from current practice. It may also, as D. Smith (1979) notes, lead to a loss of probation credibility in both the prisoners' and prison staff's eyes; to say nothing of the problem of reducing officers' knowledge of the routine of the prison and thereby extending the prison officers' discretion.

The different routines and duties of the respective services are then a cause of everyday problems. As Foucault has suggested, institutions such as Victoriana are subject to

> a whole micro-penality of time (lateness, absences, interruption of tasks), of activity (inattention, negligence, lack of zeal), of behaviour (impoliteness, disobedience), of speech (idle chatter, insolence), of the body (incorrect attitudes, irregular gestures, lack of cleanliness), of sexuality (impurity, indecency).
>
> (Foucault 1977: 178)

Within such a system inmates are ridiculed and experience injustices. I witnessed a member of staff, clearly enjoying the power, swearing at an inmate. The probation officer with me found it 'disgraceful' that this routinely took place and prisoners would be punished were they to retaliate. Writing about a young man who was found hanging in his cell at Victoriana, another inmate has written:

> For 16 weeks now I have been locked in this cell 23 hours a day. The depressingly repetitive regime goes on day after day, week after week. In theory, the confinement can only last for one month at a time; but like the South African banning order it can be renewed from month to month ad infinitum. . . . Despite the official realisation of the damage caused by solitary confinement . . . six months' segregation is frequent, and in excess of a year not unknown.
>
> (M. Leech 'Letters', *Guardian Weekly* 28 May 1989)

The regime itself becomes a cause of inmates' problems and in reacting to the symptoms of these problems, probation officers were subject to its forms. Their role then becomes one of the ameliorating adverse reactions of inmates to their environment as opposed to performing rehabilitative functions. Goffman has termed this process 'looping' whereby

> an agency that creates a defensive response on the part of an inmate takes this very response as the target of its next attack.
>
> (1968: 41)

Thus, even if long-term relationships between probation officers and inmates are possible, the institution never ceases to impinge in significant respects and circumscribes the type of work which can then be performed.

Occupationally speaking, probation officers are also personally subjected to this micro-penality. I left a team meeting and walked with a probation officer down to a wing. When we entered, the assembled prison officers looked at their watches. 'Did you see them?' the probation officer asked, showing evident frustration at the prison officers' reactions. The timing of the routines of the two services is the subject of conflict. Probation officers may start work in the morning at 8.15 am and not arrive on the wings until 9.30 am. The prison officers believe that they do not do any work up to that point because they are not visible on the wings. Weekend work on reports (not infrequent) goes unnoticed.

The upper office provided a forum for probation officers to escape from the gaze of this regime. Here, the mood changed for officers were no longer visible to the prison staff and jokes were made of the day's events. The position of this office, as with space in general within an institution, is significant. Foucault's (1977) 'analytic space' is tempered by the lack of prison officers to look at their watches and make remarks about probation practice. In this 'back region' (Goffman 1969) an impression of familiarity is maintained which is 'inconsistent with the impression of self and team-mate one wants to sustain before the audience' (Goffman 1969: 129). On the wings, behaviour changed and probation officers were visible to the prison staff and inmates; they were then judged by the criteria of others and subject to their decisions. For instance, even when the wing meetings took place, probation officers tended to find out about them only the day before and then, if probation was on the agenda, it was 'last, when everyone has had enough'. This machine of routine and discipline is not to be downplayed, nor is it to be exaggerated. In response to this situation, ideas from probation officers have emerged:

> We should seek to counteract the deformation of individuals and assert the dignity, worth and responsibility of prisoners, without seeking to sustain the legitimacy of imprisonment.
>
> (Stone 1985: 65)

Occasionally probation officers assist inmates with the help of prison staff in Victoriana. The tactic is to win over prison officers. Individually some prison officers are pro-welfare, but tend collectively to be anti-welfare. For instance, a probation officer received a phone call from an inmate's wife. His mother, to whom he was very close, was gravely ill after a heart attack. However, his wife did not want him told unless he could get home leave. The officer knew the prisoner well: he made tea on the wing and might have 'cracked with the news'. After checking with the hospital, in case the prisoner was pulling a 'flanker', the wing manager was contacted to see what the chances of a visit would be (the probation officer was using his knowledge of 'the party line on the wing'). The next day the inmate was in a car with two prison officers (uncuffed) and off to visit his mother. He returned at 2 am the next morning. That same day he came into the wing office to thank the probation officer. It was approaching lock-up time and he wanted to know how his Mum was. She was, the officer ascertained, comfortable and a temporary victory had been gained over 'the machine' by 'the welfare'.

One probation officer commented that 'You don't do any social work here'. However, the above incident – the provision of practical help – is not to be underestimated. Everyday complaints – such as the inmate who dropped his dentures on an officer's desk and said 'Look at that!' – clearly mean, in the words of one officer, that 'ongoing work is sadly a victim of some of these pressures'. Another officer wanted to undertake group-work on alcoholism, but could not because he did not have the time.

The institution impinges on what some may term real social work in prisons. This extends to everyday administration which includes easy access to files, making phone calls and recording information about clients. All of these are rendered difficult in institutional settings. Files on inmates cannot be kept in wing offices due to the risk of unauthorized readings and only one wing office had a direct outside telephone line, making it difficult to contact people outside. The prison staff even objected to keeping telephone directories in wing offices – which were always locked – in case inmates found their addresses. A lot of information, for instance summaries of parole interviews, were therefore recorded on dictaphones for writing up in the upper office or at home. (However, the tapes have short recording times and on more than one occasion this information was recorded over by accident.)

'Going in to Victoriana'

The above working conditions affect the way probation officers view the prospect of secondment to Victoriana. I asked an officer about her feelings of being seconded (usually for a minimum two years) to the prison: 'We spend most of our careers trying to avoid it!' Another officer, recognizing that he would eventually be seconded, decided to volunteer to enter the prison setting because he felt 'psychologically prepared'. His application was rejected, but he was seconded a few months later and found the experience 'the most traumatic happening' of his career. Despite this, he thought he had adjusted quickly to the prison routine. However, he was surprised when a few months later he was sitting with friends at home and someone asked his wife if he was depressed and she replied 'Yes!' Until that point he had not been aware of the change in his mental state brought about by his career move. This officer's feelings have now changed. While secondment to a prison is not to be taken lightly, it is still widely believed that to 'serve one's time' is a necessary move up the probation career ladder.[3]

'Town' and 'New' prisons

In the case of Victoriana, prison staff tend to be collectively anti-welfare, which inhibits work on both occupational and institutional dimensions. This occurs either by active non-cooperation, or a selective interpretation of rules. I shall now examine the work of probation officers in two other prisons. These I have called 'Town' and 'New' prisons.

'New' prison

This is a modern prison. The buildings are recent, open-planned and widely spaced, being of no more than two storeys with the paths between them running through well-kept flower beds and grass.

There are no walls on the outer perimeter, but a large wire fence. The prison houses approximately 112 category 'C' inmates on four wings and also has a Vulnerable Prisoner Unit (Rule 43) with fifty-six inmates (eventually increasing to a hundred). Each wing and the unit has a probation officer attached to it.

The first thing I noticed in approaching the prison – aside from the contrast with Victoriana in architecture – was an inmate, unsupervised, tending the gardens outside. In addition, the offices on the wings were larger and brighter than those at Victoriana, which helps to temper Hugman's criticisms that

> Institutionalized, office-block warrens have nothing to do with *service*: they stifle, cramp, depersonalize, limit and debase human encounters.
>
> (Hugman 1980: 136, original italics)

The SPO's office is in the administrative block, which also houses clerical staff (of which the service was short here) and governors.

I arrived on a wing – after the probation officer had unlocked only two doors, one of which was the probation office – and was taken to see the wing manager. Immediately he greeted the officer and without a second glance at me, nodded to the door to indicate I should shut it. He began to relate the story of the night's events and was briefly interrupted so I could be introduced. I was told that if there was anything I wished to ask, he would be 'only too willing' to speak to me. My entry into this prison was very different from that of Victoriana.

The corridors of the wings had formica floors and low ceilings which prevent voice echo and 'makes for a good atmosphere'. Inmates come in for lunch at 11.30 am and eat in either their cell or the canteen, whichever they prefer. I spoke to two prisoners in one of their cells – the door of which was open – about the prison. One had served seventeen years in various prisons, experiencing racism wherever he went. 'New' was the best prison he had been in; at least there was 'no shit on the walls'. When I left his cell, I walked past one of the wing offices. A prison officer was writing capital letters on the bottom of a prisoner's letter so that he could read it. 'Fresh Start', it seemed, had found an outlet in this prison.

The relations between the two services were genial. One or two officers would not be 'won over', but as a group they were sympathetic to probation work. A probation officer was also contrasting New with another prison, remembering with surprise how after only being in New for a week, a prison officer asked if he wanted to join them for a weekend fishing trip. Another prison officer asked me how I was getting along and said quietly about the officer I was with: 'They come to see me about everything'. He then laughed: 'The truth is I go to see them!' A communal canteen adds to these good relations between the two groups and is situated outside the prison gates. During one lunch, a probation officer and the SPO were sitting with the governor, who then insisted on playing a game of pool. We then walked back to the prison gates and the governor stopped to talk to an inmate tending the gardens.

The ambience of New prison therefore contrasts sharply with Victoriana. The architecture is part of the explanation, but so too is the security category and beliefs of staff. I was told that the prison was cheaper to run than Victoriana and prisoners are offered choices about the activities they wish to undertake. This, in the words of one governor, was 'more like the real world'.

Security is important, but not to the same extent as Victoriana. Telephones are unlocked from filing cabinets in the offices, but the number of doors to unlock does not match the emphasis on containment. However, being category 'C' does create its problems. The inmates may have been in the system for a long time and are waiting to get out. As a result, they could also get knocked back to category 'B'.

I joined a 'lifers' group' attended by local magistrates. The discussion centred on the constant scrutiny they all found themselves under and the difficulties of mixing with short-term inmates who may cause trouble – thereby having an effect on their chances of getting out. A representative of Home Office P2 division, in charge of lifers, had recently visited. The inmates had asked him that if they kept out of trouble how long would it be before some of them got out? Apparently he just smiled and did not answer. To them it indicated they wouldn't! They related stories of knock-backs, particularly in Victoriana. Clearly these grievances create work for the service as they had an effect on the psychological states of long-term inmates.

Women probation officers

The team in New was described to me as older and possessing certain attitudes. While it consisted of both female and male officers, it is important to remember women probation officers face peculiar difficulties in an all-male setting. As one female officer said: 'They think because you're a woman you're not intelligent'. One prison officer in particular allegedly 'hated women probation

officers'. This routine downgrading of women's skills and experiences transpired in several ways, despite the liberal rhetoric of
many of its perpetrators. As Hilary Walker has written:

> it is important for probation officers to examine the assump-
> tions they are making about women in their work and to *carry
> any conclusions into practice.*
>
> (Walker 1985: 80, original italics)

This does not occur only in the prison service; some probation
officers told me they would not want to work with women and
overt sexist comments were not infrequent.[4]

In Victoriana, prison officers insist that a woman probation
officer has an office whose door has a window, which they gather
round when interviews take place. Their motivation for this is
questionable; their justification is that it is for security purposes.
Such gender issues clearly influence the extent to which a probation officer can perform her duties free from harassment.

A probation student told me the prison officers in Victoriana had
said to her it was not the work for a woman. Their advice was to 'get
herself a man' and 'settle down'. Another probation officer worked
with a sex-offender with whom she felt particularly uneasy. She did
not know exactly what her unease was due to; it was 'just a feeling'.
Another officer, a male, was also in the room when she was relating
the story to me. He felt she should not deny her feelings otherwise
'you get too distant and professional'. Indeed, some argue that the
concept of professionalism depends not just on spurious ideologies
of objectivity (Wilding 1982), but the extent to which the profession
is dominated by men (Hearn 1982). In an all-male institution, these
feelings, while bringing a common humanity to the work, are
frequently degraded as signs of personal weakness which create
additional pressures in the execution of tasks.

'Town' Prison

Typicality is usually the justification invoked for the external
validity of selected observational settings. In this sense New prison
may not be typical: a new prison with good sanitation; not overcrowded; reasonably spacious and with prison staff who tend to be
sympathetic *and* have the time for welfare considerations. 'Town'
prison on the other hand is, like Victoriana, an old prison. However,
it is also a local prison and suffers from overcrowding; expectations
about what can be achieved in local prisons change. In these

settings, day-to-day welfare issues tend to take priority over longer-term social work in prisons. These issues were alluded to, albeit in a veiled manner, by an internal Treen Circular advertising Town's SPO post:

> Colleagues will know that H.M. Prison 'Town' is a somewhat over-crowded local prison of Victorian construction with a high throughput of remand and sentenced prisoners. It is the role of the Probation Department to keep rehabilitation high on the list of priorities and also to provide a social work service to prisoners.

Under the title 'Probation service not happy with its lot', *The Independent* (13 June 1988) reported on probation work in Wormwood Scrubs. On one wing, over 50,000 remand prisoners pass through every year. Nearly 55 per cent are estimated to stay for less than twenty-four hours: 'probation officers only have time to respond to practical requests for help'. While Town does not have problems on the same scale, they are similar in form.

The team consists of four probation officers and an SPO. The SPO has an office outside the wings and adjacent to the administrative staff (a source of some tension, given the distance from the rest of the team). One officer has a separate office and the others are located in one large office on a wing in which 'it is impossible to write', so tape recorders are used. Association time for inmates includes playing darts, table tennis and watching films, all of which take place just outside the office. Therefore these officers are more visible and in demand than their counterparts in the other prisons. Shaw's comparative study of social work in two prisons found an advantage of such visibility was the increased accessibility of officers, yet 'the welfare officer was also more vulnerable' (M. Shaw 1974: 97)

The office, while providing some back region sanctity, still had prisoners knocking on the door with constant demands, despite a suggested but impractical policy to prevent this without a request. Problems concerned small everyday matters or what Shaw (1974) calls 'first-aid on demand'. These problems are, as one officer said, 'trivial things, but important to them while they are in here'. Most of the work is about 'offering practical help with a smile on your face'. This situation is compounded by so many inmates who are recently sentenced or await trial. Such disruption to an individual's normal 'economy of action' (Goffman 1968: 45) means these requests for everyday items or needs, which outside were taken for granted, have to be made through the prison routine. This understandable disruption to normality places an extra burden on the service, which is different in form from that for long-term inmates.

The nature of prisoners' applications varies: getting in contact with visitors; asking the probation to contact friends and relatives to tell them of court appearance times, or arranging discharge grants. One prisoner whose wife was pregnant asked an officer what it was like to have a baby. However, work pressures and the turnover of inmates constantly militates against assisting with anything but this 'drip, drip, drip' of everyday requests. Officers believed these tasks were important, but as one officer said, they do not necessarily require a trained professional. She added: 'But who else would do it for the money?' The Chaplain told me that he got 'asked for everything in here'. This ranged from men wanting 'a bit of baccy' to those who wanted to talk about their 'dead Grandad'.

These constant pressures have a profound effect on the probation staff. An officer walked into the office, shut the door, leant against it and exclaimed: 'It's a bit much out there!' Just by walking to see an inmate, she found herself approached by several others and while I witnessed nothing but a sympathetic ear and the promise of help, there is a limit to what can be achieved. During one team meeting the officers noted how those in the field had 'certain buffers' from their clients. The only relief from these pressures, in the prison, is through the co-operation of the other prison staff. However, the extent to which they are able to help is rendered problematic by the peculiar pressures of local prisons. For example, aggrieved remand prisoners who are entitled to refuse work; overcrowding (no cell I visited had fewer than two beds); high turnover of prisoners and many now serving full, not short-term sentences in the institution. Officers in the field, who used to supervise parolees from Town several years ago, noted how few there used to be. Now probation officers in Town write several parole reports a month.

Discussion

Prison routine is the criterion by which probation's task is defined and circumscribed. It is the environment in which their duties have to be executed. However, it is not their task and philosophies which predominate, but those of control and containment. Thus, one probation officer who talked about the military machine echoed the words of Foucault that power 'becomes a machine that no one owns' (1980: 156). However, the mediation of these forms by groups within the prison setting, tempers this structuralist analysis. By becoming intransigent (Goffman 1968), fighting back (Cohen and Taylor 1972), and being opportunistic (R. King and Elliot 1978), the regimented machine is transformed by prisoners and also the probation staff:

> The point is not just that human beings resist being treated as automata, something which Foucault accepts; the prison is a site of struggle and resistance. Rather, it is that Foucault's 'bodies' are not *agents*.
>
> (Giddens 1984: 154, italics added)

The black prisoners in Victoriana had walked around with white handkerchiefs dangling out of their back pockets and the prison officers became agitated (I was warned to 'look out for the racism' on my first day); the prisoners persisted. This reaction was obtained by the power of symbolism: every time the black prisoners sat down they were 'putting their arses on the whites'. One probation officer went out of his way to help the black prisoners because 'everybody else is such a bastard to them'. He told a prison officer that he didn't like a black inmate 'firstly, because he's cleverer than you and I and secondly because he's black'. However, while his corner was being fought by the probation officer, this same inmate showed me the psoriasis he suffered from on his chest and scalp. He had a satisfactory herbal cure for this, but the prison medical authorities did not approve of alternative medicines.

For the probation officers the rules of the prison system can also provide a resource. One probation officer said if a prisoner makes a request 'all I have to do is say the prison doesn't allow it'. In this sense, Garfinkel's (1967) emphasis on actors' accomplishments in social settings is worthy of consideration. Indeed, calling a prisoner a 'moaner' is an example of what Sacks (1974) has called a Membership Categorization Device: that is, certain activities are taken by probation officers to be typical of certain clients; in this case, those who constantly wish to complain. To this extent probation officers in prisons exercise discretionary judgement. However, at the same time restraints exist on working practices via the dominant issues of control and security, as interpreted and enforced by uniformed prison staff. Indeed, in the Home Office Circular (1967) already mentioned, nine of the twenty-one functions listed have to do with prison management and not helping offenders as such; a point not lost on writers on the subject (D. Smith 1979; Glastonbury, Bradley and Orme 1987). These institutional constraints, together with the inmates' reaction to a total institution (Goffman 1968), act to affect the agenda of probation/inmate interactions in the occupational dimension of their work. As a result, the social work function in prisons, as popularly conceived in casework, can be rendered both inadequate and ineffective.

This situation, as with the Home Office and probation service's reactions in general, leads to what I shall call a quantitative politics. Instead of facing these difficulties, there exists the ability to subsume political and value questions surrounding work in the probation service (and criminal justice system as a whole), under a number of quantitative indices to measure workloads and performance. In this way technical solutions, such as more clients and greater throughput, are offered to value questions – what are we doing this for and what purpose is it serving. Thus, in the face of the constant daily demands of prisoners in one of the prisons – where ongoing therapeutic work became a victim – an SPO urged the officers to 'put something in your part C's' (the record of client contacts) just in case a Home Office inspection took place. At least then a record of client contact would exist. This was required of officers, despite the recognition that they had busy, demanding and full days, coping with the problems imprisonment creates for inmates and the environment for the execution of their duties on an everyday basis.

Summary

In macro policy terms, SNOP accorded a low priority to through-care on the part of the inmates' 'home' probation officer. In reaction, NAPO wrote:

> the Home Office's attitude to through-care is dangerously short-sighted and dominated by misplaced notions of cost and effectiveness.
>
> (NAPO 1986: para. 20)

On several occasions I heard seconded probation officers phone field officers, urging them to keep in touch with the inmate. They usually replied they would do as much as possible, but their areas did not prioritize such work. Certainly many probation officers do not appreciate the difficulties their prison counterparts have to endure. One officer told me her behaviour would change now that she realized what it was like inside. However, this area of work suffers in relation to both shared working between the seconded and home probation officer and within the institution (see McDermott and King 1989). In policy terms, ambivalence rules over the expectations and purposes of prisons and this reflects itself in probation practice while the official rhetoric of shared working is not in line with operational practice. These tensions are being exacerbated by ever increasing numbers of petty non-violent offenders being given custodial sentences, with little likelihood of a change in this trend. Despite this, criticisms of our prison system seems to fall on deaf ears. When it reaches its mark, the point of the argument is missed. It is well put by Louis Blom-Cooper:

> The argument here is not that no one is ever deterred by the prospect of punishment, nor that prisons do not contain some people who would otherwise be outside committing crimes; it is that, except in the most serious cases, any such effects are likely to be heavily outweighed by the damaging effect of imprisonment.
>
> (Blom-Cooper 1988: 34)

At the end of the day in an institutional world where welfare plays second fiddle to the containment functions of imprisonment what can 'the welfare' realistically be expected to achieve? Ultimately changes in these settings depend not just on the active co-operation of the prison authorities, but on something even greater: the general question of the nature and purpose of our penal system as a whole. Until that occurs, amelioration, currently worthy in itself, seems to be the only effective *and* general goal the probation service can implement. In the meantime, in prison probation work, the 'normalizing' and 'corrective' sectors of the penal system, continue to blur with the 'segregative' (Garland 1985) and thus confuse purpose.

Looking back: conflicts in modes of working

professionals, whilst attending to technological aspects of their work, typically ignore the wider social issues. In this respect they are vulnerable to deskilling and erosion of control over their work.

(K. Shaw 1987: 775)

To be effective in intervention, social workers need a knowledge of the political economy of the society in which they work. . . . The crux of the matter is that social workers are in business to challenge in social terms the doctrine of the survival of the fittest, to do more than ensure that those at the end of the queue get support, care and some priority.

(J. Cooper 1987: 68)

For heuristic purposes, I have separated the issues of practice, organization and environment in order to understand how each interrelates. Chapter 3, which examined the interpretation of policy and the reaction to this process from the staff of the Treen Probation Service, found that an implementation gap existed between management and the front line of the service. When examining perspectives on autonomy and accountability and the front-line working environment, staff believed in the need for organizational autonomy for probation work to be effective, while the nature of the working environment necessitated a degree of occupational discretion in order to render it manageable. These differences therefore place policy change in direct conflict with front-line staff and their working environment.

This book has a central theme: intra-organizational issues cannot be fully divorced from environmental ones. Therefore, in summary I wish to draw together the areas of practice, policy, politics and history of the service, which necessitates a blurring of their boundaries. However, I wish to add a caveat: that is, as long as the pertinent issues I have identified remain, so too will the type of conflicts. This contention is particularly important when reflecting on the implications of the government's White Paper *Crime, Justice and Protecting the Public* (Home Office, 1990a). The *form* of policy is similar to those issues already discussed in Chapter 2: 'just desserts' (1990a: para. 1.6) is high on the agenda. Also, in order to implement the justice model of corrections there has been an increase in central control of the probation service. Therefore, it comes as no surprise that the government published a Green Paper one week after the White Paper. *Supervision and Punishment in the Community: A Framework for Action* (Home Office 1990b) aims to remove the 20 per cent local government funding and fully fund local services from central government; amalgamate smaller areas for stronger management; privatize certain aspects of service provision; create a fund for voluntary work with offenders; and move to a new model probation officer, with less emphasis on social work. My contention is that the net results of their implementation will be to exacerbate the problems I have raised. In this process, these problems may become redefined, but will nevertheless remain.

Looking back

The policy dimension

The management of change is smoother in a rational-choice model of analysing organizations (Simon 1947; March and Simon 1970). The underlying assumption is that organizational members pursue a collective goal; policy change then relates to questions of means, not ends. However, this does not characterize the probation service where disputes over means and ends predominate. This has profound implications for the implementation of policy given that 'Any evaluation of "efficiency" has to begin by taking ends as given' (Beetham 1987: 53).

It was probation management who staff believed had the most

influence over the formation of policy in an environment shaped by the government and Home Office. Nevertheless, its implementation was then rendered problematic by the gap between probation management and the front line: in K. Young's (1977; 1981) formulation, policy-makers' and officials' definitions of the situation did not inhabit common ground and in managing change there could be no assumption about consensus within the organization. Also, management were not believed to control the actual content of probation work. These differences then infuse policy with political potential which, in turn, is compounded by the political component of that policy itself. As the White Paper states: 'Preventing re-offending and protecting the public from serious harm should be the objectives of the probation service' (Home Office 1990a: para. 1.9). This penal philosophy stands in contrast to the humanitarian tradition of the service.

These environmental changes have clear implications for the management of change in the service:

> once politics are introduced into a situation, it is very difficult to restore rationality . . . it is very hard to restore the kind of shared perspective and solidarity which is necessary to operate under the rational model.
>
> (Pfeffer 1981: 32)

The process of organizational decision-making then alters in form and increasingly involves an anticipatory component. In Treen, managers attempted to anticipate internal conflict in the implementation of policy, as well as the external intentions of Home Office policy. The agenda and discussions within probation management meetings, the Senior Consultative Group (SCG) and sub-area management meetings reflected this. While this potential was acknowledged by management, implementation fell on the shoulders of SPOs who were incorporated into the new culture of policy changes with its emphasis on targeting, monitoring and budgets. As a result, while management is 'itself a political activity' (Pfeffer 1981: xi), it now deals with a more volatile climate. Thus, although caution should be used in employing what Morgan (1986) calls a political metaphor of organizations – if you look hard enough you can always find political activity – the combinations of the external and internal politics of change has created peculiar pressures on the management of the service.

The policy process also alters the traditional components of probation work. In the implementation of policy, management now attempt to influence what was traditionally thought to be an organizationally autonomous probation officer. This involved accommodating to such changes by subsuming their political components under a technical-rational mode of administrative behaviour. Measurement, budgets, objectives and the pursuit of effectiveness – all of which form part of Home Office policy – can so easily become ends themselves. The questions which SPOs asked in the policy process – 'Why are we doing this?' – were then transformed into 'Can it be measured?' If the logic of this process was then questioned during the SCG, the resort was to fatalism: 'This is the way the Home Office want it and this is the way it has to be'.

On occasion, a theoretical analysis entered the process. Nevertheless, it was not as a transcendental justification for policy prescriptions, but related to attempts to reduce the anxiety of staff in times of rapid organizational change. Thus, by default, it did not address the reasons for their anxiety. The consequence of this was to become another administrative means of bracketing the political dimension. This was to affect employee morale which, it should be remembered, is not achieved:

> when the organisation meets the requirements of machine-logic. As a matter of fact, what may appear to be logical from a purely technical standpoint may run directly counter to the personal and social demands of employees.
>
> (Worthy 1967: 39)

Technical-administrative considerations in the policy process are bolstered by Home Office and government initiatives. Yet it could be argued that resorting to effectiveness management actually reduces the uncertainty of management in a human service organization. It is a gradual process of change in managerial focus and if accepted uncritically, it can be seen to possess its own set of justifications. Indeed, the method appeared to offer several things at once: a means of checking on front-line performance; of placating the service's political masters and potentially gaining additional staff if playing by Home Office rules. It then becomes

> difficult to fault the system as far as it goes. But it reveals a touching faith in the capacity of systems of accountable management to cope with the pathological uncertainty and disorder of public administration.
>
> (Gray and Jenkins quoted in Humphrey 1987: 27)

Effectiveness management, as pursued by the Home Office and government, has an underlying rationale which cannot be ignored when considering the changes outlined in this study.

The logic of effectiveness management

Increased effectiveness and efficient use of resources are the underlying justifications for most of the policy changes discussed in this study. While a limited amount of research has been conducted into the area of organizational effectiveness, of those studies completed, Humphrey (1987) offers the following summary.

First, it is not the criteria of effectiveness themselves, but the manner of their dissemination which effects performance; hence the feeling of SPOs that 'Planning for Action' was not a consultative document but a tablet of stone. Second, the use of effectiveness criteria can have unintended consequences. Dysfunctional decisions can then occur in the process, particularly in organizations such as the probation service which have non-financial objectives. Thus, during the policy process one conflict was noted between the service's overall aim of crime prevention and a focus on statutory clients in order to gain additional resources. Third, given this problem in organizations with non-financial objectives, surrogates are used as measures of performance. In the case of the service this has included, for example, the numbers of social inquiry reports written, the numbers of offenders occupying a hostel and the ratio of probation officers to statutory clients. However, their adoption can create further difficulties (as noted in Chapter 6) between quality and quantity of work and great care is required in their formulation. Further, in using these surrogate measures the issue of whether an objective has been achieved is clearly based on subjective criteria. Therefore, during the policy process this subjective dimension manifested itself on several occasions as disputes between management expectations and SPOs questioning the feasibility of their implementation. In particular, this arose during one meeting when an ACPO was asked 'Where did you get this target from?' 'Plucked from the sky', his gesture symbolized. Management are then tempted, if performance does not match to an objective, to resort to a narrow view in relation to its achievement, when organizational problem-solving may lie in a more global view of the organization, including its environment (see Humphrey 1987: 53–5). This also created conflict in the policy process when SPOs questioned the validity of targets, especially when management did not specify *how* they were to be achieved. Hence, when looking at improvements in court sentencing practices, SPOs translated the problem as one of court decision-making being out of step with public opinion (an environmental dimension), rather than a question of improving the practice of probation officers as the policy process implied (a more narrow practice dimension).

From the above points and the findings of this study, five factors may be concluded as arising in the relationship between the Financial Management Initiative (FMI), the probation service in general and Treen's response in particular (and, it should be added, other public sector organizations).

First, management by objectives in organizations with non-market criteria is highly problematic, while its uncritical adoption will almost certainly lead to dysfunctions in relation to its aims. The result is, as the SCG process demonstrated, policy formulation takes place:

> in the context of a diffusion of objectives between political concerns, interest group demands, professional and other provider groups as well as budgetary restraints.
>
> (Cousins 1987: 54)

Second, the technical discourse which surrounded the setting of objectives limited dissent by subsuming the SPOs' *political* questions about the limits of organizational control and the feasibility and desirability of policy, under the SCG's *administrative* considerations: form-filling, paper-work and times allotted to tasks.

Third, the resort to such managerial methods has a much more important component to it in relation to service development. While some managers may feel they are riding a political storm, they may also be creating another one. Methods of quantitative measurement which are currently used not only have the capacity to reduce front-line contact with clients, due to demands on their time, but also alter the *way* organizational problems are perceived by management. The result is what Cohen (1985; 1988) calls the obsession with 'what works' with a self-fulfilling prophecy attached to it: if measures don't work then there needs to be more and better ones, rather than questioning the whole enterprise itself.

Fourth, the quantitative measurement of output, which informs managerial decisions, resulted in tensions – as my fieldwork indicated – between standardized methods of data collection and the everyday identification of client need at the front line. The consequence of the management response, under external pressure, was an increase in a bureaucratic mode of control which tries to achieve 'predictability through the specification of how people in the organization should behave and carry out their work' (Child 1984: 160).

Finally, the overall result of this process implied a corresponding movement, in serving the criteria of its political masters, from a problem-solving service to a performance organization (Mintzberg 1979). The client's problems are not then considered central, but impression management for the government and Home Office is. Hence, a recent Treen Circular on 'Objectives, Priorities, Tasks and Targets' noted a need for actual targets: 'not so much for our own professional consumption as for *wider consumption*' (italics added). The conflict between problem-solving for the client (at the front line) and performance for the Home Office (administrative and budgetary considerations) thus created a tension between front-line work and administrative demands.

These factors do not simply stem from a conflict of values, but from the nature of the front-line working environment. As noted, there were criticisms of the policy process in that policy tended to stop at the specification of exactly *how* policies were to be implemented. Precise specification would have clearly infringed on spheres of occupational discretion and created further conflict over the boundary maintenance of work (see Chapter 5). However, it also reflected two further problems which the implementation of policy neglects at its peril.

First, in relation to what I have called the binding ethos of the probation service – the identification of an occupational desire to help clients. If changes in occupational practice are not in tune with the working environment, both their legitimacy and efficiency are then questioned. Their acceptance was not so much dependent on their content but 'the consequences or likely results of their application' (Offe 1984: 135). Therefore, as staff believed policy was moving away from a primary concern with helping the client, resistance resulted.

Second, this resistance can be effective given the need in the working environment (identified in Chapter 6) for a degree of occupational discretion in managing a probation work setting. Attempts to monitor the work of front-line personnel cannot then exact substantive accountability when its methods are not in tune with this environment.

The consequences of the above manifested themselves in Chapter 5. Front-line personnel felt formally but not substantively accountable to probation management, the Probation Committee and the Home Office, because they were considered remote from front-line work. Further, they also believed in the need for occupational discretion in carrying out their daily work. As Chapters 6 and 7 indicated, front-line personnel are constantly responding to client problems and those presented by the environment, such as the courts and the institutional criteria of the prison system. The implications are that probation activities must be monitored by their results 'rather than by the direct supervision of those activities themselves' (Giddens 1987: 163). However, a very fine line must be drawn – for the methods used by the front line in achieving these results can be subversive of formal organizational authority. Staff can easily fill in spaces in forms if that is what is required. The result is an internal quantitative politics which I referred to at the end of Chapter 6. To check on such practices fully, require highly Draconian measures which would then be dysfunctional in both practice and organizational dimensions.

This has been constructed as a problem in implementing the alternatives to custody industry. One answer for the Home Office in pursuing court-led credibility for community-based alternatives to custody has been to introduce a series of guidelines which then limit the probation officer's discretion in administering an order. The other answer is to assume more control of local organizations – as shown by the recent Green Paper proposals (Home Office 1990b). Social inquiry reports (SIRs), for example, are constructed in an officer's sphere of discretion which is informed not only by a particular ethos, but also by environmental circumstances. It is not surprising therefore that the White Paper (Home Office 1990a), in seeking punishment in the community and thereby an alteration in the courts' practices, speaks of a need for SIRs to be efficient, quick and economic in their production and that 'it makes sense to have a standard format' (1990a: para. 3.11). However, such moves towards standardization fail, along with past attempts to alter practice, to understand the daily contingencies of probation work. Policy assumes, in avoiding any threat to the independence of the courts, that a probation officer is empowered to change the practice of others. This fundamentally ignores the fact that their working environment is variable, dependent and not predictable.

It cannot be disputed that the probation service has benefited in monetary terms from the law and order industry – albeit one at odds with its philosophy. The means for it to continue benefiting is to increasingly play by rules the government and Home Office set. As one respondent in the survey noted: 'He who pays the piper . . .'. This is the logic of the situation in which probation management finds itself. This is not to suggest that they are victims and cannot ameliorate the worst excesses of Home Office and government policy in their own spheres of discretion; as Lloyd (1986) noted, there were variations in local responses to SNOP. However, times have since changed.

As this study moved from the policy to the practice dimension, a different set of concerns emerged. The organizational dimension had an indirect effect, but the working environment had a direct one.

The practice dimension

Due to changes in organizational demands, an increasing occupational uncertainty has emerged at the front line. Added to these are daily uncertainties which emerge from the working environment. Not only can these pressures be observed, but also they were found to vary according to the setting in which the work takes place. This means that the settings are not themselves predictable or uniform: the twin concepts which official policy seeks – emphasized in the White Paper (Home Office 1990a). In order to manage them, they required a degree of front-line discretion. At the same time, the potential for eliciting the client's co-operation also varied. It is in these two vital respects – a variability in the potential to control clients and the management of settings necessitating front-line discretion – that the assumptions of policy are inappropriate to everyday work with offenders in the community.

In day centres and hostels staff were more visible to clients, which led to different demands being placed upon them. Contingent-practical issues meant that in day centres, hostels, community service, prisons and one-to-one work, negotiations needed to take place between staff and clients. However, its exercise needed to take account of situationally expedient factors, as well as being mediated by the binding ethos of staff towards helping clients. The majority of these considerations revolved around the immediate material and emotional circumstances which clients face on a daily basis. As a result, there are consequences for traditional concepts of probation practice. Like the police court missionaries who saw drink as the impediment to the righteous life, contemporary probation staff who adhere to the diagnostic ideal must first deal with an individual's practical circumstances such as housing, DSS claims and employment opportunities. As the degree of client deprivation increases and policy continues to drive a wedge between people's social circumstances and their criminal acts, dealing with these becomes not a means to an end, but the constant task of any individual or organization which is involved in resettlement, rehabilitation or even punishment in the community.

This is not just a one-way equation. Like probation management in relation to policy, it is too simplistic to consider probation officers as victims of their environments. It was clear that front-line staff experienced discretion in varying degrees (as outlined in Chapters 5 and 6). For instance the Divorce Court welfare officer, in comparison with other spheres of probation work, was empowered by a process which enabled an outlet for the binding ethos. Indeed, from what I have called these spheres of discretion emanate the values of a conservative service. In relation to women offenders one study has concluded that

> the practices of probation officers serve to disadvantage women by an endorsement of a model of family life which involves the oppression and exploitation of women.
>
> (Eaton 1986: 61)

A similar point may be made in relation to black offenders (see Crow 1987). However, these issues cannot be considered as simply relating to the practice dimension – as the training of probation officers frequently implies – but also an environmental and political one. For example, the SCG discussions centred on the difficulty of challenging magistrates' background assumptions to alter their sentencing practices. Indeed, if during the research overt challenges to institutionally biased practices had been undertaken by probation officers, they may not have achieved the best possible outcome for the client. Such challenges may even exacerbate the problem by antagonizing the magistrates.

Because of these difficulties, a process of anticipatory decision-making also took place at the practice dimension and evolved from considerations of the courts mode of working. This emerged in Chapter 6 as a concern with the credibility of probation in the local court and a conflict between stand-downs which the court required and the officer's belief in the need for a full SIR: realizing that the court would make the order anyway, the officer had to be content with the limitations of a stand-down report. Courts' institutional practices are therefore reproduced by intentional occupational practice. This results, as an officer in Steeple noted, in unintended consequences: offenders may be 'up-tariffed' in attempts to gain credibility for community-based disposals and the courts' practices are never overtly challenged.

The management of settings within these spheres of discretion therefore had not only interactional effects, but also organizational and environmental consequences. Interactionally apart from the humanitarian, there was also a pragmatic payoff: such methods of working were more likely to elicit the client's co-operation. This helped to make the setting work, by not simply imposing a counter-productive and uniform mode of simple punishment to which there was no apparent constructive end. As a result, it was clear that the setting necessitated front-line workers adopting what has been referred to as a 'pragmatic commitment to control' (Fielding 1984: 162).

In the pressures which emerged from daily work with clients, we can understand the charged nature of opinion and differences expressed in the questionnaire – both of which had organizational consequences. Because of its demands, it is possible to understand not only why front-line probation work seemed far removed from policy suppositions about control over clients, but also why management was not then believed to control the content of work. As Chapter 4 uncovered, front-line staff expressed formal accountability to some groups, but not substantive accountability due to their distance from front-line work. They also exhibited a belief in autonomy from the organization, but less so than from the clients, with whom they are in daily contact. These beliefs result from the experiences of daily practice, which not only reinforce the binding ethos, but also led to conflicts between practice and policy, particularly where the latter seemed both ineffective, out of touch and inappropriate to daily contact with clients.

Probation practice involved, in the main, uncertainty. The traditional one-to-one with clients was itself dependent on the environment directly and the organization indirectly. It directly depended on the type of court to which the officer worked, on the nature of the client's offence and problems and the setting in which work normally took place with the offender. Indirectly the organizational effect was one of time – in filling in forms, attending meetings and generally furnishing administrative ends. Staff then considered this a distraction from the core task of trying to help the offender. Further, the increased level of 'fire station probation' meant more time was spent in reacting to situations, some potentially and actually threatening. In turn, this varied with the visibility of staff in the work setting, which itself implies less certainty and therefore less control over the content of work. This meant ancillaries were often able to perform such work equally as well and, as noted, were frequently left in charge of day centres and hostels. This has repercussions at two levels. First, occupationally speaking it questions the traditional probation officer role in these settings; second, under Home Office pressure to economize it also provides a temptation for the organization to employ more ancillaries, who are – as was noted by one meeting in the course of this study – cheaper.

There are other consequences for work in these settings. In the accounts of staff concerning the worst aspects of their work, many related to stress. As Brown notes 'the work environment is the most significant influence in staff burnout' (1987: 17). Nevertheless, he argues that its resolution is to be found in organizational design, rather than individual stress-reducing techniques. Thus, visibility in day centres, hostels and prisons, the lack of satisfaction in community service as merely administrative, plus having to deal with the constant practical problems of clients and furnish administrative demands, have all featured in this study. Further, as this research has found, this is exacerbated by those supervisors who concentrate on administrative tasks to the exclusion of supportive ones. In this sense, the expectations of the policy process that SPOs will assume more administrative responsibilities can only compound this problem.

There is a further dimension which generates change in the organizational and practice dimensions: as punishment becomes more the service's province, it is also more administrative in nature. After all, both the White and Green Papers (Home Office 1990a, 1990b) aim to reduce the discretionary components of probation work. As this emphasis increases, it alters the focus of organizational decisions. Ancillaries may perform these new duties equally as effectively as the diagnostic and counselling components diminish correspondingly – as is already the case in community service. Probation officers may be content with ancillary workers (as Chapter 4 indicated) as long as they remain in specified roles. However, the power they possess to maintain these boundaries of work is derived from the organization and its environment. Policy changes, in pursuit of court-led credibility, seek punishment of offenders which officially limits the potential for certain forms of practice. Practice innovation in the face of these changing pressures is then an appropriate response. This means, as ancillaries are increasingly at the front line of probation, the boundaries of work will be more difficult to maintain. In addition, when management increasingly means predictability, it is unlikely that such innovation will be encouraged. The consequences may be for more officers to see ancillaries as a threat, even though they also possess the binding ethos.

Because of these different influences on everyday work at the front line, there are significant differences between a facilitating and elite professional. The former characterizes a probation officer who not only acts according to an occupational ethos, but also is acted upon by the environment in ways which limit the scope for the officer's working practice. It is to a more general understanding of this process, in relation to both practice and the organization, that I now turn.

Understanding 'vulnerability' to change

The probation service has experienced considerable change in its relatively short history and it is therefore important to understand the power base of the occupation and organization. It is surprising, given the degree of change, that the ideology of professional practice, with exceptions, often considers itself to take place in a social and political vacuum; thereby ignoring the environmental and organizational influences I have just discussed. When these factors challenge it, it is rarely prepared, while the resources which it can mobilize in its defence vary according to the nature and status of the occupation. For probation officers, traditional diagnostic counselling of an individual suggests – and to some still does – the potential of offering a technical solution to what may be the results of a social and/or political problem. In this respect, there are obvious parallels with the management of the service resorting to administrative methods in responding to change. However, the result of constantly responding to social and material needs, at the front line, has the effect of repoliticizing probation work. This places it, once again, in conflict with the so-called administrative rationale of policy. This, for example, has found its outlet in increased union-based, as opposed to professional-based, representation of service members. Hence, there were splits between groups within NAPO at the end of the 1970s and beginning of the 1980s. Conflicts between official policy and the environment of front-line practice then result in increasing identification with the offender. Thus, in terms of the Social Fund NAPO noted

> Confidential information must not be passed on to the DHSS without specific instructions from the client in writing. *This is compatible with the role of the probation officer as a representative of the client in dealings with the Social Fund.*
>
> (*NAPO Newsletter* April 1988: 2, italics added)

However, these conflicts must also be considered alongside the history of the probation service which further assists in the understanding of its vulnerability to change.

Both in terms of its organization and in its professional self-conception, the service has been state facilitated, that is, its rise depended upon the state assuming increasing responsibility for its emergence. As Chapter 1 charted, there was a move from evangelical voluntarism to public therapeutic-based practice. Garland's (1985) 'compromise' then found state-sponsored expression, enabling the rise of a therapeutic probation discourse. The form of service organization became what Johnson (1972) refers to as state mediated:

> a powerful centralised state intervenes in the relationship between producer and consumer, intitially to define what the needs are.
>
> (Johnson 1972: 46)

Under this umbrella of state sponsorship, professional discourses on rehabilitation flourished. It defined the needs of offenders and the subsequent practices – as long as the compromise remained relatively unchallenged. However, it is now challenged by a government in which the dominant political discourses which surround offending, emphasize the notions of individual responsibility and something intrinsically bad about criminals in comparison with non-criminals. The social practices which follow from such an emphasis return us to the concept of punishing individuals – one at odds with the diagnostic ideal. The reaction by NAPO has been to a more overt and fundamental political challenge to government policy.

The response to this change, as I have argued, is differentially addressed by groups within the service. On the one hand, the administrative frame of reference is able to de-politicize the implications of policy by translating them into questions of means, not ends. On the other, the power of probation officers was based on their knowledge of practice; in this sense knowledge and power are implicated (Foucault 1980). Yet this was dependent for its support on a now challenged compromise. Indeed, if probation officers' training leads to a binding ethos which makes the administration of punishment less effective, it is not surprising that the government, through the Green Paper (Home Office 1990b) proposals, wish to alter the knowledge part of the equation by exerting more control over the content of this training. In addition, if changes in training are not effective in administering punishment in the community, the fiscal card is also played with the prospect of privatizing aspects of the service. As a result, the changes that I have outlined have left the service in a state of flux regarding its purpose and peculiarly vulnerable to blinkered and politically inspired change. With exceptions (see McWilliams and Pease 1990), few have addressed the implications of this for maintaining the unique position of the service within the criminal justice system.

Fundamental conflict therefore exists within the service – if its practitioners are willing to face it. We have seen this manifest itself in terms of two competing modes of working. First, there is the administrative mode, which is to act in such a way as to placate its political masters thus conforming 'with politically pre-established formal-legal rules' (Offe 1985: 315). Second, while this appears rational in a bureaucratic sense, it is not to those who work at the front line. They are responding to another environment. Not to that which the political master sets, but one which necessitates responding to the needs of offenders and which is rational in terms of the everyday demands made upon them. In this sense, the administration of the service, which entails the implementation of the alternatives to custody industry, is put in direct conflict with front-line work. Thus, if policy is to achieve real change, whatever its political component, it must first understand the working environment of that which it seeks to change. In the case of the service, this environment is not uniformly predictable, nor is the service empowered in the way policy assumes to alter the practices of others – especially the courts. At the practice level, staff are frequently forced to operate a 'fire station policy' and most of the time, as the second part of this study indicated, probation marches

Postscript: looking forward

There is one question still to be addressed. What about the future of the probation service? Lengthy and detailed replies to this question reflected a strong feeling of uncertainty amongst probation personnel. While written before the recent White and Green Papers (Home Office 1990a, 1990b), they still refer to the same tensions which I have indicated throughout this book and which the proposed legislative changes can only compound. I wish, therefore, to end by presenting the reader with the visions of those who are routinely engaged in probation work. This is an activity which, I hope, has been further understood as a result of this research.

The responses were reminiscent of the two scenarios for the future of the probation service which Peter Raynor (1985) posed at the end of his study. One service is more coercive and authoritarian, the other places more of a value on the rights of the offender in a more libertarian and participatory society. That said, there were only two replies which felt that the authoritarian road was one which the probation service should pass down.

Accounts centred on the question of relationships with clients. In particular, they mentioned the issue of care and control, being pessimistic in their forecasts. One person simply said 'more control', while another noted that the service would be under increasing pressure to 'adopt a more controlling role in an increasingly divided society'. The present social and political climate was believed to exacerbate this situation. As a result, the service would become increasingly divided into controlling and helping parts, which would be at odds with its value base:

> In the current social and political climate it could easily fragmentalise. The danger exists that to prevent this happening, the service could become increasingly repressive.

The law-and-order lobby would place additional pressures on the service in terms of social control and particularly electronic monitoring:

> This will involve officers on tasks which they may feel are unacceptable, which they have not been trained for and which are at odds with the value base on which traditional service work is based.

This may lead to:

> More accountability, leading to more constraint. More concern with restraints on individuals leading to a quasi-prison officer's role.

The consequences are being felt already:

> our autonomy is being more and more eroded and accountability is tightening up, which I don't think makes for particularly creative work.

Replies also centred on reasons for policy changes and how this will alter the service's role:

> Because of prison overcrowding we may be asked to exercise more control over clients which will inevitably effect our social work role.

The organizational consequence of this vision will be: More monitoring, less social work, therefore less job satisfaction. This will mean, as one officer put it, that the service needed to be:

> vigilant in resisting the excesses of the 'value for money' approach to the job. It would be relatively simple to replace the present service with a mechanistic organization which merely seeks to ensure offenders observe the rules of supervision. I would not want to work for such a service.

The future was therefore also considered alongside personal decisions about continuing to work for the service. There were visions of less autonomy; more control of officers; a reduction in job satisfaction; less of a rehabilitative approach, unless sold well; the possible privatization of sectors of work; an increase in monitoring for managerial purposes who, as a body, will 'become more powerful and abstract'. Further, more non-professional officers taking on controlling tasks; an increase in occupational stress; more work with higher-tariff offenders; the full introduction of electronic tagging; an enlarged bureaucracy and an increasingly stretched service:

> Under these circumstances I would leave the service, as I joined to practise social work.

Other officers simply envisaged a change of employment:

> If it continues in the present vein I will leave the service and attempt to find a job in the voluntary sector where I can value what I do. I feel unable and unwilling to change and become a controlling, monitoring agent of the government which is what I foresee.

Spelling out their vision, the importance of resisting more control and promoting social work values, this officer concluded:

> I want to remain a counsellor to those people who find the increased stresses of a modern society a little too much at times.

Aside from the scenarios of pessimism and qualified optimism – if the service can manage to hold on to its ethos – the answers also reflected the themes of reflection and resolution. To probation officers, ancillaries and some SPOs, these were expressed as concerns over practice restraints and changes in their roles. To others, also including a few POs, they reacted to the question in terms of what may be done, in policy terms, to alleviate the situation:

> If the Probation Service is not to become a more mechanistic and controlling agency, there must be increased attention to the quality of service provided.

More staff co-operation and a 'more realistic down-to-earth approach to the work' would then be required. This could mean: more concern with victims, crime prevention, diversion from custody, inter-agency work, etc. More teamwork and shared working, loss of individual pure autonomy but greater opportunities for officer development and satisfaction with greater sharing.

This future could provide 'a more comprehensive range of services, perhaps in closer collaboration with other agencies'.

Two answers also focused on a need for pro-active work and not simply responding to the whims of Home Office and government: 'Our future lies in the control of the Courts and public opinion'. The service may even be:

In centres on the 'patch' in the heart of the community (not tucked away in clinical offices from the reality of the clients' world). More Day Centres and liaison with the Courts, solicitors and Crown Prosecution Service, to reduce custody. A move to more preventive work and one-to-one casework confined to a few with very specific problems.

In one answer, the alternatives to custody industry even opened up 'new opportunities for the service'. Client participation in service delivery by way of opinion surveys, would be a feature of the future. However, this would be a possibility only if the service did not become a 'more mechanistic and controlling agency'. If this happened, the service would be too repressive. In this sense, replies referred to the US Probation Service in order to illustrate their concerns over the care/control dilemma. One officer echoed the sentiments many expressed in one form or another:

The service will become more repressive, more a tool of a reactionary government, so there is a need to re-assert social work values. If the service does not show a care to clients more Probation Officers will change occupation. We should strongly resist coercion and not become a carbon copy of the USA who neither care nor help, but are another arm of the law forcing clients to tow the line society has decided for them.

The state of flux that the service finds itself in and an ambivalence in responding to the growing problems it faces, were reflected in these accounts. While most were pessimistic a few were cautiously optimistic. Indeed a significant minority of replies, in speculating upon a bleak future of the service, felt that they would seek alternative employment. Increased control of offenders, more monitoring of work practices and the increased erosion of autonomy, plus becoming agents of government, all added to these feelings. Some believed that the service would change, perhaps becoming more community based and moving into more preventive work – leaving casework tasks for only the most needy of offenders. However, this was qualified and depended on the service not becoming a mechanical, controlling agency. Nevertheless, it was significant that notes of pessimism came from the front line. While a few members of staff were cautiously optimistic, optimism, it seemed, tended to be the prerogative of a few senior probation officers and probation management.

Appendix: research design

I began my research by meeting different people within the organization and asking them about their roles and beliefs about probation and the direction of the service; these were informal meetings which arose when the opportunity was presented. I also attended specific meetings, for example I went to a Probation Committee meeting (it meets three or four times a year) two months after starting the research. This period of familiarization was supplemented by attending team meetings and taking the opportunity to explain the purpose of the research to service members.

Following this, the research was triangulated: 'the combination of methodologies in the study of the same phenomena' (Denzin 1978: 291). This permitted me to examine the organization and its work patterns using a range of methods, thereby recognizing the limitations of different types of research. Hammersley and Atkinson (1983) note the limitations of ethnography, using examples which include the study of large organizations.

Following a pilot survey and the period of familiarization, an extensive self-completion questionnaire was sent to senior probation officers for distribution to members of their teams, who were specified in an accompanying letter. These included ancillaries and probation officers, as well as the SPOs themselves. Members of probation management (ACPO and above) were sent questionnaires separately. Secretaries, sessional supervisors and volunteers were excluded from the questionnaire, but interviewed during fieldwork. Allowing for retirements, job movements and sick-leave, there was a 70 per cent response rate. Given the time required to complete the questionnaire, this was a good rate of return (exceeding the average for the majority of postal questionnaires). Moreover, the possibility of bias in interpreting non-response was reduced as a result of subsequent fieldwork.

Following the return of the questionnaires I embarked on further observation and interviews. The former included team meetings; senior management meetings; a major policy process (see Chapter 3) and periods in different probation settings. This was supplemented by the unobtrusive method (Webb *et al.* 1966) of documentary research by the use of policy documents: Home Office Inspectors' reports; minutes of meetings; staff Circulars and policy documents (as well as numerous telephone calls).

The observation had to be selective due to time restraints. This required a subjective adequacy (Bruyn 1966: 180–5) which involves, among other factors, spending time in social settings for the purposes of enhancing understanding. I concentrated on specific areas, broadly paralleling the method of theoretical sampling which Glaser and Strauss (1967) suggest. These included a rural team, two urban teams, three day centres, a probation hostel, a civil work team, prison teams, court work and meetings at different levels of the organization. Other settings were also attended when the opportunity arose and the research need dictated; all of which gave me an opportunity to gain a wider insight into the workings of the service. In this sense, there can be no doubt that the openness, not only of the probation personnel I spent time with, but also of probation management (ACPO and above), in particular the CPO, was pivotal.

A particular criticism which can be levelled against this research – aside from questions of design and execution – is in respect to its external validity: the applicability of its findings to other probation services. I would argue that the pressures and constraints I have identified – both at a policy and practice level – are similarly experienced in other areas. One exception to this is the issue of race and racism. Treen has an anti-racist policy but, at the time of writing, has only one member of staff from an ethnic minority. Apart from the prisons in the area, Treen has few black clients in

Notes

1 An evolving organization and occupation

1 This approach draws upon Foucault's genealogical analysis, that is it examines how the probation service evolved within the context of penal and political thought at the time. However, it should be emphasized that this does not assert a 'master reality' or posit a 'unilinear development' (see P. Young's cautionary notes, 1983: 98–100); instead the formation of the probation service is viewed as the outcome of struggles between various forces. In this way history becomes important as a history of the present.

2 For an extended discussion of these issues see Garland (1985: ch. 1).

3 See Bochel (1976: ch. 1).

4 As Garland (1985: 4) notes, however, there is some dispute regarding this.

5 Now named the Howard League, 'which exists to promote constructive proposals for reform in the criminal justice process; to consider the principles on which penal polices should be based and to spread information about the effect of current practices' (Howard League 1987b: 1; see also 1987a: 13).

6 On the precept that there is nothing new, just that which is forgotten, the 1922 Geddes Committee on National Expenditure not only recommended a reduction in government grants, but also opposed percentage grants, considering that their amounts were determined by local authorities over whom central government

exercised no control. It appears there is historical precedent for the 1980s challenge to local democracy and the call for an economic probation service.

7 At the Report Stage of the Bill concern was expressed with regard to the interests of the ratepayers. The Bill was amended to include agreement between the local authority and the Probation Committee who, if failing to agree, would refer the matter to the Home Secretary for settlement.

8 The success of occupations in seeking professional status is considered by some authors to be predicated upon, amongst other traits, their knowledge base. The description of attributes of a profession has been used by authors as a datum against which to measure the professional status of occupations (Greenwood 1957; Barber 1963) but is fraught with theoretical and methodological problems (see Saks 1983; May 1989).

9 NAPO had lobbied for this to become part of their duties, owing to not only their long tradition in the courts, but also the feeling that probation officers had the expertise relating to such conflicts and could, therefore, make an important contribution to this area.

10 Although the relative number of those placed on probation declined during these years, between 1938 and 1962 the absolute number of indictable offences known to the police rose from 228,220 to 743,713, thus provoking concern regarding the crime problem (see the *Report of the Departmental Committee on the Probation Service*, Home Office 1962: 28).

11 For an extended discussion of these issues see Jones (1986: ch. 6).

12 It is important to note at this stage that probation officers normally dealt with what Foucault has termed the juridical subject who had temporarily suspended the social pact and thus required correction through training. The prison, on the other hand, primarily exercises control, through a series of rules and orders, for the subject's obedience (1977: 128–9). In probation discourse this manifests itself as a tension between care and control. During 1981 NAPO actually voted on the withdrawal of seconded probation officers from prison establishments – a motion which never came to fruition due to the lack of consensus on the matter.

13 Provisions for paroles for those serving more than eighteen months are given by CJA 1967, s. 60. The provision for those serving a minimum of six months is given by CJA 1982, s. 33. These recommendations followed the White Paper *The Adult Offender* (Home Office 1965). Despite NAPO's belief that the service did not have the resources to undertake this work – probably due to a need to relieve the pressures on prisons – this was implemented on 1 April 1968 and during the period 1961 to 1971 the percentage of offenders supervised by the service on after-care increased from 13.5 to 26.4 per cent of offenders.

14 A Home Office Circular of 1966 had considered the importance of supervision of casework and recommended a ratio of one senior

officer to five officers, while also urging the use of Assistant Principal Probation Officers to assist the Principal and the 'strengthening of administration' (Home Office Circular 225/1966, *Structure of the Probation and After-Care Service*). It also noted areas of more than thirty-five officers may benefit from an assistant. The Morison Committee had also recommended the appointment of a principal officer in areas of six or more officers and the supervision by senior officers if the principal's other duties suffer as a result of carrying her on his own caseload and supervising officers (Home Office 1962: paras 216–20).

2 Change and conflict

1 Also the Younger Report on *Young Adult Offenders* (Home Office 1974) stated: 'Neither practical experience nor the results of research in recent years have established the superiority of custodial over non-custodial methods in their effect upon renewed offending: this is still an open question' (quoted in Haxby 1978: 150).

2 For instance, Whittaker (1979) notes that Bean's approach seems to imply officially defined criminals are no different from the rest of the population. While some authors who incorporated the labelling approach may have implied this, it was used by those from very different theoretical backgrounds and was never intended to be a unified theory. On this last point see Plummer (1979).

3 Quoted in Radzinowicz and King (1979: 15).

4 Home Office *Criminal Statistics*, 1989.

5 Reported in the *NAPO Newsletter* February 1988.

6 Penal Policy File no. 29 page 146, in the *Howard Journal of Criminal Justice* May 1988: 27 (2).

7 It should be noted the incoming 1979 Conservative Government implemented the 1978 Edmund-Davies Report on police pay, adding another £550 million to expenditure on law and order.

8 The Home Secretary gave these figures in the House of Commons on 18 April 1988, reported in *NAPO* Newsletter May/June 1988.

9 Kavanagh (1983: 155) urges caution in interpreting government expenditure as indicative of government functions. While understanding such caution, the present government's expenditure on law and order is taken to be indicative of their approach towards the crime problem.

10 Personal communication to the author from NAPO's Research and Information Officer.

11 For a brief account of the Kent Control Unit see Spencer and Edwards (1986).

12 The Report's proposals included first, that clients should no longer need to give their consent to a probation order, and second, that probation officers should have the power to detain a client for

seventy-two hours if they thought it *likely* they would commit an offence.

3 Implementing policy change

1 The 1983 Home Office *British Crime Survey* concluded that its findings conflicted 'with the widespread belief that the public are impatient with the leniency of the legal system' (Hough and Mayhew 1984). Further, M. Wright notes in summarizing public and victim surveys: 'a substantial number of people are beginning to say "use reparative sanctions instead of punishment"' (1987: 107).

2 In relation to victims and courts' facilities there is also considerable variability (see Shapland and Cohen 1987).

3 One such form is the Home Office Form 20. This includes the probation area code; sex of offender; previous history (including any sentences); type of supervision; its length; the offence itself; the court; supervision additional requirements and reasons for termination of the order. Each option is pre-coded for the officer to complete and to be subsequently analysed by Home Office software.

5 At the front line

1 There were two psychiatric reports. One was based on one interview which found nothing wrong with the client 'psychiatrically' speaking, but 'psychologically' wrong and in the last paragraph recommended a secure unit at a mental institution. The second report, requested by the defence, found nothing wrong with the client.

2 As Weston notes, a stand-down report should be used only to form initial impressions and not as a substitute for a full inquiry (1987: 99).

3 This use of unintended consequences does not assume some functional need of the social system for the purposes of social order. This would not explain why these activities exist: 'only an interpretation of intentional activity does that' (Giddens 1984: 295). For an exposition of this position see Giddens (1984: 293–7).

4 For a discussion of the issues which surround divorce work in the probation service see Ahier (1986).

5 The dominant conceptions of family life are discussed in P. Abbott and Wallace (1990: ch. 4).

6 In prisons

1 While studies exist on the experiences of inmates in institutions (see Goffman 1968; Cohen and Taylor 1972), relatively few, with the exception of Davies (1974), M. Shaw (1974) and Jepson and Elliott

(1985), have systematically examined the work of probation officers in prison establishments.

2 During the Tory Party Conference in 1983 the then Home Secretary, Leon Brittan, said prisoners who were convicted for terms of over five years for offences involving either drugs or violence were likely to get parole only in 'exceptional circumstances'.

3 The prison where I spent most of my time draws officers from its own sub-area. Therefore the possibility of working in the institution remains, as I discovered during the research, on the minds of many officers.

4 However feminist analysis is increasingly finding its way into social work practice. For example, see Hanmer and Statham (1988).

Bibliography

Abbott, A. (1981). 'Status and strain in the professions', *American Journal of Sociology* 86 (4): 816–35.

Abbott, P. and Wallace, C. (1990). *An Introduction to Sociology: Feminist Perspectives*, London: Routledge.

ACOP (1988). 'More demanding than prison', Wakefield: Association of Chief Officers of Probation.

ACOP/CCPC/NAPO (1987). 'Probation – the next five years', a joint statement by the Association of Chief Officers of Probation, Central Council of Probation Committees and National Association of Probation Officers, London: ACOP/CCPC/NAPO.

Adler, M. and Asquith, S. (eds) (1981). *Discretion and Welfare*, London: Heinemann.

Ahier, B. (1986). *Conciliation, Divorce and the Probation Service*, Social Work Monograph, Norwich: University of East Anglia.

Alexis, M. and Wilson, C. (eds) (1967). *Organizational Decision-Making*, Englewood Cliffs, NJ: Prentice-Hall.

Audit Commission (1989). *The Probation Service: Promoting Value for Money*, London: HMSO.

Bailey, R. and Brake, M. (eds) (1975). *Radical Social Work*, London: Edward Arnold.

Baldwin, J. and Bottomley, A. (eds) (1978). *Criminal Justice: Selected Readings*, London: Martin Robertson.

Bale, D. (1988). 'Summing up for the defence', *Probation Journal* 35 (1): 17–19.

Barber, B. (1963). 'Some problems in the sociology of the professions', *Daedalus*: 67.

Barclay, P. (1982). *Social Workers: Their Roles and Tasks*, London: Bedford Square Press.

Barker, K. and Sturges, J. (1986). *Decision-Making in Magistrates' Courts*, London: Fourmat Publishing.

Bean, P. (1976). *Rehabilitation and Deviance*, London: Routledge & Kegan Paul.

Beaumont, B. (1985). 'Probation: working for social change?', in H. Walker and B. Beaumont (eds) (1985).

Becker, H. (1962). 'The nature of a profession', *The 61st Yearbook of the National Society for the Study of Education* (Part 2), Chicago: University of Chicago Press.

Beetham, D. (1987). *Bureaucracy*, Milton Keynes: Open University Press.

Bennett, W. and Hokenstad, M. (1973). 'Full-time people workers and conceptions of the "Professional"' in P. Halmos (ed.) (1973).

Bentham, J. (1830). *The Principles of Morals and Legislation*, various editions.

Blom-Cooper, L. (1988). *The Penalty of Imprisonment*, London: Prison Reform Trust and Howard League.

Bochel, D. (1976). *Probation and After-Care: Its Development in England and Wales*, Edinburgh: Scottish Academic Press.

Boswell, G. (1982). *Goals in the Probation and After-Care Service*, unpublished PhD thesis, University of Liverpool.

——(1985). *Care, Control and Accountability in the Probation Service*, Social Work Monograph, Norwich: University of East Anglia.

——(1989). *Holding the Balance Between Court and Client*, Social Work Monograph, Norwich: University of East Anglia.

Boswell, G. and Worthington, M. (1988). 'Reflecting probation service values in management', *Probation Journal*, 35 (4): 128–30.

Bottomley, A. (1973). *Decisions in the Penal Process*, London: Martin Robertson.

——(1979). *Criminology in Focus*, Oxford: Martin Robertson.

Bottoms, A. (1987). 'Limiting prison use: experience in England and Wales', *Howard Journal of Criminal Justice* 26 (3): 177–202.

Bottoms, A. and McWilliams, W. (1979). 'A non-treatment paradigm for probation practice', *British Journal of Social Work* 9 (2): 159–202.

Box, S. (1987). *Recession, Crime and Punishment*, London: Macmillan.

Brake, M. and Bailey, R. (eds) (1980). *Radical Social Work and Practice*, London: Edward Arnold.

Brandon D. and Jordan W. (eds) (1979). *Creative Social Work*, Oxford: Basil Blackwell.

Brody, S. (1976). *The Effectiveness of Sentencing: A Review of the Literature*, Home Office Research Study no 35, London: HMSO.

Brown, P. (1987). 'Probation officer burnout: an organizational disease/ an occupational cure, Part II', *Federal Probation* September: 17–21.

Bruyn, S. (1966). *The Human Perspective in Sociology*, Englewood Cliffs, NJ: Prentice-Hall.

Bryman, A. (1988). *Quantity and Quality in Social Research*, London: Unwin Hyman.

Burt, C. (1925). *The Young Delinquent*, London: London University Press.

Carlen, P. (1976). *Magistrates' Justice*, Oxford: Martin Robertson.

Carlen, P. and Powell, M. (1979). 'Professionals in the magistrates' courts: the courtroom lore of probation officers and social workers', in H. Parker (ed.) (1979).

Carr-Saunders, A. and Wilson, P. (1933). *The Professions*, Oxford: Clarendon Press.

Child, J. (1984). *Organization: A Guide to Problems and Practice*, London: Harper Row.

Christie, N. (1982). *Limits to Pain*, Oxford: Martin Robertson.

Clegg, S. and Dunkerley, D. (eds) (1977). *Critical Issues in Organisations*, London: Routledge & Kegan Paul.

Cohen, S. (1975). 'It's all right for you to talk: political and sociological manifestos for social work action', in R. Bailey and M. Brake (eds) (1975).

——(1985). *Visions of Social Control*, Oxford: Polity Press.

——(1988). *Against Criminology*, New Brunswick, NJ: Transaction.

Cohen, S. and Taylor, L. (1972). *Psychological Survival: The Experience of Long Term Imprisonment*, Harmondsworth: Penguin.

Coker, J. (1988). *Probation Objectives: A Management View*, Social Work Monograph, Norwich: University of East Anglia.

Collier, P. and Tarling, R. (1987). 'International comparisons of prison populations', *Home Office Research Bulletin* 23: 48–54.

Cooper, D. (1982). 'The Seebohm Transition', in G. Glastonbury, D. Cooper and P. Hawkins (eds) (1982).

Cooper, E. (1979). 'Social work and domestic proceedings', in H. Parker (ed.) (1979).

Cooper, E. (1987). 'Probation practice in the criminal and civil courts', in J. Harding (ed.) (1987).

Cooper, J. (1987). 'The future of social work: a pragmatic view', in M. Loney, *et al.* (eds) (1987).

Cordell, K. (1988). *The Origins and Development of Deutschlandpolitik*, unpublished PhD thesis, Plymouth Polytechnic.

Corrigan, P. and Leonard, P. (1978). *Social Work Practice Under Capitalism*, London: Macmillan.

Cousins, C. (1987). *Controlling Social Welfare: A Sociology of State Welfare, Work and Organisation*, Brighton: Wheatsheaf.

Crawforth, J. (1987). 'Efficiency and effectiveness: FMIS and the deployment of resources', in *Research, Information and Practice in the Probation Service: Proceedings of the Third National Probation Research and Information Exchange Conference*, Sheffield: Midlands Regional Staff Development Unit, 57–61.

Croft, J. (1978). *Research in Criminal Justice*, Home Office Research Study no 44, London: HMSO.

Crow, I. (1987). 'Black people and criminal justice in the U.K.' *Howard Journal of Criminal Justice* 26 (4): 303–14.

Curran, J. (ed.) (1984). *The Future of the Left*, Cambridge: Polity Press.

Daullah, M. (1989). 'Racism, probation and promotion prospects', *NAPO News* February: 8–9.

Davies, Martin (1974). *Prisoners of Society: Attitudes and After-Care* London: Routledge & Kegan Paul.

——(1976). 'A tale of two perspectives: defensive or developmental', *Probation Journal* 23 (3): 86–9.

——(1978). 'Social inquiry for the courts', in J. Baldwin. and A. Bottomley (eds) (1978).

Davies, M. and Wright, A. (1989). *The Changing Face of Probation*, Social Work Monograph, Norwich: University of East Anglia.

Davies, Michael, (1988). *Staff Supervision in the Probation Service*, Aldershot: Avebury.

Day, M. (1987). 'The politics of probation', in J. Harding, (ed.) (1987).

Day, P. (1981). *Social Work and Social Control*, London: Tavistock.

Denzin, N. (1978). *The Research Act: A Theoretical Introduction to Sociological Methods*, 2nd edn, New York: McGraw-Hill.

Dingwall, R. and Lewis, P. (eds) (1983). *The Sociology of the Professions: Lawyers, Doctors and Others*, London: Macmillan.

Downes, D. (1983). *Law and Order: Theft of an Issue*, Fabian Tract no 490, London: Fabian Society.

——(1988). *Contrasts in Tolerance: Penal Policy in the Netherlands and England and Wales*, Oxford: Oxford University Press.

Downes, D. and Rock, P. (eds) (1979). *Deviant Interpretations: Problems in Criminological Theory*, Oxford: Martin Robertson.

Drucker, P. (1955). *The Practice of Management*, London: Heinemann.

Dunsire, A. (1978). *Implementation in a Bureaucracy*, Oxford: Martin Robertson.

Durkheim, E. (1957). *Professional Ethics and Civil Morals*, London: Routledge & Kegan Paul.

Eadie, T. and Willis, A. (1989). 'National standards for discipline and breach proceedings in community service: an exercise in penal rhetoric?', *Criminal Law Review* June: 412–19.

Eaton, M. (1986). *Justice for Women: Family, Court and Social Control*, Milton Keynes: Open University Press.

Epstein, I. (1970). 'Professionalization, professionalism and social work radicalism', *Journal of Health and Social Behaviour* 11: 67–77.

Esland, G. and Salaman, G. (eds) (1980). *The Politics of Work and Occupations*, Milton Keynes: Open University Press.

Etzioni, A. (ed.) (1969). *The Semi-Professions and their Organisations: Teachers, Nurses and Social Workers*, New York: Free Press.

Faulkner, D. (1984). 'The future of the probation service', in *Probation: Direction innovation and Change in the 1980s: Proceedings of a Professional Conference*, London: NAPO.

Faulkner, D. (1989). 'Future of the probation service: a view from government', *Justice of the Peace* 153 (39): 625–6.

Fielding, N. (undated). *The Training of Probation Officers*, Occasional Paper 2, Guildford: University of Surrey, Sociology Department.

——(1984). *Probation Practice: Client Support Under Social Control*, Aldershot: Gower.

——(1988). *Joining Forces: Police Training, Socialization, and Occupational Competence*, London: Routledge & Kegan Paul.

Findlater, D. (1982). *The Ancillary Worker in the Probation Service*, Social Work Monograph, Norwich: University of East Anglia.

Finkelstein, E. (1989). *The Enforcement of Rules in the Prison Setting*, unpublished Ph.D. thesis, University of Bristol.

Fisher, R. and Wilson, C. (1982). *Authority or Freedom? Probation Hostels for Adults*, Aldershot: Gower.

Forsyth, P. and Danisiewicz, T. (1985). 'Towards a theory of professionalization', *The Sociology of Work and Occupations* 12 (1): 59–76.

Foucault, M. (1977). *Discipline and Punish: The Birth of the Prison*, London: Allen Lane.

——(1980). *Power/Knowledge, Selected Interviews and Other Writings 1972–1977*, edited by C. Gordon, Brighton: Harvester.

Fullwood, C. (1987). 'The probation service: from moral optimism, through penelogical pessimism into the future', Manchester: Greater Manchester Probation Service.

Garfinkel, H. (1967). *Studies in Ethnomethodology*, Englewood Cliffs, NJ: Prentice-Hall.

Garland, D. (1985). *Punishment and Welfare: A History of Penal Strategies*, Aldershot: Gower.

Garland, D. and Young, P. (eds) (1983). *The Power to Punish*, London: Heinemann.

Giddens, A. (1984). *The Constitution of Society*, Oxford: Polity Press.

——(1987). *Social Theory and Modern Sociology*, Oxford: Polity Press.

Glaser, B. and Strauss, A. (1967). *The Discovery of Grounded Theory*, Chicago: Aldine Publishing.

Glastonbury, B., Cooper, D. and Hawkins, P. (1982). *Social Work in Conflict: The Practitioner and the Bureaucrat*, Birmingham: British Association of Social Workers.

Glastonbury, B., Bradley, R. and Orme, J. (1987). *Managing People in the Personal Social Services*, Chichester: John Wiley.

Goffman, E. (1968). *Asylums: Essays on the Social Situation of Mental Patients and Other Inmates*, Harmondsworth: Penguin.

——(1969). *The Presentation of Self in Everyday Life*, London: Allen Lane.

——(1972). *Interaction Ritual: Essays on Face-to-Face Behaviour*, Harmondsworth: Penguin.

Gouldner, A. (1970). 'Cosmopolitans and locals', in O. Grusky and G. Miller (eds) (1970).

——(1971). *The Coming Crisis of Western Sociology*, London: Heinemann.

Greenwood, E. (1957). 'Attributes of a profession', *Social Work* 2: 45–55.

Grusky, O. and Miller, G. (eds) (1970) *The Sociology of Organisations*, New York: Free Press.

Hall, R. (1969). *Occupations and the Social Structure*, Englewood Cliffs, NJ: Prentice-Hall.

——(1975). *Occupations and the Social Structure*, 2nd edn, Englewood Cliffs, NJ: Prentice-Hall.

Hall, S. (1979). 'Drifting into a law and order society', Cobden Trust Memorial Lecture.

——(1980). 'Popular democratic *vs* authoritarian populism', in A. Hunt (ed.).

Hall, S. and Jacques, M. (eds) (1983). *The Politics of Thatcherism*, London: Lawrence & Wishart.

Halmos, P. (1970). *The Personal Service Society*, London: Constable.

——(ed.) (1973). *Professionalization and Social Change*, Sociological Review Monograph no 20, University of Keele.

Hammersley, M. and Atkinson, P. (1983). *Ethnography: Principles in Practice*, London: Tavistock.

Hankinson, I. and Stephens, D. (1986). 'Ever decreasing circles', *Probation Journal* 33 (1): 17–19.

Hanmer, J. and Statham, D. (1988). *Women and Social Work: Towards a Woman-Centred Practice*, London: Macmillan.

Hardiker, P. (1977). 'Social work ideologies in the probation service', *British Journal of Social Work* 7 (2): 131–54.

Harding, J. (ed.) (1987). *Probation and the Community: A Practice and Policy Reader*, London: Tavistock.

Harris, R. (1977). 'The probation officer as social worker', *British Journal of Social Work* 7 (4): 433–42.

——(1989). 'Probation officers still social workers?', *Probation Journal* 36 (2): 52–7.

Harris, R. and Webb, D. (1987). *Welfare, Power and Juvenile Justice*, London: Tavistock.

Haxby, D. (1978). *Probation: A Changing Service*, London: Constable.

Head, M. (1988). 'Alternatives to custody: implications for policy and priorities in the probation service', presented to a day conference, University of Hull, 26 February.

Hearn, J. (1982). 'Notes on patriarchy, professionalization and the semi-professions', *Sociology* 16 (2): 184–202.

Holdaway, S. (ed.) (1979). *The British Police*, London: Edward Arnold.

Home Office (1961). *Report of the Inter-Departmental Committee on the Business of the Criminal Courts (The Streatfield Committee)*, Cmnd 1289, London: Home Office.

——(1962). *Report of the Departmental Committee on the Probation Service (The Morison Committee)*, Cmnd 1650, London: Home Office.

Home Office (1963). *Report of the Advisory Council on the Treatment of Offenders and the Organisation of After-Care*, London: Home Office.

——(1965). *The Adult Offender*, Cmnd 2852, London: Home Office.

——(1967). *Roles and Functions of Seconded Probation Officers*, Home Office Circular no 130, London: Home Office.

——(1968). *Report of the Committee on Local Authority and Allied Personal Services (The Seebohm Committee)*, Cmnd 3703, London: HMSO.

——(1970). *Report of the Advisory Council on the Penal System: Non-Custodial and Semi-Custodial Penalties (The Wootton Report)*, London: HMSO.

——(1972). *Report of the Butterworth Inquiry into the Work and Pay of Probation Officers and Social Workers*, Cmnd 5076, London: HMSO.

——(1974). *Young Adult Offenders: A Report of the Advisory Council on the Penal System (The Younger Report)*, London: HMSO.

——(1980). *Report of the Working Party on Management Structure in the Probation and After-Care Service*, London: HMSO.

——(1984). *Probation Service in England and Wales: Statement of National Objectives and Priorities*, London: Home Office.

——(1985). *Report of the Working Group on the Review of the Role of the Probation Service in Adult Establishments*, London: Home Office.

——(1986). *Social Inquiry Reports*, Circular no 92, London: Home Office.

——(1987). *Efficiency Scrutiny of Her Majesty's Probation Inspectorate (The Grimsey Report)*, London: Home Office.

——(1988a). *National Standards for Community Service*, London: Home Office.

——(1988b). *Punishment, Custody and the Community*, Cmnd 424, London: Home Office.

——(1988c). *Tackling Offending: An Action Plan*, London: Home Office.

——(1988d). *The Parole System in England and Wales (The Carlisle Report)*, London: HMSO.

——(1990a). *Crime, Justice and Protecting the Public*, Cmnd 965, London: HMSO.

——(1990b). *Supervision and Punishment in the Community: A Framework for Action*, Cmnd 966, London: HMSO.

Horton, C. and Smith, D. (1988). *Evaluating Police Work: An Action Research Project*, London: Policy Studies Institute.

Hough, M. and Mayhew, P. (1984). *Taking Account of Crime: Key Findings from the Second British Crime Survey*, London: HMSO.

Howard League (1987a). *Justice 2000: Criminal Justice for a New Century*, London: Howard League.

——(1987b). *Submission to the Committee Undertaking the Review of the Parole System*, London: Howard League.

Howe, D. (1986). *Social Workers and their Practice in Welfare Bureaucracies*, Aldershot: Gower.

Hudson, B. (1987). *Justice Through Punishment: A Critique of the 'Justice' Model of Corrections*, London: Macmillan.

Hughes, E. (1971). *The Sociological Eye: Selected Papers*, Chicago: Aldine-Atherton.

Hugman, B. (1980). 'Radical practice in probation', in M. Brake and R. Bailey (eds) (1980).

Humphrey, C. (1987). *The Implications of the Financial Management Initiative for the Probation Service*, Manchester University, Department of Accounting and Finance.

Hunt, A. (ed.) (1980). *Marxism and Democracy*, London: Lawrence & Wishart.

Hurd, D. (1988). 'Full Speech by the Home Secretary to the 105th Conservative Party Conference, Brighton', London: Conservative Central Office.

Jarvis, F. V. (1972). *Advise, Assist and Befriend: A History of the Probation and After-Care Service*, London: NAPO.

Jepson, N. and Elliott, K. (1985). *Shared Working Between Prison and Probation Officers: A Study Conducted in Adult Prisons in England and Wales*, London: HMSO.

Johnson, T. (1972). *Professions and Power*, London: Macmillan.

——(1980). 'Work and power', in G. Esland and G. Salaman (eds) (1980).

Jones, D. (1986). *History of Criminology: A Philosophical Perspective*, New York: Greenwood Press.

Jordan, W. (1984). *Invitation to Social Work*, Oxford: Martin Robertson.

Kakabadse, A. and Worrall, R. (1978). 'Job satisfaction and organisational structure: a comparative study of nine social service departments', *British Journal of Social Work* 8 (1): 51–70.

Katan, J. (1973). 'The attitudes of professionals towards the employment of indigenous non-professionals in human service organisations', in P. Halmos (ed.) (1973).

Kavanagh, D. (1983). *Political Science and Political Behaviour*, London: Allen & Unwin.

Keynon, S. and Rhodes, P. (undated). 'A study of job satisfaction in the probation and after-care service', Loughborough University.

King, D. (1987). *The New Right: Politics, Markets and Citizenship*, London: Macmillan.

King, J. (ed.) (1969). *The Probation and After-Care Service*, 3rd edn, London: Butterworths.

——(ed.) (1979). *Pressure and Change in the Probation Service*, Cambridge, Institute of Criminology: Cropwood Conference Series no 11.

King, R. and Elliott, K. (1978). *Albany: Birth of a Prison – End of an Era*, London: Routledge to Kegan Paul.

Klegon, D. (1978). 'The sociology of the professions: an emerging perspective', *Sociology of Work and Occupations* 5 (3): 259–85.

Larson, M. (1977). *The Rise of Professionalism: A Sociological Analysis*, Berkeley: University of California Press.

Leeson, C. (1914). *The Probation System*.

Le Mesurier, L. (1935). *A Handbook of Probation and Social Work of the Courts*, London: NAPO.

Leys, C. (1984). 'The rise of the authoritarian state?' in J. Curran (ed.) (1984).

Lipsky, M. (1980). *Street Level Bureaucracy*, New York: Russell Sage Foundation.

Lloyd, C. (1986). *'Response to SNOP': An Analysis of the Home Office Document. 'Probation Service in England and Wales: Statement of National Objectives and Priorities' and the Subsequent Local Responses*, Cambridge: Institute of Criminology.

Loney, M., Bocock, R., Clarke, J., Cochrane, A., Graham, P. and Wilson, M. (eds) (1987). *The State or the Market: Politics and Welfare in Contemporary Britain*, London: Sage.

Lynch, B. (1976). 'The probation officer as employee', *Probation Journal* 23 (2): 48–51.

McDermott, K. and King, R. (1989). 'A fresh start: the enhancement of prison regimes', *Howard Journal of Criminal Justice* 28 (3): 161–76.

MacLeod, D. (1988). 'Bale's "Risk of Custody" Scale: some critical comments', *Probation Journal* 35 (1): 15–16.

McWilliams, W. (1980). 'Management models and the bases of management structure', Discussion Paper Series no 26, Sheffield: South Yorkshire Probation Service Research Unit.

——(1983). 'The mission to the English police courts 1876–1936', *Howard Journal of Criminal Justice* 22: 129–47.

——(1985). 'The mission transformed: professionalisation of probation between the wars', *Howard Journal of Criminal Justice* 24 (4): 257–74.

——(1986). 'The English probation system and the diagnostic ideal', *Howard Journal of Criminal Justice* 25 (4): 241–60.'

——(1987). 'Probation, pragmatism and policy', *Howard Journal of Criminal Justice* 26 (2): 97–121.

——(1989). 'An expressive model for evaluating probation practice', *Probation Journal* 36 (2): 58–64.

McWilliams, W. and Pease, K. (1990). 'Probation practice and an end to punishment', *Howard Journal of Criminal Justice* 29 (1): 14–24.

Manning, P. (1979). 'The social control of police work', in S. Holdaway (ed.) (1979).

March, J. and Simon, H. (1970). 'Decision-making theory', in O. Grusky and G. Miller (eds) (1970).

Marshall, T. (1963). *Sociology at the Crossroads and Other Essays*, London: Heinemann.

Mathieson, D. (1979). 'Changes in the probation service: implications and effects', in J. King (ed.) (1979).

——(1987). 'This is the heart of probation', *Justice of the Peace* 18 July: 458–60.

Mathieson, T. (1983). 'The future of control systems – the case of Norway', in D. Garland and P. Young (eds) (1983).

Mawby, R. (1980). 'The state of probation: views from within', *Social Policy and Administration* 14 (2): 268–85.

—— and Gill, M. (1987). *Crime Victims: Needs, Services and the Voluntary Sector*, London: Tavistock.

May, T. (1989). 'The sociology of the professions: the theoretical and methodological issues', *Journal of Critical Social Research* 3 (1).

—— (1990). *Probation: Politics, Policy and Practice* (Ph.D. thesis), Plymouth: Polytechnic South-West.

Millard, D. (1977). 'Constraints and strategies', *Probation Journal* 24 (1): 2–9.

Millard, D. and Read, G. (1978). 'Teamwork and the unitary model', in G. Read and D. Millard (eds). (1978).

—— (eds) (1978). *Teamwork in Probation*, Birmingham: Probation and After-Care Service, Midland Regional Development Office.

Mills, C. W. (1940). 'Situated accounts and vocabularies of motive', *American Sociological Review* 6: 904–13.

Mintzberg, H. (1979). *The Structuring of Organizations*, Englewood Cliffs, NJ: Prentice-Hall.

—— (1983). *Structure in Fives: Designing Effective Organisations*, Englewood Cliffs, NJ: Prentice-Hall.

Monro, P. (1989). 'Can't the courts cope?' *Community Care* 23 (6): 26–8.

Morgan, G. (1986). *Images of Organization*, London: Sage.

Morrison, A. (1984). 'National objectives and service values', *Probation Journal* 31 (3): 110.

NACRO (1988). 'Punishment, custody and the community: a response to the Green Paper by the National Association for the Care and Resettlement of Offenders', London: NACRO.

NAPO (1966). 'Seniority in the probation service', Probation Paper no 4, London: National Association of Probation Officers.

—— (1981). 'The provision of alternatives to custody and the use of the probation order', London: NAPO.

—— (1986). 'Community-based through-care: the case for the withdrawal of seconded probation officers from prisons', London: NAPO.

Noscow, S. and Form, W. (eds) (1962). *Man, Work and Society: A Reader in the Sociology of Occupations*, New York: Basic Books.

Offe, C. (1984). *Contradictions of the Welfare State*, edited by J. Keane, London: Hutchinson.

—— (1985). *Disorganized Capitalism*, edited by J. Keane, Oxford: Polity Press.

Orme, J. (1988). 'Can workloads be measured?' *Probation Journal* 35 (2): 57–9.

Parker, H. (ed.) (1979). *Social Work and the Courts*, London: Edward Arnold.

Parry-Khan, L. (1988). *Management by Objectives in Probation*, Social Work Monograph, Norwich: University of East Anglia.

Pearson, G. (1975a). *The Deviant Imagination*, London: Macmillan.

——(1975b). 'Making social workers: bad promises and good omens', in R. Bailey and M. Brake (eds) (1975).

Pease, K. (1981). *Community Service Orders: A First Decade of Promise*, London: Howard League.

Perrow, C. (1967). 'A framework for the comparative analysis of organizations', *American Sociological Review* 32: 194–208.

Pfeffer, J. (1981). *Power in Organisations*, London: Pitman.

Pitts, J. (1988). *The Politics of Juvenile Crime*, London: Sage.

Plummer, K. (1979). 'Misunderstanding labelling perspectives', in D. Downes and P. Rock (eds) (1979).

Pointing, J. (ed.) (1986). *Alternatives to Custody*, Oxford: Basil Blackwell.

Radzinowicz, L. (1958). 'Preface', in *The Results of Probation*, Cambridge Centre for Criminological Research.

——(1966). *Ideology and Crime: A Study of Crime in its Social and Historical Context*, London: Heinemann.

Radzinowicz, L. and King, J. (1979). *The Growth of Crime: The International Experience*, Harmondsworth: Penguin.

Rawson, S. (1982). *Sentencing Theory, Social Enquiry and Probation Practice*, Social Work Monograph, Norwich: University of East Anglia.

Raynor, P. (1984). 'National purpose and objectives: a comment', *Probation Journal* 31 (2): 43–7.

——(1985). *Social Work, Justice and Control*, Oxford: Basil Blackwell.

——(1988). *Probation as an Alternative to Custody: A Case Study*, Aldershot: Gower.

Read, G. (1978). 'What Kind of Organisation? Notes on a working conference 23–27 October', Birmingham: Midlands Regional Staff Development Office.

Rees, S. (1978). *Social Work Face to Face*, London: Edward Arnold.

Rein, M. (1970). 'Social work in search of a radical profession', *Social Work* 15 (2): 13–28.

Rock, P. (1973). *Deviant Behaviour*, London: Hutchinson.

Rodger, J. (1988). 'Social work as social control re-examined: beyond the dispersal of discipline thesis', *Sociology* 22 (4): 563–81.

Rumgay, J. (1988). '"Probation – the next five years": a comment', *Howard Journal of Criminal Justice* 27 (3): 198–201.

Sacks, H. (1974). 'On the analysability of stories by children', in R. Turner (ed.).

Saks, M. (1983). 'Removing the blinkers? A critique of recent contributions to the sociology of the professions', *Sociological Review* 31 (1): 1–22.

Sarri, R. and Hasenfeld, Y. (eds) (1978). *The Management of Human Services*, New York: Columbia University Press.

Schein, E. (1985). *Organizational Culture and Leadership*, San Francisco: Jossey-Bass.

Schon, D. (1971). *Beyond the Stable State*, New York: Random House.

Scull, A. (1983). 'Community corrections: panacea, progress or pretence', in D. Garland and P. Young (eds) (1983).

Shapland, J. and Cohen, D. (1987). 'Facilities for victims: the role of the police and the courts', *Criminal Law Review* January: 28–38.

Simon, H. (1947). *Administrative Behaviour*, London: Macmillan.

Shaw, M. (1974). *Social Work in Prison*, Home Office Research Report no 22, London: HMSO.

Shaw, K. (1987). 'Skills, control, and the mass professions', *Sociological Review* 35 (4): 775–93.

Smith, A. (1776). *An Enquiry into the Nature and Causes of the Wealth of Nations*, Edinburgh: Adam and Charles Black.

Smith, D. (1979). 'Probation officers in prison', in D. Brandon and W. Jordan (eds) (1979).

Smith, G. (1981). 'Discretionary decision-making in social work', in M. Adler and S. Asquith (eds) (1981).

Spencer, N. and Edwards, P. (1986). 'The rise and fall of the Kent Control Unit: a local perspective', *Probation Journal* 33 (3): 91–4.

Stern, V. (1987). *Bricks of Shame: Britain's Prisons*, Harmondsworth: Penguin.

Stone, N. (1985). 'Prison-based work', in H. Walker and B. Beaumont (eds) (1985).

——(1988a). *Probation Law*, Social Work Law File – Part 3, Norwich: University of East Anglia.

——(1988b). 'Parole: revamp or revoke', *Probation Journal* 35 (1): 10–14.

Strauss, A. (1978). *Negotiations, Varieties. Contexts. Processes and Social Order*, San Francisco: Jossey-Bass.

Tawney, R. (1921). *The Acquisitive Society*, London: Allen & Unwin.

Taylor, I., Walton, P. and Young, J. (1973). *The New Criminology: For a Social Theory of Deviance*, London: Routledge & Kegan Paul.

——(1975). *Critical Criminology*, London: Routledge & Kegan Paul.

Thomson, D. (1987). 'The changing face of probation in the USA', in J. Harding (ed.) (1987).

Toren, N. (1969). 'Semi-professionalism and social work', in A. Etzioni (ed.) (1969).

Turner, R. (ed.) (1974). *Ethnomethodology*, Harmondsworth: Penguin.

Vanstone, M. (1985). 'Moving away from help?; Policy and practice in probation day centres', *Howard Journal of Criminal Justice* 24 (1): 20–8.

Vanstone, M. (1988). 'Values, leadership and the future of the probation service', *Probation Journal* 35 (4): 131–4.

Vanstone, M. and Seymour, B. (1986). 'Probation service objectives and the neglected ingredients', *Probation Journal* 33 (2): 43–8.

Vass, A. (1984). *Sentenced to Labour: Close Encounters with a Prison Substitute*, St Ives: Venus Academica.

——(1988). 'The marginality of community service and the threat of privatisation', *Probation Journal* 35 (2): 48–51.

Vollmer, H. and Mills, D. (eds) (1966). *Professionalization*, Englewood Cliffs, NJ: Prentice-Hall.

Walker, H. (1985). 'Women's issues in probation practice', in H. Walker and B. Beaumont (eds) (1985).

Walker, H. and Beaumont, B. (1981). *Probation Work: Critical Theory and Socialist Practice*, Oxford: Basil Blackwell.

——(eds) (1985). *Working With Offenders*, London: Macmillan.

Webb, E., Campbell, D., Schwarz, R. and Sechrest, L. (1966). *Unobtrusive Measures: Non-Reactive Research in the Social Sciences*, Chicago: Rand McNally.

Wells, T. (1989). 'Children Bill: the implications for Divorce Court welfare officers', *Family Law* June: 235–6.

Weston, W. R. (1987). *Jarvis's Probation Officers' Manual*, 4th edn, London: Butterworths.

Whittaker, W. (1979). *Probation in the Balance*, unpublished MSc thesis, University of Cardiff.

Wilding, P. (1982). *Professional Power and Social Welfare*, London: Routledge & Kegan Paul.

Willis, A. (1986a). 'Alternatives to imprisonment: an elusive paradise?' in J. Pointing (ed.) (1986).

——(1986b). 'Help and control in probation', in J. Pointing (ed.) (1986).

Worthy, J. (1967). 'Organizational structure and employee morale', in M. Alexis and C. Wilson (eds) (1967).

Wright, A. (1984). *The Day Centre in Probation Practice*, Social Work Monograph, Norwich: University of East Anglia.

Wright, D. (1979). *The Social Worker and the Courts*, London: Heinemann.

Wright, M. (1987). 'What the public wants: surveys of the general public, including victims', *Justice of the Peace* 14 February: 105–7.

Young, A. (1976). 'A sociological analysis of the early history of probation', *British Journal of Law and Society* 3: 44–58.

Young, K. (1977). '"Values" in the policy process', *Policy and Politics* 5 (3): 1–22.

——(1981). 'Discretion as an implementation problem', in M. Adler and S. Asquith (eds) (1981).

Young, P. (1983). 'Sociology, the state and penal relations', in D. Garland and P. Young (eds). (1983).

Index